Mentoring

Perspectives on School-Based Teacher Education

Edited By

Donald McIntyre, Hazel Hagger
and Margaret Wilkin

KOGAN
PAGE

London • Philadelphia

First published in 1993

Kogan Page Limited
120 Pentonville Road
London N1 9JN

© Donald McIntyre, Hazel Hagger, Margaret Wilkin and named contributors, 1993

British Library Cataloguing in Publication Data

A CIP record for this book is available from the British Library.

ISBN 0 7494 0678 X

Typeset by Books Unlimited, Nottm – NG17 1AL.
Printed and bound in Great Britain by Clays Ltd, St Ives plc.

Contents

Notes on Contributors

Geof Alred is a Lecturer in the School of Education, University of Durham.

James Calderhead is Professor of Education at the University of Bath.

Pie Corbett is Primary Articled Teacher Course Leader, Cheltenham and Gloucester College of Higher Education.

Anthony d'Arbon is Professor in the Division of Secondary Education, Australian Catholic University, MacKillop Campus, Sydney.

Richard Dunne is a Lecturer in the School of Education, University of Exeter.

Bob Elliott is Associate Professor of Education, Queensland University of Technology, Brisbane.

Sharon Feiman-Nemser is Associate Professor at the National Center for Research on Teacher Learning, College of Education, Michegan State University.

David Frost is a Lecturer in Education at Christ Church College, Canterbury.

John Furlong is Professor of Education at University College, Swansea.

Phil Gardner is a Lecturer in the Department of Education, University of Cambridge.

Gareth Harvard is a Lecturer in the School of Education, University of Exeter.

Peter Lucas is a Senior Lecturer in the Division of Education, University of Sheffield.

Trisha Maynard is a Research Associate in the Department of Education, University College, Swansea.

Michelle Parker is a researcher at the National Center for

Research on Teacher Learning, College of Education, Michigan State University.

Richard Smith is a Lecturer in the School of Education, University of Durham.

Les Tickle is a Senior Lecturer in the School of Education, University of East Anglia.

Chris True is a Lecturer in the Division of Education, University of Sheffield.

Diana Wright is Principal Lecturer in Education, Cheltenham and Gloucester College of Higher Education.

Ken Zeichner is Professor in the Wisconsin Center for Education Research, School of Education, University of Wisconsin-Madison.

Introduction

The aim of this book is to encourage, and to contribute to, serious and constructive thinking about initial teacher education in schools. None of the authors contributing to this book suggests that school-based initial teacher education is sufficient on its own; indeed, some argue strongly against this. But the premises of the book as a whole, however, are that moves towards school-based initial teacher education have to be accepted, that there are indeed good arguments for welcoming such moves and, especially, that school-based initial teacher education therefore requires serious, critical, scholarly and constructive attention. For too long, although not at all by accident, the bombastic, ignorant and negative arguments of the extreme right have been allowed to set the agenda. Anti-intellectual, ill-informed and destructive, they do not merit reasoned debate, but only contempt. The serious arguments for school-based initial teacher education are much more constructive ones, based on experience within teacher education, research into the processes of teachers' learning and socialization, and a developing understanding of the multi-faceted nature of experienced teachers' expertise. The time for a more constructive, serious and critical agenda is overdue: there is an urgent need for scholarly debate to contribute to practical decision-making.

The particular focus of this book is on *mentoring*, since it is clear that the quality of school-based initial teacher education will depend crucially on the work of teachers in the role of mentors. What that role is or should be, and what 'mentoring' means, are far less clear. The authors of at least two chapters of this book have found it helpful to go back to the classical roots of the term; certainly, Homer's wise mentor and his relationship with his protégé Telemachus offer an attractive and thought-provoking model for the teacher-educators of tomorrow. More precise 'operational' definitions of mentoring certainly cannot be taken for granted, and discussion which does so is almost certain to lead to confusion.

It is worth emphasizing this point because the term 'mentor' has rapidly become widely used over the last two or three years in discussions of initial teacher education in the United Kingdom. It has been imported to education from other diverse occupational contexts, and generally from the United States, and has carried with it diverse connotations, varying widely in, for example, the formality of the relationships implied, and the extent to which these are seen as managerial, or teaching, or counselling relationships. Jacobi (1991), discussing the various contexts and ways in which the term has been used in recent years, quotes two earlier writers to demonstrate that this is a persistent problem; she writes:

> Although many researchers have attempted to provide concise definitions of *mentoring* or *mentors*, definitional diversity continues to characterize the literature.... A review of these varying definitions supports Merriam's (1983) contention that:
>> 'The phenomenon of mentoring is not clearly conceptualised, leading to confusion as to just what is being measured or offered as an ingredient in success. Mentoring appears to mean one thing to developmental psychologists, another thing to business people, and a third thing to those in academic settings.' (p. 169)
> Wrightsman (1981) also noted the diversity of definitions of mentoring within the psychological research literature and discussed the problems that result from the lack of consensus:
>> 'With respect to communication between researchers ... there is a false sense of consensus, because at a superficial level everyone "knows" what mentoring is. But closer examination indicates wide variation in operational definitions, leading to conclusions that are limited to the use of particular procedures.... The result is that the concept is devalued, because everyone is using it loosely, without precision....' (pp. 3–4)
> ... variation in operational definition continues to plague mentoring research and has almost certainly devalued the concept for application in 'hard' research. (Jacobi, 1991, pp. 506–8)

It is with an awareness that we cannot take for granted either consensus or clarity about the meaning of 'mentoring' that this book has been written. Not only are there important open questions about what can best be done by mentors and by school-based initial teacher education more widely, and about what potential advantages, limitations and dangers there are in different versions of mentoring; there are also complex related questions about the concepts which will be most helpful in differentiating among different versions of mentoring and in teasing out what is most feasible, most effective and most valuable in different circumstances.

One aspect of the openness with which this book has been conceived is the broad view taken of 'school-based initial teacher education'. Sharon Feiman-Nemser and her colleagues explicitly ask whether the mentoring scheme which they studied in California was concerned with *education*; that fundamental question is clearly quite generally important. In deciding about the range of situations with which the book should be concerned, however, the editors have been glad to have contributions grounded in a variety of contexts. Some of these, like the Oxford Internship Scheme and several versions of the Articled Teachers Scheme, are far from fully school-based; others, such as the California mentoring scheme and also the induction programme studied by Les Tickle, are fully school-based but might not conventionally be included within the category of 'initial teacher education'. Such different contexts help to provide different perspectives from which two central questions can be considered: just how school-based should initial teacher education be? And will the conventional distinction between initial teacher education on one hand and induction into teaching on the other continue to be meaningful and useful?

We have grouped the chapters of this book into three sections according to the ways in which we see them as contributing to consideration of current moves towards school-based initial teacher education in the United Kingdom. First, there are three chapters which help to put these moves into historical, cultural and comparative context. Second, there are five chapters which focus primarily on what school-based initial teacher education *should* be concerned with, on what mentors should do and how they should do it. Finally, there are five further chapters based on research into what happens in diverse school-based initial teacher education situations and concerned with what can be learned from these investigations. These three themes provide the framework within which we can best introduce the individual chapters.

Contexts of Mentoring

At the time of writing, the most immediate context within which schools and teacher education institutions have to consider mentoring is that provided by Circular 9/92 of the England and Wales Department for Education which 'introduces new criteria and procedures in England and Wales for the accreditation of courses of initial teacher training (ITT)' (DfE, 1992, p. 1), one of the main principles of which is that 'schools should play a much larger part in ITT as full partners of higher education institutions (HEIs)' (loc. cit). The Circular specifies that student-teachers should spend a minimum of 24 weeks in 36-week full-time secondary PGCE courses 'on the premises of partner schools', and that 'the contribution of partner schools to teacher training should be recognized through transfer of resources from HEIs.' (ibid., p. 4).

These requirements will accelerate to some degree, and may introduce greater uniformity in, trends initiated and sustained by professional teacher educators during the last two decades (Wilkin, 1990). They also reflect a political initiative which probably takes some account of the strident voices of the extreme right to which we earlier referred. Indeed, it would not be difficult to interpret the initiative as having nothing to do with a concern for the quality of teacher education but as being merely one part of a general move to isolate schools from all professional support agencies (including local education authorities, a professional inspectorate and higher education institutions), so as to leave them more completely exposed to market forces. In these circumstances, when the government initiative could be entirely explained *either* as an educationally concerned reflection of informed thinking among professional teacher educators *or* as conformity to an ideology grossly serving the interests only of the wealthy and the unscrupulously self-seeking, we have to be extremely cautious about how we interpret it and react to it.

Such cautious interpretation may be facilitated by taking account of aspects of the wider context within which current moves are situated. This is, we believe, achieved by the three chapters in Part I.

Phil Gardner's elegant and scholarly historical chapter reminds us that, a century ago and less, school-based initial teacher education was being seen not as the solution to our problems but, on the contrary, as the unsatisfactory, outdated old practice which had to be replaced by something better. He shows how, despite concerns expressed by some wiser voices, the opportunity to achieve a balanced partnership between schools and training institutions was missed as the dominance of one was replaced by the dominance of the other; and he warns against the dangers of a similar mistake being made now.

Margaret Wilkin's equally scholarly chapter ambitiously seeks to relate current developments in the thinking and practice of teacher education to the wider *cultural* context in which these are occurring. She is surely right to warn us against thinking in a narrowly insular way, whether in focusing on our own professional arguments within teacher education or in responding defensively to political initiatives. She offers a valuable lead in trying to understand our problems and the ways our practices are changing in wider cultural terms. While assimilating teacher education problems and trends to the much more general ideas by which modernism and postmodernism are characterized could easily result in oversimplification, the analogies provoked by this broader perspective may add new dimensions to our thinking and offer new insights into our problems.

The third chapter which helps to contextualize current British moves towards school-based initial teacher education is Tony d'Arbon's revealing account of developments in Australia. It is especially thought-provoking that in a country which has experienced the development of a dominant ideology similar to Britain's, government initiatives towards school-based teacher education have clearly been informed by sophisticated understandings of professional research and experience. That might encourage us in Britain not to interpret over-pessimistically the implication of our own government's initiatives. This case-study of the planning of an internship scheme in Australia also reminds us of valuable opportunities for cross-national learning at the level of course planning and student-teachers' learning.

Conceptions of Mentoring

We have already emphasized the diverse meanings which the term 'mentoring' can carry. There is no doubt that this semantic diversity reflects a similar diversity of conceptions of what mentors in teacher education should do. At this early stage in the development of largely school-based initial teacher education, such diversity is to be welcomed provided that the different conceptions are made explicit, that their relative merits are vigorously debated, and that the outcomes of these debates have a major influence on policy and practice. It is just such explicitness, debate and subsequent influence to which we seek to contribute in this book.

Of course, policy and practice are not likely to be determined on the basis of intellectual debate alone, however well informed. Different conceptions of mentoring are likely to reflect different interests, and it is those which reflect powerful interests that are likely to prevail unless their limitations and weaknesses are forcefully made public. It is important to recognize that there are peculiar dangers of this kind in the move towards school-based initial teacher education.

To pursue this point briefly, conceptions of mentoring may perhaps be categorized as being primarily concerned with staff management, with counselling, or with education; these broadly different conceptions are likely to reflect the different interests of those who hold them. The interests of schools, at least from the perspective of their senior managements, are likely to be best served by a staff-management emphasis in mentoring, with a concern that beginning teachers should be socialized into the culture and practices of the school, and that they should fit in effectively. The interests of beginning teachers, from their own perspective, are likely to be best served by a counselling emphasis in mentoring, through which they can be helped to cope with their own problems, to clarify their own concerns, and to plan how to pursue these. While some tensions are to be expected between the interests of school managements and those of beginning teachers, it is not difficult to envisage a mentoring role which combines counselling and socialization concerns; indeed it seems inevitable that both of these concerns should have some place in a mentor's work.

It would surely be difficult to argue, however, with the view that mentors' primary concerns should be with the professional education of beginning teachers. But whose interests in the school context are likely to be served by such a primary emphasis in mentoring on professional education? The answer is not obvious, and the consequent threat to the quality of school-based initial teacher education is a serious one.

The chapters in Part II are concerned with conceptions of mentoring in which the primary emphasis is on professional education. Within that broad framework, there is plenty of scope for disagreement, for example on the basis of different understandings of the knowledge, expertise or other qualities required for good schoolteaching, of different views of the learning processes involved in the development of these qualities, or of different beliefs about how experienced teachers can facilitate learning. For instance, the mentor's role is likely to be a minimal one if, like Lawlor (1990), one believes that, beyond a good understanding of the subject to be taught, teaching is the same kind of relatively simple skill as driving a car. On this view, mentors need only provide a few helpful hints and tips and organize the extensive practice required. In contrast, all the chapters here take the view that teaching is a very complex and difficult undertaking, dependent on the development of many kinds of qualities and abilities, and that therefore helping people to learn to teach is also a complex and difficult task. Despite such common ground, however, the five chapters have very diverse concerns.

The chapter by Trisha Maynard and John Furlong properly comes first in the section since its major concern is with the processes of learning to teach and with the complexities and limitations of mentoring which follow from an informed understanding of these learning processes. Complementary to this is the concern of the section's second chapter with what practising schoolteachers are best placed to contribute to initial teacher education and with how they can best make such contributions. On the basis of their experience in the Oxford Internship Scheme, Donald McIntyre and Hazel Hagger explore the versions of mentoring which in their view take fullest advantage of teachers' expertise and the circumstances of their work.

Richard Smith and Geof Alred eloquently warn against overly mechanistic views of mentoring and in their chapter highlight some of the aspects of teaching and of learning to teach which cannot easily or usefully be systematised. Their powerful advocacy of 'the civilizing function' of mentoring, of the importance of the mentor 'standing for' a conception of teaching and of education, of 'knowledge that extends beyond the instrumental', of mentors passing on 'a sense that education, and good teaching, are something of a mystery' and 'worthy of contemplation', and of the importance of the 'mentor's self-knowledge', provides a persuasive and attractive vision of what good mentors might be able to offer and of what could be learned from them.

In quite striking contrast to Smith and Alred's emphatic rejection of systems, Richard Dunne and Gareth Harvard describe a very fully elaborated system of mentoring, which they view as a central element in a teacher education course planned in the light of interacting methodological, pedagogical and psychological models. For them, mentoring is provided only in part by practising schoolteachers, and also in part by university-based supervisors. Their conception of mentoring is distinctive also in the careful precision both of its operationalization and of the rationale which they offer for it.

David Frost, in the final chapter in Part II, picks up and develops one of Smith and Alred's themes, that of the need for mentoring in schools to be concerned with knowledge that goes beyond the merely instrumental. His argument is an important one. While, as he acknowledges, university seminars provide the established context for the exploration of educational value issues, and considerable success can be achieved in academic contexts in leading student-teachers to articulate and examine their own previously taken-for-granted values, it is the values embedded in their classroom practices which most need critical examination. For that, the help of mentors is crucial.

Realities of Mentoring

However reasonable or laudable our ideas for mentoring may be, it is what happens when mentors are at work that matters. As yet we have very little basis for knowing what it is possible for mentors to do, what objective and subjective conditions are necessary to make different things possible or likely, or what effects mentors' activities have, or are likely to have, on beginning teachers' learning. We need to build up a knowledge base from which an understanding of the realities and possibilities of mentoring can be gradually developed.

There are, as always, two main kinds of questions: theory-testing questions and theory-generating questions. Theory-testing questions will mostly be asking whether or not the preconceptions and hopes built into our planned programmes and practices have been justified; better yet, if our evaluations have been well planned, *which* of these preconceptions and hopes have at least not been falsified? Where we are fortunate, which will usually mean having the help of critical friends, these questions will extend beyond asking about what happens, and even beyond asking about the consequences of what happens, and will include questions about the worth of what happens and of what was meant to happen.

Theory-generating questions will be mostly those seeking to make sense of what mentors and their charges do, and why, and with what consequences. The importance of these questions relates to the need suggested earlier to find the concepts which will be most useful for thinking about mentoring activities and programmes.

The five chapters which make up Part III – the final section – make a substantial contribution to the building up of a knowledge base about mentoring. We are delighted to have as the first of these the chapter by Sharon Feiman-Nemser, Michelle B. Parker and Ken Zeichner, the only transatlantic contribution to the book. Their study of a Californian mentoring programme includes an examination of what by British standards is a rather thorough training programme for mentors and also case studies of several mentors at work. Their analysis leads them to ask the fundamental question: is this an *educational* programme for beginning teachers?

The second of these largely empirical papers, by Bob Elliott and James Calderhead, is concerned with the activities of mentors in the context of an Articled Teachers programme. Against the background of a succinct review of research-based insights into beginning teachers' learning, they explored mentors' understandings of their roles, of what they were trying to achieve, and of the ways in which their activities were likely to foster useful learning. Perhaps the most striking feature of their findings is the diversity of the understandings they reveal as informing mentors' practices.

The third chapter is by Les Tickle, who explores the perspectives of teachers in their first year of employment on the opportunities for learning which a mentoring system offers them. He shows clearly the daunting multiplicity of conditions which mentors have to fulfil in order to provide learning opportunities which are experienced as valuable by beginning teachers, opportunities which are appropriately offered, appropriate in substance and appropriate in their timing.

The chapter by Peter Lucas and Chris True is different from the others in that the two authors collaborated to investigate their learning from each other in a mentoring relationship. They do not pretend to have discovered any simple truths in this way. On the contrary, their claim is to have reached new understandings of the dangers of over-simplifying, for example by being over-ready to regard as illegitimate student-teachers' ways of apparently 'explaining-away' their own weaknesses.

Finally, the chapter by Pie Corbett and Diana Wright is written from their perspective as people developing and running an initial teacher education programme heavily dependent on mentoring. We decided that this should be the chapter to finish the book because it is about practitioners seeking to develop their practice for the future through systematically investigating their present practice. The title indicates their concern with 'the selection and training of mentors', but they report that 'the term "training" soon became one that we questioned.' That seems to us such an important insight that our own last word will focus on it.

The Way Forward

The overall picture which the empirical studies reported here provide of school-based initial teacher education is one of complex needs and of practice which falls very far short of meeting them. That should not, however, be a cause for alarm or despondency. It should simply remind us that we have yet to learn what is possible, how it can best be done, and under what kinds of circumstances. More particularly, mentors in schools do not know how to do the job because it is not only a demanding one but also quite different from anything they have done before, while people based in universities do not know how to do the job because it is quite different from anything they have done or studied. There are no experts on how to do the job of mentoring in initial teacher education.

Thus mentors urgently need to learn how to do the job: there is nobody qualified to train them. In these circumstances, there is every danger of it seeming that one person's preferences are as good as another's and that trial-and-error learning is the appropriate way forward: the postmodernist scenario painted by Margaret Wilkin in Chapter 2 would be realized and the idiosyncratic differences found by Bob Elliott and James Calderhead would become the norm. We hope, however, that the chapters in Part II have demonstrated that there are many good reasons – relating for example to effective learning, to making the most of what experienced practising teachers have to offer, and to educational values – for believing that one person's initial ideas about mentoring are *not* as good as another's, and that we can learn in much more coherent and productive ways than by trial and error.

In the development of skilled educational mentoring, mentors themselves will have to play the central roles. There is, however, a great deal to be done by mentors, and by others in supporting roles, in order to theorize better about what is possible and how, to try new ideas out, to investigate, and to reflect on what happens. The opportunities to develop coherently theorized practical approaches to initial teacher education, guided by research and reflection on experience, have never been greater.

Donald McIntyre
Hazel Hagger
Margaret Wilkin

REFERENCES

Department for Education (1992) *Initial Teacher Training (Secondary Phase)* (Circular 9/92) London: DFE.

Jacobi, M (1991) 'Mentoring and undergraduate academic success: a literature review', *Rev. Educ. Research*, **61**, 4, 505–32.

Lawlor, S (1990) *Teachers Mistaught*, London: Centre for Policy Studies

Merriam, S (1983) 'Mentors and protégés: a critical review of the literature', *Adult Education Quarterly*, **33**, 161–73.

Wilkin, M (1990) 'The development of partnership in the United Kingdom', in M. Borth, J. Furlong and M. Wilkin (eds) *Partnership in Initial Teacher Training*, London: Cassell.

Wrightsman, LS (1981) 'Research methodologies for assessing mentoring', presented at the Annual Conference of the American Psychological Association, Los Angeles (ERIC Document Reproduction Service No. ED 209 339).

Part 1
Contexts of Mentoring

1 The Early History of School-based Teacher Training

Phil Gardner

> The part of the field which we are to examine has long been a battleground for the expert, and many questions call for discussion. What, for example, should be the purpose of professional training? – its character and duration? Where should it be given, and by whom?... At what age should it commence? – and is a system of apprenticeship desirable? (Lance Jones *The Training of Teachers in England and Wales*, 1923)

The principle of systematic initial training for teachers was a new one in the early nineteenth century. It was an idea whose currency widened with the inception of mass elementary schooling and which was not thereafter seriously challenged.[1] The form and content, and more fundamentally, the purpose of such training have, however, been extensively debated from the early blueprints of Lancaster, Bell, Stow, Kay-Shuttleworth and Coleridge through to the more familiar models of our own day.

These debates might be interpreted in two ways. On the one hand, there is the perspective of the contemporary educationist, concerned principally with the application and development of training policy. From this point of view, the business of teacher training constitutes a search for the most effective arrangements for the preparation of classroom teachers. To the extent that this perspective has a dimension of change, it is of periodic reform attended by implicit assumptions that the search has been, or is about to be, more or less successfully resolved.[2] Indeed, the notion of progress must be a central one in any account of the development of the teacher training process. Yet beneath the changing policies for professional preparation for the classroom, there lie the deep continuities of classroom life itself. Any reading of the classroom logs of today's trainee teachers alongside the recollections of, say, Phillip Ballard or FH Spencer or Abel Jones, from the turn of the century demonstrates this in a particularly vivid way.[3] Even more telling are the columns of the teachers' press from the late nineteenth century onwards. No modern teacher could fail to browse through these sources, with their endless, familiar stories of stress, fatigue, injustice and conflict over recurring issues, without feeling that he or she is treading in professional footsteps already worn deep by earlier generations.[4] Teacher training itself forms part of this continuing repertoire, with reforms characteristically consisting of the rearrangement or redistribution of a number of key elements which have, to one degree or another, been present from the earliest days of teacher training. Of these, perhaps the most important has been the relation between the place of training which is based in the classroom, and that which is based in the training institution. History records how the balance between the two sites has shifted over the last century and a half, with each shift leaving an image in professional and political consciousness which could be raised in support of further change in one direction or another. Thus for example, the attacks on institutional training as variously remote, limited or overly-theoretical which, in differing contexts, were raised in the 1890s, in the 1960s and in the early 1990s; and, on the other hand, the dangers of a school-based apprenticeship model – the spectre of the pupil-teacher– adverted to by many in the 1880s, the 1920s, by some in the 1970s, and by others today.[5]

In broad terms, it might be said that until the final decade of the nineteenth century, training based within the school enjoyed an effective practical hegemony. By the end of the 1920s however, a new college-based primacy was firmly in place. The intervening years, as we shall see, have a particular significance as a period of tension and transition between the sites of school and training institution which in some respects mirrors that of our own age.

The history of the teaching profession and its concerns – as opposed to the history of education itself – has, to date, been but poorly explored. It offers us a rich resource of collective experience which needs to be attended to more respectfully and exploited more thoughtfully. That is why present-oriented perspectives on the significance of training debates in the past cannot stand alone. They have to be informed by a second understanding; that of the historian. The historical perspective has no interest in rummaging through the past for idealized or timeless policy models. Instead, it seeks to understand changes and continuities in teacher training contingently, as expressions of particular moments in time. Thus, for example, whilst it may be useful to conceptualize school-based 'apprenticeship' as one broad model of training, it is considerably less helpful to invoke a 'return to the pupil teacher system'. The characteristics of that essentially nineteenth century system belong to a particular time, which has passed.[6] Moreover, the historical approach understands that, whatever the apparent familiarity of this or that aspect of training in the past, the meanings ascribed to it, and to training as a totality, change over time. Such changes cannot be understood simply as responses to purely educational pressures. Reform of teacher training needs also to be set within the context of much broader social, political and religious debates over the direction and purpose of educational change.

In seeking to address these wider problems, policy formulators have always been faced with a simple but intractable truth. The classroom, recognized as the critical productive site of all educational enterprise was – and remains – beyond the continuous control of church or state. Only the teachers were – and are – continuously there. For the interest of church and increasingly of state, an enduring problem, therefore, has been to ensure that the teachers operated as effective agents of a higher authority. This was a central purpose behind the state's entry into the sponsorship and certification of teacher training in 1846. From that moment, effective forms of training, together with regular inspection by the recently-formed HMI, were envisaged not simply as mechanisms to improve the quality of schooling, but also to regulate and direct the daily activity of the teacher in the classroom. Since 1846, this is a capacity which the state has utilized in varying degrees according to perceived need and which it has never relinquished.

State-sponsored training, however, had a reverse side. It did not only promise to lever up the quality and effectiveness of schooling and to offer closer control over the teachers. Paradoxically, it also carried the potential to exercise an independent effect upon those who were trained. It conveyed new knowledge and skills and, perhaps more important, a shared sense of professional identity. From very early on, it was clear that the concerns of the newly-trained profession were unlikely to remain those simply of humble and trusty servants of the classroom. The experience of being trained might do something more than simply to inculcate approved behaviour. In particular, training exposed the ambivalent class position of the elementary teacher.[7] Over time, it released new collective concerns for higher social status, for better material reward, for enhanced professional autonomy and for the satisfaction of personal ambition. In short, the trained teachers began to produce their own tunes to march to. This was a danger of which Kay-Shuttleworth, the architect of the pupil-teacher system, was aware. The safeguard he advocated was the encouragement of humility and self-sacrifice in the form of a sub-professional missionary ideology for teachers.[8] This was to be built into the structure of the training process through the new teacher training colleges founded, mainly from the 1840s, under the auspices chiefly of the established church and organized as semi-monastic total institutions. Such closely organized insitutional training was to be the guarantor not of particular standards of personal competence and classroom practice, but of moral commitment. Official support for institutional training – though there were never sufficient college places – was unwavering. The contrast with the scepticism for institutional training of the 1990s is instructive. Today, official perceptions of institution-based training have long since ceased to be of professional quietism, and the prospect of training delivered in schools and by teachers is seen no more as educationally or socially damaging.

In the short term, the reasons for these changes can be seen to have been accelerated by the implications of the contractual and curricular constraints placed upon the profession at work in the second half of the 1980s, but there is a much longer perspective within which change needs to be set.

At the start of the nineteenth century, any form of specific preparation for teaching was virtually unknown. Schools were either controlled by the churches or were private in character and could therefore be established by any individual. In the latter case, qualifications to teach depended not on formal certification but on the *de facto* recognition of proficiency accorded by paying customers. In essence, this depended upon the demonstration by the teacher of appropriate teaching skills. These consisted in a particular level of academic knowledge – gained from an elementary schooling in the case of teachers of 'inferior' private schools and from a university education in the case of most middle- and upper-class private schools – and the ability to manage effectively a classroom to ensure the transmission of this knowledge. This latter quality was acquired, or not, by trial and error. Some succeeded, others did not.

The first attempts to produce trained teachers did not concern themselves with the middle- and upper-class echelons; these would not figure substantially until well into the twentieth century. The most pressing early concerns for formalized training were seen to attach to those who, in the words of Derwent Coleridge, were to become 'the teachers of the people'.[9]

Initially, such training was typically based not in purpose-built colleges, but in schools. These were the schools organized from the earliest years of the nineteenth century upon the innovatory and voguish monitorial principles associated with Lancaster and Bell. The form of such training was normally very short, often lasting no longer than a month or two. The majority of the adult trainees were already serving teachers who were sent to be trained in the principles of the system. This is a centrally important point, the residual significance of which was to mark the course of training for the rest of the century and beyond. Trainees came to the monitorial schools not to learn to teach in any reflective, still less theoretical, sense. They came instead to learn a mechanical system and to pick up tips for its practical implementation; to internalize a closely prescribed form of knowledge transmission and schoolroom organization. In the oft-quoted words of Bell,

> It is by attending the school, seeing what is going on there, and taking a share in the office of tuition, that teachers are to be formed, and not by lectures and abstract instruction.[10]

So, alongside the ranks of pupils who were learning through the system, sat the trainees observing its operation and learning to replicate it. This notion of effective teaching as the replication of set principles was to be a very powerful one, finding many echoes, for example, in the professional memories of the last generation of pupil teachers, trained in the first three decades of the twentieth century.[11] In these memories, the description 'a good teacher' is habitually used in a rather precise sense, to denote a constellation of fixed attributes and shared meanings in a way which would make little sense to practitioners at this end of the century.

The central problem for this early form of monitorial school-based training lay in the paucity and generally poor quality of trainees. Those who were prepared to undergo training, however brief, as mature students were always going to be few. In 1838, for example, JC Wigram, the Secretary of the Anglican National Society calculated that at the society's 46 'training schools', other than its larger metropolitan central schools at Baldwin's Gardens, there were not more than 100 trainees in attendance at any one time.[12] Where could a more constant supply of recruits be found? Despite the ambivalent social status later attached to it, elementary school teaching was perceived to be an occupation which was fundamentally appropriate to those of working-class origin. But how could bright working-class children, leaving school at the very latest before the onset of their 'teens, be attracted to a profession which could not offer training or employment until they had reached early adulthood? How, in other words, could clever working-class children – prospective teachers of the future – be identified, corralled and preserved from other more immediately lucrative occupations whilst they waited to attain the age of 18?

The solution, of course, came with the introduction of Kay-Shuttleworth's pupil-teacher scheme, announced in the Committee of Council on Education's Minutes of 1846.[13] Their Lordships were aware of

> the very early age at which the children acting as assistants to schoolmasters are withdrawn from school to manual labour and the advantages which would arise if such scholars...were apprenticed to skilful masters, to be instructed and trained, so as to be prepared to complete their education in a normal school.[14]

Here was a system which was to be the backbone of teacher supply and training for the rest of the century.[15] The system was in part borrowed from schemes already operating on the Continent, and in part a development of the role of the monitorial system's monitors – the squads of juvenile helpers who, as agents of the solitary teacher, supervised a mechanical or catechetical process of learning.

It is very important to recognize that, as the 1846 Minutes make clear, the pupil-teacher system was not intended to comprise in itself a complete system of professional preparation. It was above all a supply mechanism, designed to bridge the gap between the age of 13, when a pupil-teacher signed his or her indentures, and the age of 18, when he or she was old enough to enter a training college. The desirability of a professional college-based training for teachers was made clear from the outset:

> The apprenticeship of a pupil-teacher has never been contemplated as sufficient in point of preparation for the office of schoolmaster or schoolmistress. The Minutes of 1846 explicitly advert to the further training of apprentices in a normal school.[16]

The purposes of the school-based, pupil-teacher phase and the subsequent college-based phase were seen as fundamentally distinct, with the first concentrating on mechanical classroom skills and the second on personal education and moral reformation. If there were no element of apprenticeship, then however learned he or she might be, a teacher could never fare so well as former pupil-teachers who,

> reared in the atmosphere of schools are exceedingly preferable to the best instructed men who are not familiarized, by daily habitude, with the minutest details of school management.[17]

Conversely, the dangers of training which was wholly school-based, which was not rounded off by the elevating and civilizing experience of college, were recognized. The dangers were two-fold, though both related to the ultimate problem of professional control over the teaching force. In the first place, a programme of training located only in the schools would be likely to lead to a circumscribed, practice-oriented professional culture. The danger here was not the narrowness *per se* of this culture, but that it would be formed and would develop solely under the control of the teachers themselves.

Ultimately such a culture, confident in its commanding craft expertise in the classroom, might seek to extend its professional independence. To a degree, this turned out to be the case, most notably of course through the agency of the National Union of Elementary Teachers, formed in 1870, and through the long subsequent campaigns for professional autonomy through a registration council, for the opening of the inspectorate to experienced teachers and for higher professional status.[18]

In the second place, college training was desirable for the symbolic distance it established between the teachers and the working-class parents and pupils who would be their clients. In traditional forms of working-class schooling, teachers – themselves members of the working class – shared a cultural closeness with their users and were highly susceptible to their demands.[19] For policy-makers who sought large-scale social reformation through education, this kind of closeness between teacher and client needed to be weakened. While there was no question that teachers would continue to be drawn primarily from the working class, policy-makers saw some utility in actively encouraging the ambivalent social status of the schoolteachers – hovering between the class of their origin and the class of their aspiration – which was to be such a central strand in the social history of the profession. This is very clearly expressed in the words of an 1853 circular to HMI on the subject of pupil-teachers:

> These young persons are drawn for the most part from very humble homes; they have learnt the routine of teaching, and a few elementary subjects, in the day schools where they have first served their apprenticeship; but the first, and very often the last, point in their career at which they are brought into intimate and domestic contact with persons of superior cultivation, and are obliged to conform to a higher standard of manners and habits, is in the normal college.[20]

It is not surprising that the college-trained elementary teacher, stuffed with useless facts and full of airs and graces, was often a figure of some contempt not just to working-class clients but also to middle-class secondary teachers who inhabited a different professional world.[21] In essence, the two phases of the elementary teacher's training, first as a pupil-teacher in school and then as a student in college, were designed to answer very particular goals. From the perspective of the trainee the two experiences were effectively separate, with no systematic attempt during the standard two years of college training to develop the preceding four or five years of school-based work.

During the pupil-teacher phase, the apprentice embarked upon a course in which continuing personal education, delivered by the head-teacher of the school, was combined with classroom observation and practical experience of teaching. At the close of each year of the apprenticeship, progress was monitored by examination by a visiting HMI. The history of education is not, however, devoid of innovations which have made a greater show as rhetoric than reality, and the pupil-teacher scheme was no exception to this.[22] In many cases, the trainee's education was neglected and he or she effectively became a full-time, if temporary, addition to the staff of a school. Pupil-teachers were often pitched in at the deep end, finding themselves at the age of 13 or 14 as teachers of children who, a year or two earlier, had been their playmates. It was a difficult baptism, but a surprising number of trainees, under the eye of their mentors (often several classes would be operating in the same curtain-divided schoolroom) and with their practical model in mind and on show, seem to have picked up the mechanical skills of classroom discipline and rote learning without much difficulty. One of the very few to record this experience was FH Spencer, later to become Chief Inspector with the LCC, who in 1886 embarked on his career as a pupil-teacher in Swindon:

> A pupil teacher was precisely what the name implies, The pupil teacher was the pupil of the headmaster in things academic, and he was a teacher. No doubt the theory was that he was trained to teach. In fact, he taught as best as he could, his practice being based on what he remembered of how he had been taught, and on those tricks of the trade picked up from those among whom he worked. In these respects at fourteen he was like the normal public-school master of twenty three. In the circumstances of those times the system was not without its advantages. You sank or swam. Either you could 'hold' a class of thirty, fifty or sixty boys or you could not....So far as the academic side was concerned, my pupilage was largely a fraud.[23]

At the conclusion of his or her apprenticeship, the pupil-teacher might, if results in final examinations were good enough, go on to take one of the limited number of places available at a training college and, thence, the teacher's certificate. For those who did not, the process of training was over, and they might seek permanent employment as uncertificated assistants at lower rates of pay than their certificated colleagues.[24] Within the limitations of their narrow training and the modest expectations of elementary scholarship, it is clear that many uncertificated teachers were extremely proficient classroom practitioners. Yet the very narrowness of their craft skills was, by the close of the nineteenth century, coming to be regarded – by many within the profession as well as without – as a barrier to educational advance.

Spencer, who went on to take his certificate at Borough Road College, was clear about what was lacking from his school-based training:

> ...teaching hard five-and-a-quarter hours every day, and subconsciously absorbing the craftsmanship of the trade, I was without proper intellectual discipline or any scholarly criteria, or any standard of comparison except with two fellow pupil-teachers of the same vintage as myself...but I soon realised by occasional intercourse with others outside my elementary school that there were lamentable deficiencies about my kind and me.[25]

What, above all else, bright working-class youngsters like Spencer lacked was access to a form of personal education in advance of the merely elementary. All existing forms of secondary education, other than that which could be provided in a teacher training college, were closed to them. As a result, the normal sequence of professional preparation which we have come to expect in an age of wider educational opportunity had, in effect, to be undertaken in reverse. Practical, school-based work had to come first and personal education second, if at all. By the time that pupil-teachers arrived in college, they were experienced practitioners of classroom craft and recognized as such. The accent in their school-based training, as another former pupil-teacher, PB Ballard, pointed out, had been on the pupil-teacher as teacher rather than pupil.[26] The college did not expect much to develop the pedagogical aspect of their skills. The few lectures which Spencer received at Borough Road in school management and psychology were supplemented only by the occasional criticism lesson and no more than six weeks' schools practice over two years. The rest of the time was devoted to academic subjects other than education.[27]

The dramatic expansionary effects of the 1870 Act put increasing pressure on both the quantity and the quality of the supply of trained teachers. By the turn of the century, a strong current for reform was running. The Minority Report of the Cross Commission of 1888 and the Report of the 1898 Departmental Committee on the Pupil Teacher System signal the direction of the current.[28] It was moving away from the pupil-teacher and towards a new emphasis – more familiar to today's teacher-trainers – on a reformulated college-based

29

training, following on from a full personal education in a secondary school. By the early 1920s the change was substantially in place and in 1923 Lance Jones could write of '...the convenient and customary division between preliminary education to the age of seventeen or eighteen and the later stages of preparation...'.[29]

If, on the surface, the direction of this current for change is not difficult to identify, the submerged eddies at its margins are harder to read. A number of powerful factors were at work in this complex moment of change. In the first place, there were the general pressures for improvements in opportunity within the elementary system itself, which were to lead by increments along a tortuous route through the campaign for higher grade schools, through limited public scholarships from the elementary sector to the secondary, and ultimately to the formal linkage of the two systems in 1944. Within this growing movement for 'secondary education for all', the debate about the preparation of teachers was at the forefront. The goal was to postpone or even to eliminate the preliminary school-based training of prospective teachers in favour of a fuller secondary education. Initially, in the 1880s and 1890s, such efforts were focused on attendance at the pupil-teacher centres being developed in the larger urban areas.[30] Here, traditional school-based apprenticeship was combined with academic study at the secondary level. With a series of Board of Education regulations in the first decade of the twentieth century, however, the latter element of the work of the centres was annexed by the grammar schools and the former postponed.[31] Local secondary scholarships for bright elementary pupils were made available to those who pledged themselves to a subsequent teaching career. These provided a new, academic bridge to span the gulf between elementary school and college. The old, practical bridge – the pupil-teacher scheme – which Kay-Shuttleworth had constructed to cross the same gulf, fell into disuse. By the 1920s, only a handful of elementary pupils from isolated rural areas were using it.[32]

As the pupil-teacher system began to totter, so the purpose of the training colleges had to change. In some degree, the vestiges of the missionary function lingered as, in some places, perhaps they still do. But no longer did the colleges need to act as the belated providers of the secondary education their students should have had. So what would the new function be? With less time now needed for academic education, there would be scope for the introduction of some elements of education theory. This was certainly the case with the new non-residential day training colleges, associated with the universities and university colleges, which began to appear in the 1890s. The day training colleges called a new, more intellectually challenging tune, in which the older colleges strove to join.[33] The higher education association of the new colleges, and the scope that they offered to able students to study for a degree as well as for the teacher's certificate, brought a theoretical aspect to professional preparation which had been lacking in the old system. Henceforth there was to be '...less emphasis on details of "school method" and more attention to the underlying educational principles'.[34]

Herbert Ward, the Board of Education's chief inspector for the training of teachers in the early 1920s, summarized the viewpoint of the university training departments like this:

> ...teachers should be trained to do their work, not following blind tradition, or even immersed in the particulars of technique, but with some knowledge of the philosophical bases of teaching and of education...and if students do not get it during their year of training it is hard to come by in later years. We will try to be as practical as we can, and we are sincerely anxious to give our students adequate experience in actual teaching. But we cannot be satisfied to remain on the level of technique.[35]

Without the impetus of the new day training institutions, the old residential college was, by comparison,

> ...never likely to produce an organised body of educational theory....The training college existed to train, that was its business and that is what it claimed to do. In the broader aspects of education it was uninterested. The day training college, also, set out simply to train, but it proceeded to establish the systematic study of education as appropriate work for a university....[36]

This move away from practical experience was marked, but significantly, the justification could still be couched in terms of enhanced classroom effectiveness:

> Any study leading to the development of the student, however intensive or intellectual that study may be, is a direct and definite contribution to the training of the child, and therefore has a 'professional' value.[37]

Yet there was another responsiblity for the colleges in the post pupil-teacher era. The whole matter of school-based practical experience now fell to the college. For the first time, substantial numbers of students – academically better qualified than ever before – were coming forward with no prior experience of practical teaching. Indeed, some of them had never seen the inside of an elementary school at all, even as pupils.

Under the pupil-teacher system, the culture of teaching had been located in the hands of the teachers themselves. While college principals and HMI might have been respected as influential figures, they were seen as representatives of a different educational culture, with little real understanding of classroom life. Since 1846, a traditional occupational culture had developed, based on clever working-class children for whose talents there were few other career opportunities and who, as pupils and then as apprentices, had developed an unrivalled if narrowly conceived craft expertise. With the reformation of the pattern of teacher training, this expertise was increasingly marginalized and ultimately atrophied with only the occasional sullen outburst in the teachers' press from members of what was commonly dubbed the 'Old Guard' against the annexation of their profession by the effete, unblooded new generations of grammar school pupils:

> Criticism emanates from those who have been familiar with the older forms of the Pupil Teacher system and their products. Remembering the facility which the Pupil Teacher acquired in the art of class-management, they deprecate a long separation of the young teacher from the Elementary School, and the deferring of all practical work....[38]

Older teachers clung to the notion of teaching as a constellation of definable and coherent craft skills which could only be learned through practical engagement in the classroom:

> Much adverse criticism is directed against the university-trained elementary school teacher, particularly by the older teachers in the schools who themselves went through the pupil teacher and training college treadmill. It has to be admitted that, so far as the actual technique of elementary teaching is concerned, the university sends out teachers less well qualified than the training colleges. But it is to be hoped that their longer academic training, and their broader and more philosophic treatment of educational principles and method, will render them capable of working out their own methods, which, because individual, should be more fruitful and significant than 'cut-and-dried' methods acquired during training.[39]

The extent of the decline of teacher involvement in training and the rapidity of its disappearance from the professional culture was signalled by Herbert Ward in 1928:

> I have often wondered why teachers, as a body, in elementary and secondary schools alike, do not demand a larger share in training. The trained teachers are to join their staffs...yet, in effect, they are content to entrust the training to persons who, however skilled, are at the time outside the schools.[40]

Whatever, in future, were to be the benefits of new forms of teacher education and training, any large element of control by practising teachers was not to be among them. This was a particularly acute moment of change and also of loss. More than simply the form of teacher training was changing; so was the traditional source of recruitment. For decades, the pupil-teacher system had ensured that teachers were recruited from young women and men predominatly from the working class. The new route, based on a liberal secondary education followed by college, opened the profession to more recruits from the lower middle class and effectively closed it to some within its traditional constituency, for whom the postponement of earnings often could not be borne. Here was a channel through which the social composition of the teaching force might be levered up. With the expansion of secondary schooling which followed the 1902 Act, hopes could be pinned on tapping into a new, ostensibly superior source of recruitment. As a consequence, the original reformative emphasis of college training could be relaxed, particularly as the professional domination of school-based training by the 'Old Guard' was now effectively bypassed. At the same time, the inception of the day training colleges provided a mechanism to pull teacher training into the orbit of higher education and away from its earlier, humbler locus within the schools themselves.[41]

The turn away from the old pupil-teacher tradition and the embracing by teacher training institutions of approaches enthused by the less mechanical, more child-centred perspectives of influential writers such as Edmund Holmes seemed to symbolize a devaluation of the recognized form of practical teaching skills.[42] Moreover, no routes were found to link such skills with the growing emphasis on theory in the colleges, and certainly no space for practitioners to build their own theory from their personal practice. The rejection of the pupil-teacher system for its manifest practical faults seemed also to imply a rejection of the principle of school-based experience which had been at its heart. This produced a moment in which some of the central concerns of the training college and those of the school appeared to drift apart. Movement of this kind inevitably carried within it the germs of the perception, later to develop, of the abstract world of 'theory' set against the 'real' world of the classroom. The danger was recognized from the outset by Herbert Ward: 'the study of education as an organic theory and the technical preparation for the teaching of classes do not run well together'.[43]

Ward's solution was the unification of theory with practice through institutional partnership: 'The schools should be taken into partnership even more closely than they are at present and something like a real apprenticeship...restored'.[44]

In the context of the current of change in the 1920s, Ward was realistic – and prophetic – about the likelihood of reform on these lines being implemented:

> The plea for closer association of schools with university training departments and with other training colleges will doubtless be accepted in principle. The practical application of the principle offers endless difficulties. But...if there is no advance, there is a danger lest training should become stereotyped, and the balance between theory and practice, philosophy and technique should weigh too heavily on the side of theory.[45]

The 1907 student-teacher scheme, a vestigial remnant of the old pupil-teacher system, might, in different circumstances, have offered a route towards a form of partnership. But the scheme replicated the same separation between work in the school and work in the training institution which had dogged the pupil-teacher system. The new scheme was unpopular with most teacher-trainers and with officials at the Board of Education and it withered as the 1920s drew to a close.[46]

In this climate, the decline and disappearance of practical experience as a preliminary to college training could be seen as involving no great loss. There was no sense of partnership and few in the colleges who sought it. This was a perception accentuated by a failure to expand effectively the place of practical school experience within programmes of institutional training. In this respect, the colleges continued to follow broadly the pattern they had always done, with teaching practices amounting to no more than 6–12 weeks of the two-year course. Amidst all the changing teacher training regulations of the early years of the twentieth century, the minimum teaching practice period of a total of six weeks remained unchanged. However well prepared in other respects, new generations of young teachers were now emerging from the colleges with but a tiny fraction of the practical experience of earlier cohorts.

In the critical decades of change at the close of the nineteenth century and the opening of the twentieth, the reforming pendulum was beginning its long swing from school to training institution. As it did so, it swept past the moment of partnership. A century later, with the pendulum moving in the other direction, it would be well to bear this in mind.[47]

NOTES

1. RW Rich (1972, lst ed. 1933) *The Training of Teachers in England and Wales during the Nineteenth Century* (Cedric Chivers), LGE Jones (1923) *The Training of Teachers in England and Wales* (Humphrey Milford), HC Dent (1975) *The Training of Teachers in England and Wales* (Hodder and Stoughton), R Aldrich

'The evolution of teacher education' in NJ Graves (ed.) (1990) *Initial Teacher Education. Policies and Progress* (Kogan Page) pp.12–24.

2. JL Dobson 'The training colleges and their sucessors 1920 – 70' in TG Cook (ed.)(1973) *Education and the Professions* (Methuen), p.49.

3. PB Ballard (1937) *Things I Cannot Forget* (University of London Press), A Jones (1940) *From an Inspector's Bag* (Abbrevia); (1943) *I was Privileged* (Abbrevia), FH Spencer (1938) *An Inspector's Testament* (English Universities Press).

4. M Lawn (1987) *Servants of the State* (Falmer Press), p. ix.

5. In the 1972 preface to his standard work, Rich observed in the light of the recently published James Report that 'Educational circles tend to "come full circle". Has the old pupil teacher system come to life in the second year of cycle two?', Rich, op. cit., p.xv.

6. Rich, op. cit., p.135, Spencer, op. cit., p.v.

7. A Tropp (1957) *The School Teachers* (Heinemann), pp. 33 – 4, G Grace (1978) *Teachers, Ideology and Control* (Routledge and Kegan Paul), ch.1, B Bergen 'Only a schoolmaster: gender, class and the effort to professionalize elementary teaching in England 1870 – 1910', in J Ozga (ed.)(1988) *Approaches to the Labour Process of Teaching*, (Open University Press) pp.39–60.

8. Rich, op. cit., pp.65–9.

9. D Coleridge (1862) *The Teachers of the People; a Tract for the Times.*

10. Quoted, for example, in Rich, op. cit., p.4, Dent, op. cit., p.7. See also the Rev RJ Bryce in evidence before the 1834 Select Committee on Education: 'It appears to me that the education of these schoolmasters is a thing of the same kind as if medical students, instead of studying general scientific principles to guide their medical practice, were simply to follow a physician or surgeon through the wards of an hospital and look at him while he felt the pulse and examined the symptoms of the patient, and then take notice what sort of prescription he afterwards wrote', Rich, op. cit., p.45.

11. Preliminary finding from my current research designed to construct an oral history of school teachers from the first half of the twentieth century. Scheduled for publication by Methuen in 1993.

12. PP 1837–8 VII. *Report from the Select Committee on the Education of the Poorer Classes in England and Wales*, p.255.

13. The Committee of Council on Education was established in 1839 to become the first national executive authority for elementary education.

14. *Minutes of the Committee of Council on Education,* 1846, p.2. General Minute, August 1846. The Continental usage of 'normal school' to mean a training college did not pass into common parlance.

15. For Matthew Arnold's effusive endorsement of the system, see Rich, op. cit., pp.137–9.

16. *Minutes of CCE,* 1852–3, p.22. Circular Letter no. 2.

17. *Minutes of CCE,* 1839–40, p 33. Minute of 2 February 1840.

18. Tropp, op. cit., chs. 8 and 9, G Baron (1954) 'The Teachers' registration movement', *British Journal of Educational Studies*, 2, pp.133–44, N and J Parry, 'The teachers and professionalism. The failure of an occupational strategy', in M Flude and J Ahier (1974) *Educability, Schools and Ideology* (Croom Helm), pp.160–85, PHJH Gosden (1972) *The Evolution of a Profession* (Blackwell), ch.11, P Gordon and D Lawton (1987) *Her Majesty's Inspectorate of Schools* (Routledge).

19. TW Laqueur 'Working class demand and the growth of English elementary education 1750–1850', in L Stone (ed.) (1976) *Schooling and Society,* Baltimore: Johns Hopkins University Press, pp.192–205.

20. *Minutes of CCE,* 1853–4, p.28. Circular, November 1853.

21. For example, R Gurner (1937) *I Chose Teaching*, p.58, also Rich, op. cit., p.232, Tropp, op. cit., pp.169–70.

22. Spencer, op. cit., ch.4, Ballard, op.cit., pp.23–8.
23. Spencer, op. cit., pp.75–6.
24. From its inception until 1926, the certificate examination was open, under certain conditions, to serving teachers. For statistical details of the composition of the teaching force at the turn of the century, see Lawn, op. cit., p.17.
25. Spencer, op. cit., p.86.
26. Ballard, op. cit., p.80.
27. Spencer, op. cit., p.141. Also Joint Standing Committee of the Training College Association and Council of Principals (1939) *Memorandum on the Training of Teachers*, p.6.
28. Gosden, op. cit., pp.196–7.
29. Jones, op. cit., p.37.
30. GA Christian (1922) *English Education from Within* (Wallace Gandy).
31. Jones, op. cit., p.27.
32. Gosden, op. cit., p.276.
33. Dobson, op. cit., pp.52-3, JB Thomas (1978) 'The day training college: A Victorian innovation in teacher training', *British Journal of Teacher Education*, 4, pp. 249–61.
34. Joint Standing Committee, op. cit., p.6.
35. H Ward 'The training of teachers' in J Dover Wilson (1928) *The Schools of England* (Sidgwick and Jackson), pp.221–2.
36. Rich, op. cit., p.231.
37. Joint Standing Committee, op. cit., p.22.
38. Jones, op. cit., p.45, also p.55, Dent, op. cit., p.5, A Jones (1943), op. cit., pp.52-3.
39. Rich, op. cit., p.232.
40. Ward, op. cit., p.223.
41. Dobson, op. cit., p.55.
42. E. Holmes, (1911) *What Is and What Might Be* (Constable), also RJW Selleck (1972) *English Primary Education and the Progressives 1914-1939* (Routledge and Kegan Paul), ch.2.
43. Ward, op. cit., p.222.
44. ibid., p.222.
45. ibid., p.224, Selleck, op. cit., pp.121–2.
46. NUT Report of Committee of Investigation (1939) *The Training of Teachers and Grants to Intending Teachers*, p.19.
47. A brief historical account of the development of post-war partnership training is in D Fish (1989) *Learning Through Practice in Initial Teacher Education* (Kogan Page), ch.2, also D Lawton 'Teacher education', in M Morris and C Griggs (1988) *Education – The Wasted Years? 1973–1986*, (Falmer Press) pp.160–71.

2 Initial Training as a Case of Postmodern Development: Some Implications for Mentoring

Margaret Wilkin

Introduction

Since the Conservatives came to power in 1979, initial teacher training in the UK has been subject to government intervention to a degree which would have been inconceivable during the 1960s or 1970s (Gilroy, 1992; Wilkin, 1992a). One consequence of this may be that the *cultural* dynamic of training has become obscured. The profession has become so preoccupied with responding to political initiatives that it is failing to acknowledge that teacher training is both a cultural activity in its own right (with its own integrated system of values, norms, goals, expectations, patterns of behaviour) and that like all social institutions it is also influenced by cultural features of the wider society in which it is located. The government of the day is only one potential source of pressure for change in training. A far more powerful force for change in the past has been the profession's own critical appraisal of its current practices and the conclusions reached by its members in deliberation and debate; and it is the thesis of this chapter that in the future a major influence for change in the curriculum and practices of training will be those several cultural trends in society which together constitute 'postmodernism'. This conclusion follows from a consideration of the way in which developments in training over the past two or three decades which are usually attributed either to the evolution of the internal professional culture of training or more latterly to government intervention, can be reinterpreted in postmodern terms.

One benefit of reviving an interest in the cultural aspects of training is that to do so promotes a sense of empowerment since the concept of 'culture' signifies not only reaction but active engagement by the subject. In her detailed analysis of the workings of the cultural system, Archer (1988) demonstrates the reciprocal nature of the culture-agency relationship, pointing out that as agents we have 'transformative potential' or the capacity to redefine or 'elaborate' aspects of the cultural systems in which we are located. To focus on cultural pressures for change, even when as here those pressures are societal and therefore powerful, is to introduce a sense of autonomy. But it also raises the question of how the patterns of practice, currents of belief, the priorities, values and fashions and so on which constitute our general socio-cultural world, spread throughout society and become lodged within particular social institutions in a peculiar and appropriate form. The answers to this are profound, and cannot be considered here. But it is recognized that a more thorough investigation of the relationship between the wider culture and initial training would need to consider in greater detail than is possible here the links between socio-cultural trends and institutional development, rather than rely on the demonstration of coincidence.

The following discussion is limited first to proposing that certain structural developments which have occurred as part of the trend towards school-based initial training can be regarded as postmodern in character. To suggest this is not to imply either that the polity or the profession itself has been without influence in the evolution of training during this time, or even that wider cultural currents such as that of postmodernism have exerted the major effect. It is to do no more than to acknowledge that the institution of teacher training cannot be isolated from or impervious to cultural events in society at large, and to propose that locating training within its wider cultural context may offer some useful insights concerning its current dilemmas and future prospects. If it seems to be the case that postmodernism has penetrated initial training, then the consequences of this for existing practice and particularly in this instance for the practice of mentoring become an issue for consideration. These matters will be addressed below.

Postmodernism as a Cultural Dynamic of Initial Teacher Training

The most recent government circular (DFE, 1992) which requires PGCE students (secondary phase) to spend two-thirds of their training period in school takes to new limits the trend towards school-based training which was initiated many years ago within the profession. This trend has been analysed in detail elsewhere (Wilkin,

1990). But placing students in school for a higher proportion of their training period is clearly not merely a matter of relocating them within the time at their disposal. The development of school-based training is associated with numerous other changes which for convenience can be divided into two types: those that are structural and those that could be termed 'personal' but which are perhaps more properly regarded as effective or cognitive. These two dimensions of development are interdependent but can be considered separately for analytical purposes. Due to limitations of space only those in the structural domain will be considered in this chapter. Chief amongst such developments in initial training over the last two to three decades have been:

1. *Changes in the balance of theory and practice within the curriculum.* As the time that the students spend in school has increased and practice has become prioritized within training, the disciplines of education have declined both in status and in degree. Today in most initial training courses they feature only minimally and in very dilute form.
2. *Changes in the basis of student theorizing.* The disciplines of education having been dismissed as the source of student theorizing, reflection on personal experience has today emerged as the most frequently quoted principle underpinning the learning of trainee teachers (MOTE, 1992).
3. *Changes in the nature of the relationship between teacher and tutor.* With the trend to school-based training, the relationship between tutor and teacher is becoming one of greater equality. As schools become more actively engaged in training, the authority of the teacher has increased and that of the tutor diminished and their respective responsibilities are being redefined.

These three developments are regarded as structural matters, the first being a revaluation and reweighting of the elements of the curriculum and the third a redefinition of roles. The second, that of the basis of student theorizing, refers to the *origins* of student theorizing. Here 'the basis of theorizing' is to be interpreted as the network of links that we all have with our past experiences and with the various areas of knowledge which have been made available to us in one way or another and on which we can draw in order to deal the more effectively with the challenges of current circumstances.

The changes summarized above have evolved during the years since the Robbins Report (1963). This is approximately the same period during which postmodernism is usually considered to have emerged and developed. Callinicos (1990) reminds us that the roots of postmodernism lie within three very diverse areas. The first is that of French post-structuralism which challenged our notions of truth, meaning and subjectivity; the second is the belief that we are entering a new capitalist era which is dominated by technology and hence the dissemination of knowledge rather than of goods; and the third is a reaction in the world of the arts against abstraction in painting and the international style in architecture. Huyssens (1984) suggests that these developments constitute 'a slowly emerging cultural transformation in Western societies'. For Jameson (1984) however, they remain a 'cultural dominant'. Postmodernism may therefore be seen either as a new period in our cultural history or as a major trend of some significance. Alternatively, it may be seen as the rationalization of the comfortable life-style of well-off members of the middle classes (Callinicos, op. cit.) or merely as a debate which is riven with inconsistencies (Montag, 1988).

To know the heterogeneity of its origins is to understand why the concept of postmodernism is so complex. There is no unified theory. Between them, writers on the postmodern condition cover a wide range of cultural transformations: former grand solutions to the problems of mankind are now seen to have failed and consequently the notion of legitimating values has collapsed; modern communications have promoted a wider understanding of how others live and this has led to an appreciation of the dignity of the other and the celebration of plurality; for the same reason there has been a loss of historical and geographical continuity; exposure to the media has led to a confusion between reality and illusion; boundaries between high and low culture, between different areas of knowledge and between appearance and reality have merged. Such developments can be regarded favourably or with deep misgiving for they promise either freedom and autonomy and the recognition of the rights of formerly subservient or minority groups, or alternatively a nihilistic chaotic fragmented world without guidance or goals. Postmodernism thus contrasts sharply with the preceding 'modern' era which was characterized by rationalism and order, universal laws and the domination of science.

Some problems need to be acknowledged. First, it is clearly quite impossible in a few pages to do justice to any social movement which subsumes so wide a range of topics, and necessarily the account that follows will be superficial and selective. That there are aspects of postmodernism which seem to have little relevance for initial teacher training and particularly for mentoring is acknowledged. Moreover, to pick and choose from the elaborate theoretical discussion of any one postmodern writer could be to distort the unity of his or her overall perspective. There is also the question of the theoretical status of postmodernism. Is it a theory about our current situation? That is, does it constitute a *theory* rather than exist as a loose collection of unrelated concepts and hypotheses about current Western life-styles; and can a development which originated principally in the world of the arts become a theoretical interpretation of our general social condition? The view that postmodernism *is* a general social trend is now held by a number of writers in the area (Featherstone, 1988; Harvey, 1990; Kellner, 1988). Others would disagree. For example, Honneth (1985, p.147) suggests that 'the idea has increasingly lost conceptual clarity' but that 'its suggestiveness has at the same time incessantly gained force'. Given the constraints of space which make it impossible to argue these points further, postmodernism is here being taken as a cultural trend, and this chapter offers a tentative exploration of some of the ways in which it appears to have exerted an influence in initial training.

What parallels can be drawn between the developments in initial training outlined above and the general concerns of postmodernism? It is Lyotard who identifies 'incredulity toward metanarratives' as a key characteristic of the postmodernism age. He argues that in the Western world in the past, two philosophical principles, one cognitive and one moral, have justified the practice of science. These are the attainment of universal knowledge and the attainment of universal freedom (Lyotard, 1979, pp. 31–2). As a form of knowledge, science has been regarded as superior on account of its promised ability to meet the requirements of these principles, that is, to emancipate us from ignorance and from prejudice. But these metanarratives are now perceived to be merely 'myths of legitimation'. They have lost their credibility, for modern communications have enhanced our awareness of events elsewhere and the life-styles and preoccupations of others. In addition, in this age of computerization, knowledge can be circulated. It can also be bought and sold. Knowledge, including science, is thus no longer the prerogative of any particular group or persons; the manufacturers and purveyors of knowledge are no longer privileged. It has become evident that Western intellectual codes do not represent the totality of knowledge. As Lyotard (op. cit., p.9) puts it: 'who decides what knowledge is?' Since we can no longer be certain what truth is, it has been supplanted by efficiency ('performativity') as the measure of success. In general, the values that held society together are in disarray and social coherence is achieved no longer through consensus to these overarching values but by participation in a network of localized competitive 'language-games'.

If we can accept that theorists may be given to exaggeration of their case, and if we can also agree with Featherstone (1988, p.201) who suggests that postmodernism 'does have the merit of suggesting a process with degrees of implementation rather than a fully fledged new social order or totality', then it is suggested that Lyotard's thesis on our current condition (so inadequately summarized here) has some valuable insights to offer us and that the demise of education theory in initial training as outlined above could be construed as an example of the wider social developments he portrays.

The disciplines of education can be regarded as the metanarratives of teacher training for the following reason. The practice of science is not associated with any particular set of values and thus science and values must be regarded as distinct. But this is not the case for the disciplines. Here values and practice come together. The disciplines *embody* both of Lyotard's metanarrative values. In both the area of practice, that of research, and in the process of transmission, the disciplines enhance both intellectual understanding (they 'reduce ignorance') and moral awareness. Like Lyotard's science they were the dominant forms of knowledge in their domain. They too were regarded with optimism for what they could achieve. They too were seen to fail for reasons of 'irrelevance', in fact because too much was expected of disciplinary theory, and its relationship with practice was initially misconstrued. Today, public disciplinary theory no longer enjoys superior status over the personal theories of the practitioner in the classroom, and success in training is now less frequently measured by what here might be called 'truth' – that is the student's ability to argue and defend his/her view by reference to the results of research in social science or to philosophical debate – than by competence in the classroom, or as Lyotard would put it, 'performativity'.

For Bauman (1988) a central feature of postmodernism is the fall from grace of the intellectuals. Since their traditional services are no longer in such demand, intellectuals are experiencing a status crisis. These services were the 'provision of an authoritative solution to the questions of cognitive truth, moral judgement and aesthetic taste' (p.219). The reasons that Bauman gives for the decline in the social importance of the intellectuals are first, like Lyotard, globalization. No longer can the West believe itself superior for,

> nobody but the most rabid of diehards believes that the western mode of life...has more than a sporting chance of ever becoming universal...The search for universal standards has suddenly become gratuitous (p.220)

and so our justificatory philosophies no longer have the status that they once had. Second, he argues that the State no longer needs intellectuals to legitimate its authority, because political control is possible by seduction through the media and by repression through financial deprivation. Third, he suggests that the mass media have opened up the domains formerly regarded by the intellectuals as their property and made them readily available to all. While in general intellectuals, that is, non-practitioners, have lost status under the Conservative government of recent years, it is suggested that Bauman's comments have particular relevance for the sub-system of teacher training. In the post-Robbins period, the 'intellectuals' of this system were the tutors in the disciplines of education, who provided the sort of service indicated in the quotation above and who enjoyed higher status than their methods colleagues. Today their territory has indeed been 'invaded'. The residues of the disciplines that now linger in training are becoming as much the province of teachers in schools as of tutors in sociology, psychology or philosophy.

The merging of boundaries between areas of knowledge such as that which typified the thematic approach to the disciplines during the 1970s has its counterpart in the postmodernism of Jameson (1983) as does the second structural dimension under review, that of the heterogeneous basis of student theorizing. Jameson attributes the advent of postmodernism to the progressive development of capitalism, what he terms 'the frantic economic urgency of producing fresh waves of ever more novel-seeming goods...at ever greater rates of turnover...'. As a consequence of its need to encourage spending, capitalism plunders where it can, looting examples from here and ideas from there and relentlessly combining them. This *modus operandi* is also characteristic of the postmodern media which must satisfy the demand for novelty. Thus boundaries of time and space are effaced, particularly that between low and high culture, and our sense of historical continuity is undermined. This is 'pastiche'. Pastiche picks and chooses and combines, randomly and superficially imitating other styles from the past or from elsewhere, but with all seriousness so that 'there is no feeling that there is something *normal* compared to which what is being imitated is rather comic' (op. cit., p.114). It is suggested that the reflective practice which students are now encouraged to undertake in order to generate their own practical principles of teaching may verge on pastiche as interpreted by Jameson in one respect at least: that unless reflection is undertaken in a purposeful and disciplined manner, with an awareness of the appropriate criteria for that occasion, it may readily become an indiscriminate and unstructured demand-led process, the outcomes of which will be disappointingly superficial. There are hints of this in Calderhead's (1987) study of the quality of reflection in student teachers' professional learning.

The third structural dimension – that of the merging equivalence of status of tutors and teachers – has already been implied in the above remarks but needs further brief comment. The implosion of boundaries is a fundamental theme in the work of numerous postmodern writers. For example, Baudrillard (1983) hypothesizes that the sophistication of information technology results in our lives being dominated by simulations to the extent that differences between reality and representation are eliminated. Lash (1990) interprets postmodernism as the age of 'de-differentiation', the major characteristic of which is the transgression of boundaries in the cultural sphere. That the erosion of boundaries also features in the work of Lyotard and Jameson has already been indicated. Bauman's (op.cit) concern is de-differentiation with respect to social or cultural groupings. Rather than attributing this to the spread of capitalism or to the advanced state of communications, he suggests that the decline of empire – what he terms 'the advanced erosion of that global structure of domination' (p.219) – has been the determinant.

> The era of modernity had been marked by an active superiority...This active superiority meant the right of the superior to proselytise, to design the suitable form of life for the others, to refuse to grant authority to the ways of life which did not fit that design (p.220).

These universalistic assumptions are now regarded as unacceptable and the rights of others and the value of their way of life are recognized. As Bauman (1988, p.220) says when describing postmodernism: 'The certitude of yesteryear is now at best ridiculed as naivety, at worst castigated as ethnocentric', and as Harvey (1990, p.48) puts it:

> The idea that all groups have a right to speak for themselves, in their own voice, and have that voice accepted as authentic and legitimate is essential to the pluralistic stance of postmodernism.

Changes in the relationship between teachers and tutors in initial training fully exemplify this.

It is unfortunate that there is insufficient space in which to review the changes in the cognitive-affective dimension of initial training and their postmodernist counterparts. Such a discussion would have suggested that pragmatism, loss of depth of understanding and immersion – all of them central concepts in postmodern theory – could describe the experiences of the student in school-based training, but that hedonism and fragmentation of the subject do not. That these concepts have not been discussed unfortunately necessarily eliminates them from the following section. But prior to that, a few comments on three papers given at the 1992 Philosophy of Education Society of

Great Britain Annual Conference will illustrate the extent to which postmodernism is already established in discussion among educational theorists.

A paper by Hirst supports many of the points made above. It opens by declaring that in the 1960s and 1970s the philosophy of education was dominated by

> a hard rationalism that profoundly determined its substantive content and the major educational principles for which it argued. Since then both these spells have been broken (Hirst, 1992, p.1).

It was believed that our beliefs, actions and emotions could and should be determined by reason and 'this philosophical position...provided a clear coherent framework for the formation of educational aims'. However, this rationalist approach to education was later challenged, particularly because 'there were grave doubts...about the primacy of reason', and was replaced by a more utilitarian perspective. Society then came to be seen as 'a collection of atomic individuals associating together for their personal satisfaction' (p.3). Hirst goes on to imply that we should utilize the best elements of both of these perspectives. We should give recognition to the demands and needs ('wants and satisfactions') of ourselves and others but reason should be retained as a reconciling and coordinating principle.

Smith's paper (1992, p.57) acknowledges 'the beleaguered position' of philosophy. Education is now fragmented into groups, each of which has its own language and vision. Thus a single theoretical perspective is impossible. An alternative theoretical approach is required which accommodates diversity (plurality). Smith suggests that deconstruction fulfils this requirement, since it does not aspire to a single interpretation.

Finally, a paper by Mendus was motivated by 'the apparent inability of universities to justify what they are doing to the outside world' (Mendus, 1992, p.8). She reviews the arguments of McIntyre, Bloom and Eliot, all of whom fear for the disintegration of a society which has come to lack shared standards and common assumptions, a world 'of intellectual anarchy, in which progress has been rendered impossible' (p.11). All three see the remedy for this situation in the reinstatement of standards. But as Mendus points out, it is impossible to return to an age of innocence. Instead she argues for recognizing the need to experience and evaluate competing traditions, without which conflict we cannot 'become the creators of different traditions'.

These papers refer to many of the issues raised above and are clearly illustrative of the debates of postmodernism. They cover the functional inadequacy of the grand narrative of reason when divorced from action; the dethronement of the intellectual; fragmentation of the educational community; and the need to recognize and respect the wants and needs of the other. They also offer some remedies for the cultural disintegration that postmodernism seem to promise: the need to retain a theoretical perspective, but the need for the new theory to take a different form; the importance of retaining conflicting viewpoints if progress is to be maintained and the need to be *active* creators of our own (cultural) destiny.

Implications for Mentoring

The above 'postmodern' representation of developments in initial training is but one interpretation of some of the structural changes which have characterized training courses during the last 25 years or so. It highlights the influence of culture on training rather than the influence of either the polity or the profession. Today, political intervention in training is frequent but it is also inconsistent and the profession itself is necessarily heavily engaged in responding to such initiatives. On the other hand, culture is evolutionary and has a degree of predictable continuity. The postmodern representation of the way in which training is developing may be the most reliable vision of the future that we have. Whether or not this is the case, to locate initial training within a postmodern framework provokes the evaluation of possible trends and encourages the development of policies within the constraints which these trends seem likely to impose.

Postmodernism offers us an incoherent future of relativism and fluidity, of social fragmentation and of instrumentalism. It offers theoretical paralysis since theory has been dethroned and there are no transcendent qualities or experiences to which we can appeal. But it also offers an arena in which all voices will be heard with equal favour. It celebrates difference and seems to promise the formation of a new order based on the democratic recognition of the rights of others. Modernism on the other hand offers rationally defined goals, distinctive areas of knowledge and modes of interpretation, certainty and order but also domination and oppression. In teacher training we need to find ways of retaining the best of both the postmodern world with its emphasis on plurality and democracy and the modern world with its emphasis on values, clearly defined goals and rational action.

The implication of the need for mediation between the two poles of modernism and postmodernism is clear with respect to the third of the three structural areas of teacher training discussed above, that of the roles of tutor and teacher. As training becomes school-based, numerous teachers of varied interests, experience and skill must necessarily become empowered to fully share in the training of students. The particular expertise that they as mentors have to offer must be recognized and reflected in their status as truly equal partners in training who fully share in decision-making and whose views are not just to be respected but also to be given institutional expression. Such typically postmodern developments are to be welcomed. But the fusion of boundaries between areas of knowledge which is also a characteristic of postmodernism must surely be rejected. It is essential to negotiate and then *retain* the boundaries between the roles of mentor and tutor, not to eliminate them. Both school and training institution must have distinct but interrelated and coordinated responsibilities if the curriculum of training is to be covered and if that training is to be coherent for the student (Wilkin, 1992b).

The other two structural issues concerning the role of disciplinary theory and the basis of student theorizing are far more complex. The metanarratives which justified the teaching of the sociology, philosophy and psychology of education have not been rejected but remain the aims of those engaged in the training of students. It is still the hope that during training students will become intellectually enlightened and morally aware professionals. Moreover, although it has not been possible to demonstrate it here, the collapse of the disciplines of education was due more to a failure of their (presumed) function as determinants of practice than to a rejection of their substantive content. Nevertheless, the postmodern perspective invites a reassessment of the status and role of disciplinary theory and also of public practical theory *vis-à-vis* the status and role of that theory which is the outcome of personal reflection. In the past the construction, presentation and evaluation of public theory has been the task of intellectuals operating within a certain discourse, a discourse which does not accommodate the hesitant idiosyncratic perceptions and explanations of the beginning teacher which in a postmodern world achieve their own contextualized validity. Postmodernism would grant these different forms of theory a similar status, the individual personal perspective of the student being deemed to be of no greater or lesser worth than the wider public perspective of the tutor who has expertise in the sociology of education, say. Today it is the first of these forms of theory in the guise of the personal theorizing of the 'reflective practitioner' which dominates training courses at the level of principle at least (MOTE, 1992). But both these forms of theory must be retained if training is not to become either a postmodern quagmire of relativism or a modern desert of irrelevance.

Theorizing at the personal practical level enables the student to impose order on his or her social environment and to provide explanations for successful or less than successful examples of practice. Such explanations may be highly personal and localized. Yet a thorough understanding of the current reality is not achieved by reification of that reality; rather it arises through the investigation of alternatives (Beyer, 1991). Personal theories cannot be adopted as general principles of teaching without first having been recontextualized within a wider discourse for the purpose of verification. This wider discourse may well be rational public disciplinary theory but in the postmodern era it need not be so since all theoretical perspectives are regarded as of equivalent status and hence qualify as a resource. It is no longer a question of relating disciplinary theory to practice (constantly advocated in the past but rarely demonstrated) but of relating one form of theory (personal theory) to any other form of publicly available theory which will perform the function of challenging the personal viewpoint. As Bauman (op.cit., pp.226–9) puts it, the question becomes 'how to secure communication and mutual understanding between cultures'. He goes on: 'This points, above all (to) the skill of interpretation'.

The notion of interpretation between the different forms of theory which are intrinsic to different discourses can be found in the work of several writers (Crook, 1990; Featherstone, 1985; Griffiths and Tann, 1992; Winter, 1991), and it is a conclusion of this chapter that in the future 'interpretation' in the sense in which it is to be used here – that of mediating between or interrelating two different forms of discourse – will become a major task of the mentor. For further elaboration of this concept in teacher training one can quote from the work of Griffiths and Tann (op. cit.). They wish to honour the metaphors and individual images which are characteristic of personal theorizing (the postmodern stance) yet to strengthen their values as practical principles by refining them within the domain of public theory based on rational practice (the modern stance).

> The comparison remains a difficult one. The difficulty is partly one of translation: the two kinds of theory are most easily expressed in different kinds of language. It is also one of scope: personal theories are focused on the small-scale and particular, and public ones on the large scale and universal (op.cit., pp.77–82).

The authors posit five 'levels of reflection': reaction, repair, review, research, retheorizing and reformulating. The process of action research is portrayed as 'spiralling' between these levels and the danger of superficiality if understanding remains at a single level is noted.

This model need not be reserved for formal action research. Although the term 'levels' is unfortunate here since it perpetuates the notion of hierarchies which postmodernism seeks to avoid, the 'levels' (or types) of reflection are associated with types of theory ('the last two levels...lend themselves to engaging with public theory', p.79). Here the task of mentors in collaboration with tutors will be to support and promote the learning of students as they,

> articulate their own theory, critically examine it, check it for consistency, coherence and adequacy, compare it with alternative theories and reconceptualise it in order to increase the effectiveness of their own professional thinking (p.82).

To 'interpret' in this sense is undoubtedly a demanding task. It entails engaging with the student on an intellectual journey from a particular to a general form of theorizing for the purposes of confirming or disconfirming or clarifying or extending his/her original assumptions. The outcome of this exercise cannot be foreseen or guaranteed since postmodernism equalizes the perspectives of all participants in the debate, and it may be that the view of the student remains unchallenged. High priority must be given to honouring the student's particular representation of the situation. This does not mean that it has to be accepted as 'correct', only that substantively this is the issue of interest for the student which therefore should be the focus of analysis. Extending the student's understanding may be achieved by a variety of means: questioning, the provision of appropriate reading material, consultation, involvement in group discussion or undertaking some minor research project, for example. Whichever method the mentor and student use it must be with the intention of engaging the student in a focused, disciplined (and sceptical) review of the query, problem or hypothesis which has been expressed. Only then will the dangers of drifting into the inconsequential world of pastiche be avoided.

Questions can be of the straightforward challenging kind which will oblige the student to think beyond immediate reaction or routinized assumption and to confront the need for definitions or evidence, say. Further questions should be directed to clarifying the core concern of the student's own personal theory for only then will it be possible for the mentor to identify the most useful substantive resource in this instance. Is it a *technical* (how to), *practical* (what to) or *critical* (why) concern (Kemmis, 1985)? Although disciplinary theory may be the theoretical resource most frequently used for this enlightenment, the postmodern perspective does not 'privilege' one form of theory or perception of the world above another. Hence students can make use of any alternative theoretical domain in order to sophisticate their own interpretations. Hypothetically these could include the views (either written or verbal) of their fellow students, of teachers, or of any other individuals or groups to whom they have access. But, irrespective of where the mentor encourages the student to seek those alternative viewpoints and formulations which will stimulate, challenge and perhaps help to develop his or her own assumptions, certain rational procedures associated with investigation must apply if the transition from personal theory to general principle is to be achieved. These might include, for example, the search for agreement on definitions, the marshalling of evidence, establishing criteria for measurement, and so on.

The desirability of retaining the best of the modern and of the postmodern positions was noted at the beginning of this section. The above discussion suggests that it would be difficult to do otherwise in a training of quality. Personal theorizing *per se* provides an insecure basis for practice, yet individual interpretation cannot be disregarded if participation and commitment are to be wholehearted. Although reference to the views of other individuals extends one's vision, reference to established research, for all its weaknesses, offers the sounder means of verifying one's assumptions. Whatever the resource on which the student draws for enlightenment, the procedures employed must surely be rational and universalistic. Furthermore, while reflection on personal practice should be a flexible and wide-ranging process, rigorous selection and firm judgement must also be exercised if pastiche is to be avoided. Moreover, it is crucial to avoid a postmodern confusion between theoretical levels, for to do so, as Crook (op. cit.) points out, would be to close the gap between context and goal and so deny the tension which is necessary for accountability. The notion of 'interpretation' readily subsumes the postmodern and the modern. It accommodates alternative interpretations of individual action, it relates the personal, idiosyncratic world to the general public forum, and it subsumes the tension which as Mendus (op. cit.) points out is so necessary for progress and which is so sorely lacking in the postmodern perspective.

Finally, a few brief comments on the Oxford Internship Scheme will demonstrate that postmodernism does indeed appear to have become grounded in initial training. This assessment is based on the accounts by Benton (1990) and McIntyre (1990) of the aims, principles and practices of the Scheme. The Oxford Scheme, like most others today, but in contrast to many training programmes of the 1960s which emphasized the intellectual development of the student, gives priority to the student's general competence in the classroom. School staff and university tutors are of equal status, the mentors being full partners ('co-professionals') in planning, implementing and evaluating the content, activities and procedures of the training programme. Regarding the relationship between theory and practice, the theory-into-practice model is firmly rejected. Instead it is recognized that most learners start from their own ideas and commitments (to which their personal histories have contributed) and only gradually modify these in the light of experience and as they become acquainted with the ideas of others. But none of the sources of further knowledge upon which the student is likely to draw is especially privileged either in terms of the status of its proponents or in terms of its reliability. Nor is there any expectation of consensus across these various sources of knowledge, it being recognized that teachers and tutors may hold quite different views on priorities or on matters of practice, for example. Students are encouraged to develop their personal thinking through synthesizing knowledge acquired from these various sources and tested against diverse criteria. In all these respects the Oxford Internship Scheme exhibits postmodern characteristics and the praise that the Scheme has attracted suggests that it may be influential in introducing and possibly even stabilizing a form of initial training in this country which has a postmodern bias. But in other respects, the Scheme exemplifies modernism: goals are clearly stated; the roles of tutor and mentor are distinct and rationally defined in accordance with their respective skills; the criteria against which students test their theories are universal.

Acknowledgements

I wish to thank Ruth Furlong and particularly Professor Paul Hirst for their extensive and valuable comments on the first draft of this chapter.

REFERENCES

Archer, M (1988) *Culture and Agency*, Cambridge: Cambridge University Press.
Baudrillard, J (1983) *Simulations*, Semiotext.
Bauman, Z (1988) 'Is there a postmodern sociology?', *Theory Culture and Society*, 5.
Benton, P (1990) 'The internship model', in Benton, P (ed.) *The Oxford Internship Scheme*, London: Calouste Gulbenkian Foundation.
Best, S and Kellner, D (1991) *Postmodern Theory: Critical Interrogations*, London: Macmillan.
Boyne, R and Rattansi, A (eds) (1990) *Postmodernism and Society*, London: Macmillan.
Beyer, LE (1991) 'Teacher education, reflective enquiry and moral action', in Tabachnick, R and Zeichner, K (eds) *Issues and Practices in Enquiry Oriented Teacher Education*, London: Falmer Press.
Calderhead, J (1987) 'The quality of reflection in student teachers professional learning', *European Journal of Teacher Education*, 10, 3.
Callinicos, A (1989) *Against Postmodernism*, Cambridge: Polity Press.

Callinicos, A (1990) 'Reactionary postmodernism?', in Boyne, R and Rattansi, A (eds) (op.cit.).

Crook, S (1990) 'The end of radical social theory?', in Boyne, R and Rattansi, A (eds) (op.cit.).

Department for Education (1992) *Initial Teacher Training (Secondary Phase)*, (Circular 9/92) London: DFE.

Featherstone, M (1985) 'The fate of modernity', in *Theory, Culture and Society*, **2, 3.**

Featherstone, M (1988) 'In pursuit of the postmodern', *Theory Culture and Society*, **5.**

Foster, H (ed.) (1983) *Postmodern Culture*, London: Pluto Press.

Gilroy, DP (1992) 'The political rape of initial teacher education in England and Wales', *Journal of Education for Teaching*, **18**, 1.

Griffiths, M and Tann, S (1992) 'Using reflective practice to link personal and public theories', *Journal of Education for Teaching*, **18**, 1.

Harvey, D (1990) *The Condition of Postmodernity*, Oxford: Blackwell.

Hirst, PH (1992) 'Education, knowledge and practices', *Proceedings of the Annual Conference of the Philosophy of Education Society of Great Britain*.

Honneth, A (1985) 'An aversion against the universal. A commentary on Lyotard's 'postmodern culture'', *Theory, Culture and Society*, **2**, 3.

Huyssens, A (1984) 'Mapping the postmodern', *New German Critique*, **33.**

Jameson, F (1983) 'Postmodernism and Consumer Society' in Foster, H (ed.) *Postmodern Culture*, London: Pluto Press.

Jameson, F (1984) 'Postmodernism or the cultural logic of capitalism', *New Left Review*, **146.**

Kaplan, EA (ed.) (1988) *Postmodernism and its Discontents*, London: Verso.

Kemmis, S (1985) 'Action research and the politics of reflection', in Boud, D, Keogh, R and Walker, D (eds) *Reflection: Turning Experience into Learning*, London: Kogan Page.

Kellner, D (1988) 'Postmodernism as social theory: some challenges and problems', *Theory, Culture and Society*, **5.**

Lash, S (1988) 'Discourse or figure? Postmodernism as a regime of signification', *Theory, Culture and Society*, **5.**

Lash, S (1990) *Sociology of Postmodernism*, London: Routledge.

Lyotard, J (1979) *The Postmodern Condition: A Report on Knowledge*, Manchester: Manchester University Press.

McIntyre, D (1990) 'Ideas and principles guiding the internship scheme', in Benton, P (ed.) (op. cit).

Mendus, S (1992) 'All the king's horses and all the king's men: justifying higher education', *Proceedings of the Annual Conference of the Philosophy of Education Society of Great Britain*.

Montag, W (1988) 'What is at stake in the debate on postmodernism?', in Kaplan, EA (ed.) op. cit.

MOTE (Modes of Teacher Education) Barrett, E, Barton, L, Furlong, J, Galvin, C, Miles, S and Whitty, G (1992) *Initial Teacher Education in England and Wales: a Topography*, Goldsmiths College, University of London.

Nixon, J (1991) 'The politics of postmodernism', paper for the BERA Conference.

Polan, D (1988) 'Postmodernism and cultural analysis today', in Kaplan, EA (ed.) (op. cit).

Robbins Report (1963) Report to Committee on Higher Education, London: HMSO.

Rowland, S (1991) 'A few tentative thoughts on postmodernism', paper for the BERA Conference.

Smith, R (1992) 'If you can think: deconstructing philosophy of education', *Proceedings of the Annual Conference of the Philosophy of Education Society of Great Britain*.

Wilkin, M (1990) 'The development of partnership in the United Kingdom', in

Booth, M, Furlong, J and Wilkin, M (ed.) *Partnership in Initial Teacher Training*, London: Cassell.

Wilkin, M (1992a) 'The challenge of diversity', *Cambridge Journal of Education*, 22, 3.

Wilkin, M (1992b) 'On the cusp: from supervision to mentoring', *Cambridge Journal of Education*, 22, 1

Winter, R (1991) 'Postmodern sociology as a democratic education practice', *British Journal of Sociology of Education*, 12, 4.

3 Seeking a Comparative Perspective: A Case Study From Australia

Tony d'Arbon

As in England and other countries, Australia has seen a significant shift in the emphasis on the practicum in recent years. National reports on teacher education have opted for the increase of the length of the training or pre-accreditation period and there have been moves to introduce an internship. This move to extend the period in schools represents a shift from a short-term focus on the presentation of individual lessons to a longer-term assimilation and bonding process to the school and its culture.

A flurry of government reports, beginning in 1980, began to address the practicum issue and introduced the notion of extended periods in schools under a general heading of internship. These reports represented increasing moves by the Federal authorities to assume a more centralizing role in education and universities were encouraged to become more involved in the development of internship programmes. What was meant by an internship was not clearly defined. The effect of this lack of specificity was to provide higher education institutions (HEIs) with opportunities to experiment with duration, placement of students, modes of supervision, payment of supervisors and other variables, to enable HEIs to meet local needs and conditions and to be creative in devising new programmes.

Practice teaching has always involved, in a loose alliance, the institutions, the employers, the teachers, the unions and the students – each to a greater or lesser degree, depending on circumstances and personnel. Sometimes the interactions have been positive and there have been significant outcomes, including closer school-university links, staff exchanges and enthusiastic support for collaborative programmes. At other times, there has been the close guarding of territory, perceived threats against local autonomy and timidity when confronting new and novel situations.

In recent times, there have been moves to develop closer collaboration between these groups and to formalize existing arrangements which have involved participation by all groups at all levels of the planning and implementation of internship and a number of positive gains have been made. While everyone comes to the discussion table with histories of previous encounters to call on in times of need, the overall response has been very good and a co-operative atmosphere is being developed which, it is hoped, over time will develop into full partnership.

For many years, supervision of practice teaching in schools was seen as part of the professional duties or responsibilities of classroom teachers with some status or small financial allowance being provided as reward or recompense. At a time in the early 1970s when funding in universities for teacher education programmes was more generous, these allowances were significantly increased and the concept of 'master teacher' was introduced. This arrangement was later used as the basis for an industrial agreement by which all supervising teachers were to be paid for their services. Depending on your point of view, the supervising allowance may or may not be seen to be small – A\$20 per day, equivalent to £9 – but in a large teacher training institution the sum soon mounts up to be a major proportion of a departmental budget.

While there have been moves to vary this payment, the fact that it is a legal requirement means that it has to be taken into account when budgeting for the practicum. Some teachers regard the supervision of practice teaching as part of their professional responsibility and decline to apply for the payment. In these times of financial constraint, university administrators may see the sum set aside for the teaching practice as a way of easing their financial burdens by reducing the practicum by some quantum of weeks or days and using the funding thus released to reduce deficit burdens. As a result, the introduction of any programme with the possibility of increasing the number of days in school is seen as having the potential for causing budget problems in already overstretched education departments.

The Setting

This chapter describes the steps leading to the introduction of an internship and the development of a mentoring programme for secondary students in the final year of a four-year Bachelor of Education programme at Australian Catholic University – New South Wales (ACU). It is being written as the pilot internship programme has entered the second of its three phases. It reports on the developments leading up to the introduction, the implementation of the first phase, and the student evaluation. It represents the 'now and the not yet', the hopes and aspirations of the designers and their level of realization to date. As such, it is expected to be of interest and help to those developing internship programmes for their own constituencies.

The full introduction of the internship programme will begin in 1993. During 1992, the cohort of fourth year students on one of the two secondary campuses, and which for a variety of reasons is much smaller than usual – some 27 in number – is participating in a three-phase pilot programme which is the main subject of this chapter.

The development of the structure of this new internship pro-gramme and implementation strategy is detailed below. This devel-opment is obviously an evolutionary process and the proposed structure will undergo many alterations as it goes along, but its broad shape and general thrust will be much as given here.

What is Internship?

In the last several years, a number of reports and Papers of Advice to governments have indicated that there should be a new model of teacher preparation in Australia incorporating some form of intern-ship and a number of HEIs have begun pilot programmes.

Beginning with Auchmuty in 1980 and the *Report of the National Inquiry into Teacher Education*, research findings were reported and suggested that:

> students who have experienced 'continuous' teaching practice (at least in the
> final year of the three-year diploma of teaching course) feel better prepared as
> beginning teachers than those whose teaching practice was arranged in blocks
> (6.64).

Correy (1980) in the New South Wales report, *Teachers for Tomorrow,* also made passing reference to internship, noting that, 'some institu-tions had developed the idea of an *extended practicum or internship* that might last up to ten weeks (for final year students)' (p.55) (emphasis added).

Apart from these two references, no major initiatives were taken in this area until much later in the decade. Indeed, when the Review Committee which produced the report, *Quality of Education in Aus-tralia* (Karmel, 1985) identified a series of priorities, it said:

> From the Committee's perspective, pre-service teacher education can undoubt-
> edly be improved and the Commonwealth Tertiary Education Commission
> should give active leadership forthwith towards that end. However, for the next
> five to ten years, the priority should lie with inservice education (p.125).

So the situation remained until the meeting of the Australian Education Council, made up of the Federal and State Ministers of Education, in April 1989, when the Ministers established a working party to review the situation in teacher education generally and to give advice on a number of specific issues. The subsequent report, *Teacher Education in Australia* (The Ebbeck Report), released in July 1990, contained 20 recommendations, a number of which relate to the practicum and its extension into internship and associateship.

Ebbeck noted that although the concept of internship had been alluded to in several reports on teacher education over the last decade, no moves had yet been made to embody it in any teacher education programmes. He added:

> The term is sometimes used in connection with some forms of school experience in existing courses, but this is not what the Working Party would have in mind in advancing a form of *structured employment and learning* as a *central element* in the format of teacher education in the future (1990, 3.4.2) (emphasis added).

The concept has since been given some substance by the reports to the National Board of Employment, Education and Training (NBEET). In the most recent paper prepared by the Schools Council, *Australia's Teachers*, it is suggested that there be an exploration of the notion of internship which it describes thus:

> By *internship* we mean the practice of placing student teachers near the completion of their training in a school for an extended period of time (six to twelve months) under the *supervision of an experienced teacher* (NBEET, 1990, p.94) (emphasis added).

From another source, when describing the Oxford Internship Scheme, Judge (1990) writes:

> *Internship* represents a commitment to the school-based training of teachers. It is grounded in a partnership of skilled practitioners in the schools with university academics. It exploits the analogy (but not the model) of the teaching hospital in medical education. Fundamentally, it requires the integration of theory and practice.

The substance of the Australian reports was summarized in a report of the National Board of Employment, Education and Training in 1990, *The Shape of Teacher Education: Some Proposals*, in which the notion of internship was incorporated into the discussion of teacher induction.

At the Australian Teacher Education Association (ATEA) Conference held in Adelaide in July 1990, and again in Melbourne in 1991, participants were informed that internships were on the drawing board at the University of New England – Northern Rivers (Young, 1990; 1991) and since then, the University of Newcastle and other institutions have announced their initiatives in this area (Fullerton and Taylor, 1991).

Features of the discussions relating to these statements of internship are that they are embodied in considerations of the pre-service practicum. Ebbeck describes the features of a quality experience in the practicum: well-planned and coordinated with the academic course, well-supervised and well-assessed and reported (1990, 3.2.4). The introduction of a well-planned internship would overcome those features of practice teaching which Ebbeck sees as limiting, where he says:

> No matter how well-planned and executed, practice teaching which involves teaching isolated lessons over a few weeks of the year suffers the limitations that result from the lack of opportunity for the students to experience 'whole school' operation. Such experiences include not only a wide variety of inter-relationships within the school itself, but relationships with the surrounding community, a factor becoming more important as changes in the nature of schooling take effect. In addition to this, the students in a practicum have limited opportunity to develop a continuing relationship with the same group of pupils (3.2.4).

It was when a study was made of the notion of internship that a variety of understandings became apparent. This encouraged us when arriving at the ACU definition of secondary internship which picked up the ideas and sentiments expressed by the Schools Council's definition and Benton's conceptual model. All the schemes investigated addressed the issues raised in these descriptions to a greater or lesser extent. The consistent theme was some form of school-based training, adequate training for school supervisors (mentors), cooperation between the University and schools and for an extended period of time. Thus, there are many definitions and descriptions of internship from the medical model, staff development models and now the school model. All have an inductive component.

It is one of those great truths that while you can read and talk about internship, you have to go through the process to really understand it.

The Internship Model

The initial government reports urging the introduction of internship came at a time when secondary pre-service courses at the University were moving from the three-year to the four-year format. There was concern that the addition of a fourth year could well be one more year of the same and, urged by a visionary principal, the secondary teacher education division placed an internship into its programme. The restructuring of the course meant that it would take four years to run through and that, in effect, meant that there were three years to prepare for the internship and to develop, trial and implement a suitable model.

This restructuring also provided the opportunity to review current practices and to develop a new model of school-employer-union-university interaction which would maximize collaboration and help to realize the potential, benefits and possibilities of such an arrangement. A review of this type involved the examination of other internship schemes and developing a synthesis appropriate to our needs and realizable within our resources and structures.

When it became obvious that it would be opportune to introduce a pilot internship programme in 1992, it was agreed that a short overseas study visitation programme should be undertaken. In enquiries at all levels as to the best places to visit, three names kept recurring – the internship programme in the State of New Jersey in the United States, the internship programme organised through the University of Alberta in Canada, and the Oxford Internship Scheme in England. Each of these programmes had attractive features and each had been described in the literature. The New Jersey scheme had been publicized through the report of a visit of HMI (DES, 1989), the Alberta scheme through a comprehensive series of reports (Ratsoy *et al*, 1987), and the Oxford scheme through the collection of writings edited by Peter Benton (1990).

At the same time, a number of internship schemes were being developed in Australia in response to government urgings and had been reported in the proceedings of various teacher education conferences and elsewhere (d'Arbon, 1991; Fullerton and Taylor, 1991; Young, 1991). Each of these schemes had been developed to meet local needs. None had been directed towards secondary teachers, but these were one-year, end-on models, which had a primary focus. None had all the features we were seeking for ACU and we were faced with the challenge of distilling from the various models what would best suit our needs.

The definition and model of internship put forward by the Schools Council was considered to have a number of advantages, including:

- providing intending teachers with a more realistic training setting, with attendant opportunities to develop a deeper understanding of the culture of a school and to establish relationships with classes over longer periods of time;

- providing the opportunities to acquire the knowledge and skills which can only be developed 'on the job';
- providing opportunities to accept a higher level of responsibility than is possible in a shorter teaching 'round';
- influencing the structure of the training institution's programme so that theory and practice can be more effectively related, encouraging reflective practice.

It was also anticipated that there would be a number of positive outcomes such as:

- improving the quality of teachers entering the profession;
- smoother introduction to the profession seen as part of induction and career development;
- closer collaboration between universities, schools, employers and unions;
- increased access to *craft skills, contextual knowledge* and *enabling skills* of classroom teachers;
- greater attention to the blending of theory and practice;
- increased commitment to teaching as a career, reflected in greater retention rates;
- greater commitment on the part of schools for the professional development of staff, with interns being seen as the beginning of a career-long continuum.

In the end, a three-phase model was developed comprising a full-term placement in a secondary school, preceded by five days on the basis of a day-a-week. The phases were as follows.

Phase A
* Familiarization and orientation to the culture of the school (day-a-week).
* Liaison with university teacher.

Timing – The equivalent of five days in school, given six hours as a school day, the exact timing of these days to be a flexible arrangement between the school and the intern.

Purpose – Essentially, the purpose of this time is for the interns to become acquainted with the culture of the school in which they are placed, to develop a rapport and trust with the mentors, the colleague teachers, the classes they will be taking, fellow interns in the same school, the 'collegial' group and the staff of the school as a whole. There are opportunities at this time for taking part in a variety of school activities, as well as observation of and participation in the teaching of classes in the school in many different ways, including, for instance, team teaching with mentors, colleague teachers and peers.

Phase B

Teaching in a **reflective mode.**
* Focus on teaching
* Collegial activity and reflection with Catholic Education and Schools Offices+mentors+university teachers in diocesan group.

Timing – At the commencement of term 2, the intern begins full-time in school. The first four or five weeks of this time constitute Phase B.

Purpose – Phase B is a time of increasing immersion in the role of a classroom teacher. Although the interns are in school full-time, they may take one or two classes on a continual basis. There is an emphasis on observation and experimentation. While the interns are practising long-term planning with the one or two classes, they are expected to teach some other classes on a one- or two-off basis, where a variety of teaching strategies can be practised, perhaps involving other teachers or interns. These observations involve the mentors, colleague teachers, other teachers and fellow interns, and extend beyond the classroom to include all aspects of a teacher's professional duties, particularly those of an administrative nature. During this immersion time, there is an opportunity for interns to meet as a 'collegial' group.

Phase C

Teaching in **Learning Partner Mode.**
* Full practitioner
* Focus on administrative role
* Intern-mentor negotiated learning experience.

Timing – This phase takes place for the remainder of the school term following Phase B.

Purpose – During this time, the interns' duties, both in their quality and in their nature, are increased, so that they are acting as 'teacher' for some classes. The emphasis is on the implementation of long-term planning and acceptance of responsibility of *all* the duties of a teacher for some classes. There is continuing opportunity for 'collegial' meetings and an important aim of this phase is implementing strategies derived from reflections and observations arising in Phase B.

Moves Towards Mentoring

Like all committee decisions, the range of terms developed to cover the activities of the various school and university personnel in the internship represented a series of compromises, but by dint of arguing and perseverance, 'mentor' remained intact. In the end, a set of terms was defined thus:

Intern – A student in the fourth year of the Bachelor of Education – Secondary having an extended placement of one term in a school where the student has the opportunity to contribute to the life of the school as a member of staff.

Mentor – The person nominated by the school for the overall supervision of one intern. There will be one mentor for each intern in the school.

Colleague teacher – The teacher with whom the intern would work on a daily basis in the class-room, either as the 'second teacher in the room' or as the alternate teacher.

There may be more than one colleague teacher and one of the colleague teachers will also be the mentor.

University teacher – The person from the university with responsibility to the university for the internship at a particular school.

Curriculum lecturer – The person in the university with responsibility for the particular subject area(s) taught by the intern.

The use of these new terms and our insistence on their use signalled to all parties that the internship was different in intention, perceived purpose and method of operation, and echoed the Oxford position described by McIntyre (1992, p.117).

Principles of the Internship

In the discussions, it was agreed that the interns would gain maximum benefit from their school placement if they were able to have extended experience of the rhythms of the school.

Earlier, mention was made of the possibility of a six- to twelve-month placement, but this was thought to be impracticable. With the school year divided into four terms of roughly equal length, a period of one school term was chosen as more appropriate, since it was thought that this length of time would allow the interns to experience opening and closing rituals for a school term, to become aware of the way in which classroom situations could be handled long-term, to develop interpersonal relationships with mentors, and closer bonding with the school and its community.

There would be one mentor for each intern. The mentor would play a leading role in the intern's introduction to the school culture and act as guide, philosopher and friend for the period of the internship. Because the interns had been trained in two teaching methods and would be required to implement and practise both of them during the term, other teachers apart from the mentor would be involved in the specialist subject supervision of the intern and these persons were designated as colleague teachers. Their role was seen as being subsidiary to the mentors and this perception was followed through when it came to discussion of the levels of payment.

The issue of payment for the mentors and the possibility of varying the Industrial Award schedules to accommodate the new supervision model required us to consult closely with the unions. In Australia, teachers in government schools are covered by a different set of award conditions from those in non-government schools. Both sets of unions have been engaged in discussions about mentoring and in drawing up contracts between employers, the universities and the unions. These contracts set down the understandings and agreed terms between the various parties.

It was important to establish at an early stage a clear understanding that the university did not see the introduction of the internship as some form of cost-cutting. In this way, when negotiations began regarding the method of payment for the supervision of the interns, the funds which normally would have been paid for a practice teaching session for a length of time equivalent to the internship were to be 'quarantined' within the university and distributed across the supervising personnel, mentors and colleague teachers in appropriate proportions, based on perceived work value of their role. This situation will be reviewed as part of the evaluation of the pilot programme later this year.

Phase C, the assumption of full class responsibilities, takes place in about the fifth week of the internship. The actual movement between phases may vary from intern to intern and will be the subject of negotiation between the various parties. Already, experience has shown that the interns also begin this phase with different classes at different times which depend on the complexity of the teaching and other factors. In this phase, the role of the colleague teacher diminishes but does not disappear, while the role of the mentor continues.

There are two days during the internship when the interns return to the University to meet with their curriculum lecturers, other university staff and their fellow interns to discuss their progress and to establish goals for the remainder of the internship. On these days, there is also an afternoon meeting with mentors to check progress and assessments, carry out an evaluation and receive advice for the implementation of the full internship programme in 1993.

The Role of the Mentor

In the pilot internship programme, the mentor has two roles – the first as the point of reference in the school and for the day-to-day introduction into the context of the school (the guide, philosopher and friend role); the second as a colleague teacher responsible for the intern in a particular subject area.

From the outset, it was seen that the mentor played a highly significant role in the programme. The responsibilities went beyond previous demands for the practicum and mentors were asked to assume a much more active role in their association with the intern. These extra demands were detailed in their duty statements, listed below.

The mentor oversees the immersion of the intern into the school culture by:

- regular conferencing with the intern;
- reflecting with the intern on significant incidents;
- making the intern aware of school policies and role-modelling their implementation;
- sharing non-classroom activities and duties such as staff development exercises, playground supervision, administrative duties and participating in pastoral care groups;
- ensuring the social integration of the intern into the school staff and full participation in staff social activities and celebrations.

The mentor acts as a liaison between the school and the university by:

- regular meetings between the mentor and the university teacher appointed to that school to discuss progress of the intern;
- negotiating with the intern and the university on the timing of the transition of Phase B to Phase C;
- writing the final report at the conclusion of the internship;
- regularly reporting to the school principal on the progress of the internship and conveying any suggestions or advice to the university teacher.

The mentor encourages engagement with the professional culture by:

- attendance at meetings of professional associations;
- reading of professional journals;

- joining the appropriate professional association.

The mentor acts as the focus person responsible for a particular intern in the school by:

- participating in the selection of colleague teachers;
- ongoing liaison with colleague teachers;
- negotiating with peer teachers for additional colleague teachers where appropriate.

It was then left to the individual mentor and university teacher to implement these expectations. Evaluation will help to clarify the success of their outcomes.

The Role of the Colleague Teacher

The colleague teacher is responsible for the classroom supervision of the intern and for all situations. The mentor will act as a colleague teacher for one of the intern's teaching subjects.

Initially, the intern and colleague teacher are expected to operate in a team situation. This could begin as early as Phase A where the intern could operate in a 'second pair of hands' situation for group work or similar activities. In Phase B, the colleague teacher acts in the role of a normal supervising teacher for the practicum with the difference that there will be a period beyond Phase B leading to greater responsibility by the intern (with a diminishing level of supervision) for the classroom activities of a particular group of students.

The colleague teacher, the mentor and the university teacher act as a team to ensure the best mix of classroom and field experiences for the intern and opportunities for the development of special expertise and skills. This team will also negotiate as to the best time to move to Phase C, although, as has been found already, this may not be a one-step process.

Is the Internship a Reform in Teacher Education?

It is interesting to note Benton's reference to the internship as a 'reform' in teacher education (1990, p.1). A reflection on whether it is a reform or not is helpful in clarifying the perceived role of the internship in a pre-service programme, the attendant requirements for university and school staff training and, to use a term in these times of economic rationalism, of how to market the scheme.

The introduction of the internship programme at ACU was seen to have a number of purposes. The most obvious one was to provide a better quality in-school experience for students completing the fourth year of their pre-service course whilst a contributing purpose was to respond to the increasing pressure from government sources to introduce some form of extended experience in schools. An obvious spin-off was the development of a closer working relationship between the schools, employers, unions and the university, as well as a better linking of theory and practice. That this collaboration would develop into a partnership was one of the long-term aims of the internship project.

The major difference between English PGCE and the scheme described in this chapter is that whereas the English scheme comes as a one-year course at the conclusion of a liberal arts or science degree, the Australian internship comes as part of an integrated four-year Bachelor of Education. One difference between the ACU programme and the Oxford scheme is the placement of the interns. The Oxford scheme places the interns in numbers of 10 in the schools. We have restricted the pilot programme to two interns per school. At a later stage, we may be able to expand these numbers, but at this stage, it is our view that this is the maximum number the schools could reasonably take.

For secondary courses at ACU, it was a reform because it involved closer cooperation with a number of groups who saw themselves as having a stake in the outcomes of the teacher education process. It became clear that cooperation was not necessarily partnership and that collaboration was somewhere in between. If the university is going to be serious about the process of working together and invest energy and commitment, this area would have to be a matter of continuous evaluation.

Finally, the introduction of the internship into ACU has been a source of energy within the secondary division. Students have looked forward to the internship and are enjoying the experience of full involvement in schools, and the schools are committed to the programme. The test of its success will be in seeing how many schools volunteer to take interns for the full implementation of the internship in 1993.

REFERENCES

Auchmuty, JJ (Chair) (1980) *Report of the National Enquiry into Teacher Education*, Canberra: Commonwealth Government Printer.

Benton, P (ed) (1990) *The Oxford Internship Scheme*, London: Calouste Gulbenkian Foundation.

Correy, PM (Chair) (1980) *Teachers for Tomorrow: Continuity and Change in Teacher Education in New South Wales*, Report of the Committee to Examine Teacher Education in New South Wales, Sydney: Government Printer.

d'Arbon, JA (1991) 'Proposal for internship for secondary teacher education courses', paper presented at 21st Conference, Australian Teacher Education Association, Melbourne, 7–10 July.

Department of Education and Science (1989) *Teaching – It's a Vital Profession,* the Provisional Teacher Program in New Jersey, a paper by Her Majesty's Inspectorate, London: HMSO.

Ebbeck, F (1990) *Teacher Education in Australia,* a Report to the Australian Education Council, Canberra: National Board of Employment, Education and Training.

Fullerton, T and Taylor A (1991) *Pilot Year 4 Program for B.Ed. (Primary) 1991,* incorporating an internship and collaborative arrangements, University of Newcastle (NSW).

Judge, H (1990) 'The reform of teacher education', in Benton, P (ed.) *The Oxford Internship Scheme,* London: Calouste Gulbenkian Foundation.

Karmel, R (1985) *Quality of Education in Australia,* Report of the Review Committee, Canberra: Australian Government Publishing Service.

McIntyre, D (1992) 'The Oxford University model of teacher education', *South Pacific Journal of Teacher Education ,***19**, 2, 117-30.

National Board of Employment, Education and Training (1990) *Australia's Teachers: An Agenda for the Next Decade,* Canberra: Australian Government Publishing Service.

National Board of Employment, Education and Training (1990–1996) *The Shape of Teacher Education: Some Proposals,* Canberra: NBEET.

Ratsoy, E, Friesen, D, Holdaway, E and others (1987) *Evaluation of the Initiation to Teaching Project,* Edmonton: Alberta Education.

Young, WH (1990) 'An internship model: primary pre-service', paper presented at Australian Teacher Education Association Conference, Adelaide, 8-11 July.

Young, WH (1991) 'Responding to change–an imperative for Australian teacher education', paper presented at Australian Teacher Education Association Conference, Melbourne, 7–10 July.

Part II
Conceptions of Mentoring

4 Learning to Teach and Models of Mentoring

Trisha Maynard and John Furlong

Introduction

Learning to teach, as we all know but often fail to remember, is a complex, bewildering and sometimes painful task. It involves developing a practical knowledge base, changes in cognition, developing interpersonal skills and also incorporates an affective aspect. This chapter represents a preliminary examination of the ways in which teachers, acting as mentors, can most effectively help trainees in this difficult process.

Before starting to discuss the role of the mentor in facilitating the professional development of trainee teachers, it is necessary to ask a prior question – why, in principle, should school teachers themselves be part of the process? What is the rationale for the mentor's contribution? In these times of rapid change in teacher education it is more than ever necessary to have a clear and principled understanding of the rationale for each aspect of training and how it relates to other dimensions.

In order to try and answer that question we will briefly return to the research on school-based training undertaken by Furlong *et al.* (1988). In that analysis, Furlong *et al.* (p.132) distinguished between four different levels or dimensions of training which, they argued, went on in all forms of teacher training course. These levels were as follows:

Levels of Professional Training
Level (a) Direct practice

69

Practical training through direct experience in schools and classrooms.
Level (b) Indirect practice
'Detached' training in practical matters usually conducted in classes or workshops within training institutions.
Level (c) Practical principles
Critical study of the principles of study and their use.
Level (d) Disciplinary theory
Critical study of practice and its principles in the light of fundamental theory and research.

Furlong *et al.*'s argument was that professional training demands that trainees in their courses must be exposed to all of these different dimensions of professional knowledge. Moreover, courses, they suggested, need to establish ways of working that help trainees *integrate* these different forms of professional knowledge. Trainees need to be systematically prepared in practical classroom knowledge – they need to be prepared at level (a) – it is a distinctive form of professional knowledge and training can not be left to chance. But Furlong *et al.* suggested that it is only teachers who have access to that level of knowledge; it is only they who know about particular children working on a particular curriculum in a particular school. Lecturers can visit schools and give generalized advice but by definition that will always be generalized. Furlong *et al.* also argued that although individual teachers might be in a position to prepare trainees at levels (b), (c) and (d), the nature of their job meant that their greatest strength was at level (a). However, lecturers, because of their breadth of experience and because of their involvement in research, had access to other forms of professional knowledge. Training must therefore be a partnership between training institutions and schools.

Since publication, this analysis has been criticized for its notion of levels and certainly given that the term does carry overtones of a hierarchy then it would seem inappropriate – different *dimensions* of training might have been a more appropriate term. McIntyre (1990), in a lengthy critique, has also suggested that there is an implicit hierarchy in more than the language – he suggests that the model prioritizes academic knowledge at level (d) implying that – that is the only route to professional rigour. McIntyre agrees that trainees need access to different forms of professional knowledge and that the practical knowledge of teachers must be a central part of that training process. However, he suggests that different forms of professional knowledge should all be used to interrogate each other. Practical classroom knowledge – the province of teachers – should be used to interrogate more theoretically-based knowledge and vice versa.

The debate continues but where many of those writing on initial teacher education would now agree is that trainees need systematic preparation in that practical classroom knowledge and by definition that aspect of training (and we would reassert that it is only one aspect of training) can only be provided by teachers working in their own classrooms and schools. As a consequence it is necessary to move from the notion of *supervision* in school, where teachers are supervising trainees in the application of training acquired elsewhere, to the notion of *mentoring*, which is an active process, where teachers themselves as practitioners have an active role in the training process.

Since the publication of that earlier study, the benefits of school-based training have become much more widely accepted, at least in principle. In practice, however, it seems to us questionable whether an appreciation of the consequent and substantial difficulties experienced by trainees in gaining access to teachers' knowledge have yet been fully considered in many teacher education courses. In starting to think more deeply about the structuring of school-based experience and the role of the mentor, we believe that it is necessary to begin with the trainees' perspective. Their learning needs should be the foundation on which the planning of practical training should rest. To ignore the trainees' needs is equivalent to the student-teacher planning a lesson without any thought of the age, abilities or interests of the children for whom the lesson is intended.

Student Concerns and Stages of Development

What do we know of the needs of trainee teachers? An examination of research literature on the process of learning to teach confirms the common sense observation that trainees typically go through a number of distinct stages of development, each with its own focal concerns. These concerns can usefully be grouped under the following headings: early idealism; survival; recognizing difficulties; hitting the plateau; and moving on.

Early idealism

Research into the *pre*-teaching concerns of trainees has found that they are often idealistic in their feelings towards their students, identifying realistically with pupils but unsympathetic or even hostile to the class teacher (Fuller and Bown, 1975). Moreover, they often seem to hold a clear image of the sort of teacher they want to be. They are terrified of ending up like that 'miserable old cynic in the corner of the staffroom'!

Survival

Once trainees embark on their teaching experience, however, their idealism often fades in the face of the realities of classroom life and they frequently become obsessed with their own survival. It is therefore not surprising that class control and management, 'fitting in' and establishing themselves as a 'teacher' often become major issues for them.

At this stage of training, trainees frequently refer to the problem of not being able to 'see'. Student-teachers in our own research have used phrases such as 'it's all a blur', 'I can't seem to focus' and 'feeling my way'. In the early stages of school experience, time is often given for trainees to observe classroom practice but as Calderhead (1988a) confirms, this is often wasted time – they can not make sense of the noise and movement around them; they do not understand the significance of the teacher's actions – they simply do not know what it is they are supposed to be looking for. It is no wonder that at this stage trainees often express the need for 'quick fixes', and 'hints and tips' (Eisenhart *el al.*, 1991).

Recognizing difficulties

At the next stage, trainees become sensitive to the varied demands made on them and are keen to give an impressive performance. With confidence shaken, the issue of assessment often starts to predominate. As college tutors are well aware, even at quite early stages, trainees constantly make the plaintive cry of, 'Am I doing well?', 'Will I pass?' This is despite the fact that an over-concern with assessment means that they have missed the main point of the experience. In this phase, trainees also begin to focus on the issue of teaching methods and materials, referring frequently to classroom constraints or lack of resources.

Hitting the plateau

After the first few weeks when basic management and control procedures have been established, trainees are liable to 'hit the plateau'; at last they have found a way of teaching that seems to work and they are going to stick to it! However, they frequently find great difficulty, as Feiman-Nemser and Buchmann (1987) explain, in shifting the focus from themselves to others, or from the subjects they are teaching to the issue of what the pupils need to learn. There often is, as Feiman-Nemser and Buchmann point out, a vast gulf that exists between 'going through the motions of teaching...and connecting these activities to what pupils should be learning over time' (p.257).

Moving on

Trainees may eventually go on to experiment and/or show concern for pupils' learning but without positive intervention, Calderhead (1987) maintains that their level of reflection will be shallow and ineffective in promoting professional learning. (For sequences of concerns see Calderhead, 1984, 1987; Fuller and Bown, 1975). A final phase of development has been identified as occurring after approximately seven years – that of 'teacher burn-out' (Calderhead, 1984).

What are the reasons for these concerns at different stages of development? Are they warranted if, as many believe, learning to teach is just a matter of picking up practical hints and tips and gaining expertise through a process of trial and error? In the next section we examine what research tells us about a variety of processes in learning to teach: the nature of the practical knowledge trainees must acquire; the process of forming concepts; the interpersonal skills they must develop; and the affective issues they must confront. A more detailed understanding of these issues is, we argue, essential if we are to have a clearer vision of what the role of the mentor in school must be.

Learning to Teach

Developing a practical knowledge base

As we indicated above, there is now broad agreement that learning to teach demands that direct practical experience is placed at the heart of the training process. But what of the content of practical training? What exactly is it that mentors can help trainees learn through direct experience in schools and classrooms that can not be gained elsewhere? Research into teachers' practical knowledge is, as Elbaz (1983) points out, patchy and fragmented, focusing on isolated characteristics and usually approached from a negative stance. This must be due, in part, to the fact that teachers are simply not seen as possessing a body of knowledge or expertise appropriate to their work. It is thought they possess knowledge in relation to, for example, subject matter, but not practical professional knowledge (Clandinin, 1986; Elbaz 1983; Lortie, 1975; Wilson et al., 1987). We would disagree and suggest that practical classroom knowledge can usefully be understood in terms of four broad areas – the four 'Ss'. They are knowledge of 'students' (or pupils), 'situation', 'subject matter' and 'strategies'.

At the most specific level, in terms of the *students* or pupils, the trainee needs to gain a knowledge of the actual students in the class: learn their names, discover their interests, attitudes, backgrounds, and find out what they are capable of achieving. But they also need to develop a detailed knowledge of the *situation* in which they must teach. This will involve developing a knowledge of the actual classroom, school and community in terms of its ethos, demands and constraints.

Subject matter, or content knowledge, has been called the 'missing paradigm' in research on teachers' thinking, particularly at secondary school level (Shulman, 1986). Trainees may well know their subject from their own education but in becoming teachers they need to acquire a new type of subject knowledge: 'pedagogical content knowledge'. Pedagogical content knowledge involves ways of representing subjects that make them understandable to others (Wilson *et al.*, 1987). While certain aspects of lesson 'content', for example evaluation of different types of subject matter and subject specific skills, may best be explored outside the classroom situation, trainees will be dependent on their observations of particular students in particular situations to evaluate just how effective their 'representations' of the subject matter have been.

Finally, and inextricably linked to pedagogical content knowledge, trainees need to develop a knowledge of which *strategies* may be used. Not simply a theoretical knowledge of different strategies that 'may' be used, but a practical knowledge of which techniques or tactics are most appropriate to facilitate learning in each case.

In practice these four domains (students, situation, subject matter and strategies) are never 'experienced' or 'used' in isolation. While they may differ in character, both 'students' and 'situation' are largely distinct but in a sense 'given' or 'fixed', whereas 'subject matter' and 'strategies' are inseparable but more mutable and open to choice. When planning, interacting or responding to problems, trainees need to weigh up and balance considerations of these four aspects. In reality, trainees' decisions and responses will also be influenced or modified by considerations of their own 'interests' and constrained by their particular stage of development.

Developing and exposing concepts

Learning to teach, however, does not merely involve acquiring a body of new practical knowledge, it actually involves changes in cognition, the perception and memory of less-experienced teachers differing from that of 'experts' (Berliner, 1987). Trainees need to form concepts, schemas and scripts in order to make sense of, interpret and come to 'control' aspects of classroom life (Carter and Doyle, 1987). The fact that new trainees have not yet had the experience to form these concepts is associated with the problem of not being able to 'see'. Without such concepts, classrooms remain what Copeland

(1981) describes as 'a bewildering kaleidoscope of people, behaviours, events and interactions only dimly understood' (p.11).

Concepts can be held at the level of personal theory, such as concepts of acceptable levels of movement and noise in the classroom or can be generalizations abstracted from the trainees' practical knowledge base – about typical students and situations or about subject matter and strategies that are likely to work. These concepts evolve only through experience; not life experience, not from observations of classrooms, but from actually doing the business of teaching (Berliner, 1987). Since practical knowledge both at the level of the 'actual' and at the level of the 'typical' is formed through the trainee's classroom experience, this knowledge tends to be personal and largely tacit. Indeed, Sternberg and Caruso (1985) maintain that practical knowledge lends itself better to tacit or possibly mediated learning in that academic representation of this knowledge is 'poorly fit for practical purposes' (p.149). Although this means that practical knowledge can not be 'passed on' in any traditional sense, it does not, however, negate the role of the mentor. Mentors are in a unique position to be able to support trainees as they begin to form concepts about their practical work. They are also uniquely placed to expose trainees' developing concepts and help them see the implications of various ways of working. This is what Schon (1991) refers to as 'guiding their seeing'.

Helping trainees to look at their own practice is particularly important because the way in which they interpret school experience is so often influenced and 'shaped' by their own set of attitudes, beliefs and values; their life values in general and their educational values in particular. The trainees' own experience of schools and certainly the 'images' they hold of classrooms and pupils and of the sort of teachers they want to be will exert a powerful effect on their practice (see Calderhead, 1988b; Clandinin, 1986; Nias, 1989). Freeman (1991) maintains student-teachers are only made aware of their own educational beliefs when forced to articulate them in the process of teacher education. Their old perspectives interact with their new understandings and may consequently lead them to modify or change their views. Other researchers argue that beliefs about teaching are largely 'fixed' before training; student-teachers merely become more skilled at articulating and implementing the perspectives they already hold (Tabachnick and Zeichner, 1984). Whether or not they are permanent, they certainly need confronting by trainees at some stage in their training.

What we are advocating here is the importance of reflection on teaching: a notion that has assumed an important role in many teacher education programmes in recent years (Barrett *et al.*, 1992). Trainees are today constantly urged to reflect, though it is not always made explicit what reflection means or what they should be reflecting on. Studies of practice have found that too often trainees' and cooperating teachers' reflections centre superficially on issues such as whether a particular strategy 'worked', on the children's apparent enjoyment of an activity or whether specified objectives had been met (Ben-Peretz and Rumney, 1991; Calderhead, 1987) – in essence focusing on the 'safe' and not the 'challenging, on the 'existing' and not on the 'possible'.

In our view, the aim of reflection must be to learn something wider and of more significance by 'making the tacit explicit' (Freeman, 1991). Through helping the trainee to understand the underlying implications of working in particular and in different ways, mentors can be encouraging the formation of patterns of thinking. In terms of Furlong *et al.*'s (1988) model, reported above, trainees begin to work at level (c) looking at the 'practical principles' underlying their own practice and at level (d) examining the moral, political and theoretical bases of practice. It is these forms of thinking, these dimensions of professional knowledge, that are the 'link' to college-based aspects of training.

Making the tacit explicit also allows the trainee to make their developing concepts of practical knowledge and educational values known to themselves. This in turn gives them greater control over their own practice and therefore in a sense empowers them (Elbaz, 1983; Freeman, 1991). However, it may only be after basic competence and confidence in teaching is achieved, only with the help of a trusted mentor and possibly only after trainees have been 'prepared' in some way that their capacities to reflect can be developed (see Calderhead, 1987, 1989, 1991; Feiman-Nemser and Buchmann, 1987; Zeichner and Liston, 1987). This parallels Russell's (1988) idea of moving from comfort with practice to criticism of practice! One trainee in our own research who was in his first weeks of teaching practice explained that whenever the teacher asked what he had planned she would ask, '"Why?", always "why?" Those "whys" get me panicking and I begin scribbling out everything I've already planned"'. He maintained that you can get too much questioning and lose confidence. Having watched him teach we would agree with him!

The political and the personal
The practical business of learning to teach is therefore a complex and necessarily slow process. It is not possible to undertake all of the steps to effective professionalism at once. That process is often made more

complex still by other pressures that impose on trainees – the pressure of conflicting expectations as well as demands on the self. Effective school-based training needs to recognize both of these.

Trainees have often reported that they feel under pressure to adopt a similar teaching style to their mentor. This is partly in an attempt to gain credibility in the pupils' eyes – Copeland (1981) for example, suggests that student teachers find that pupils respond better to known ways of working – but also in order to gain favour with the teacher. As one student in our own research commented, 'What my teacher would really like is for me to be more like him!' This need to fit in with the teacher and with the school can put enormous pressure on the trainee (Lacey, 1977), a pressure that can be exacerbated by a further need to meet the sometimes conflicting demands of the college tutor. Fish (1989) elaborates that trainees are caught in a no-win situation. Who should they keep happy: the mentor whom they have to face on a daily basis or the college tutor whom they see less frequently but who is largely responsible for their final assessment? They can be caught between their own sense of the depth and complexity of teaching and the knowledge that their final mark can depend on a superficially impressive performance; between the teacher's possible view that learning to teach is just a matter of 'copy and practise' and the college's requirement to plan ahead and reflect...and so the list goes on (Fish, 1989; Squirrell et al., 1990; Zeichner and Liston, 1987).

Alongside the problem of sensing and adapting to conflicting expectations, the trainee also finds that teaching makes demands upon the 'self'. Teaching is a personal activity and as such exposes and makes calls upon the personality; it is an occupation that is felt as well as experienced (Nias, 1989). Fuller and Bown (1975) describe teaching as a process of constant, unremitting self-confrontation. Certainly in our research the trainees' sense of their own identity and the rift and shift between their personal and professional selves is often at the centre of their concerns.

Trainees desperately want to be liked by the pupils but are often accused of being 'over-friendly' and then react to this criticism by becoming over-controlling, stern and authoritarian; it is hard for them to find the right balance. They are, to an extent, reliant on pupils for feedback as to the effectiveness of their teaching and learn to detect, for example, signs of boredom and frustration as well as understanding and pleasure (Feiman-Nemser and Buchmann, 1987). Trainees will also detect how pupils feel about them as people; they are 'on trial' as a person (Squirrell et al., 1990). Sometimes this information can be excruciatingly painful!

In summary, we would agree with Nias (1989) when she states that teachers, among other abilities, need to process densely packed information reaching them simultaneously on many channels and respond sensitively and with accuracy; not only orchestrating their skills but, as Schon (1991) explains, dealing with and making new sense of the uncertain, unique and value-conflicted situation that their existing practical knowledge will not fit.

Models of Mentoring

If these then are some of the processes involved in learning to teach what can they tell us about the role of the mentor? What sorts of strategies and approaches should they be using in supporting trainees through these different stages? Unfortunately, if we examine the literature that already exists on the role of the mentor, most of it is extremely one-dimensional, reflecting the fact that much of the debate to date on the value of school-based training has been ideologically inspired (Furlong, 1992). From looking at current literature it is possible to identify three rather distinct models of mentoring: the apprenticeship model; the competency model; and the reflective practitioner model. As we will suggest, each of them is partial and inadequate, perhaps only appropriate at a particular stage of a trainee's development. However, taken together, we suggest that they may contribute to a view of mentoring that responds to the changing needs of trainees.

The apprenticeship model and 'learning to see'

The first model apparent in the literature is what might be called an apprenticeship model. This is an approach to learning to teach that is strongly advocated by O'Hear (1988) and the Hillgate Group (1989). In one of their more coherent passages, the Hillgate Group argue that there is a long tradition going back to Aristotle that some skills, including many that are difficult, complex and of high moral and cultural value, are best learned 'by the emulation of experienced practitioners and by supervised practice under guidance' (p.9). In the case of such skills, apprenticeship, they suggest, should take precedence over instruction.

Of course the Hillgate Group argue that their apprenticeship model is all that is necessary in learning to teach – all you need to do is to work alongside an experienced practitioner. But before we fall into the trap of dismissing their arguments out of hand, we need to recognize the truth in their observation, for it would seem to us that the work of a mentor does indeed contain elements of this apprenticeship model. Trainees need first-hand experience of real students, teaching situations, classroom strategies and subject matter. In the early stages of their training the purpose of that practical experience is to allow them to start to form concepts, schemas or scripts of the process of teaching. But in order to begin to 'see', trainees need an interpreter. They need to work alongside a mentor who can explain the significance of what is happening in the classroom. As we have argued above, trainees also need to sense and fit into established routines. They therefore also need to be able to model themselves on someone. Such a model can also act as a guide, articulating and presenting 'recipes' that will work.

It is often advocated that in the first weeks of teaching experience trainees should work with individuals or small groups of pupils. The reason this is thought to be useful is that it is believed to reduce the complexity of the teaching process. However, as trainees are mainly concerned with 'survival' issues at this stage, small-group work of this sort may only partially meet their needs. Small-group work can, for example, help them focus on the issue of differentiation. It will not, however, address their concerns with classroom management and control. Moreover, if it detaches them from the main business of the classroom, it reduces the opportunity for the mentor to act as a model and interpreter. We would suggest that at this early stage, a more appropriate strategy is for the trainee to work alongside a mentor, taking responsibility for a small part of the whole teaching process.

If we substitute the term 'collaborative teaching' for apprenticeship – a term used by Burn (1992) in describing part of her work as a mentor in the Oxford Internship Scheme – then we can perhaps start to see the power of this aspect of the mentor's role in the early stages of learning to teach. For example, Burn (p.134) lists the following as some of the advantages of collaborative teaching:

> learning to plan lessons carefully through being involved in joint planning with an experienced teacher, finding out what the teacher takes account of and identifying with the planning and its consequences;
>
> learning certain skills of classroom teaching through having responsibility for a specified component of the lessons, while identifying with the whole lesson and recognizing the relationships of the part to the whole;
>
> gaining access to the teacher's craft knowledge through observation of the teacher's actions, informed by a thorough knowledge of the planning and probably through discussion of the lesson afterwards, with a heightened awareness of having joint responsibility for the lesson.

This is precisely the sort of training that students need in the early stages of school experience when they are 'learning to see'.

The competency model – systematic training

While the Hillgate Group and their friends are urging that learning to teach can best be understood as a form of apprenticeship, others are advocating a competency-based approach. For those in this camp, learning to teach involves practical training on a list of pre-defined competences. The mentor takes on the role of a *systematic trainer,* observing the trainee, perhaps with a pre-defined observation schedule and providing feedback. They are in effect coaching the trainee on a list of agreed behaviours that are, at least in part, specified by others.

Systematic training in this country has a long history, becoming particularly popular in the 1970s with the development of interaction analysis, micro-teaching and some interest in American competency-based teacher education. We have of late, of course, seen the approach re-emerge – initially somewhat tentatively in Circular 24/89 (DES, 1989) and now much more forcefully in Circular 9/92 (DFE, 1992).

What is right about the competency approach is that after an initial period of collaborative teaching, trainees will benefit from an explicit programme of training following a routine of observation and feedback. In this second stage of learning to teach, trainees must be given control of the teaching process. Learning at this stage necessitates trainees taking responsibility; they have to learn by actually doing the job of teaching. While still adopting some of the teachers' ready-made routines, they need to be helped progressively to form and implement some of their own while continually developing and modifying their own personal concepts and schemas. In order to help this process the mentor therefore needs, at this stage of the trainee's development, to take an active role, acting as a mirror or working as a coach.

There are very many models within the literature of how mentors can best approach systematic training (see Smyth, 1991, for an up-to-date critical review). Current British regulations are prioritizing one of these: the competency model. It may well be that this aspect of the mentor's work is facilitated if they utilize a predefined list of competences, though we would re-emphasize that it is not the only approach. However, we would suggest that if the phase of collaborative teaching has been gone through it is perfectly possible and educationally advantageous to involve the trainee in discussion of which competences they want their mentor to focus on.

One common problem that trainees face is that once they have taken control, once they have established routines that work for them, they can stop learning – they can hit a plateau. At this point the mentor therefore not only needs to 'remove the structure' of support but also encourage the trainee to observe and experiment with different teaching styles and strategies. Just because trainees are ready for more explicit training in relation to their own performance it does not mean that the benefits of modelling through observation and collaborative teaching are over. The foundations for an extended repertoire continue to be best laid by working alongside and observing experienced teachers. In other words, it is not appropriate to think of these phases of mentoring as discrete entities; rather, they are progressive.

The reflective model – from teaching to learning

The final approach to mentoring currently widely advocated is the reflective practitioner model. Some would argue that calling it a model is too generous – 'slogan' might be more appropriate for as Calderhead (1989) has noted, there are great difficulties in defining what reflective teaching actually is and even more difficulty in suggesting what activities by mentors might promote its development. Indeed most courses, it would seem, try to promote the reflective practitioner by means other than involving mentors – by the way they structure the course with concurrent periods of school and college activity so that the lecturers can encourage trainees to reflect – or by particular assignments or activities such as keeping journals or undertaking IT-INSET assignments. All of these are valuable, but we would suggest that once trainees have, with systematic support from their mentor, achieved basic classroom competence, ways have to be found of introducing a critical element into the mentoring process itself. To put it more directly, if learning to teach is at the heart of training then reflection on teaching, however it is defined, must be part of that learning process.

In this final stage of practical preparation in teaching, trainees need to be encouraged to switch from a focus on their own teaching performance to a focus on the children's learning and how they can make it more effective. But to achieve this switch means more than the trainee simply extending his or her repertoire of routines. To focus on children's learning demands that trainees move beyond routines and rituals; they need to develop a deeper understanding of the learning process; thinking through different ways of teaching and developing their own justifications and practical principles from their work.

While it is common for mentors to withdraw and let the trainee get on alone once they have achieved basic competence, it would seem to us that if mentors are to facilitate this shift of focus they must continue to take an active role. However, we would argue that trainees are unlikely to be ready for this form of reflection on their own practice until they have gained some mastery of their teaching skills; they need to be ready to shift their focus from their own teaching to the pupils' learning and that can not come until they have gained some confidence in their own teaching.

Supporting trainees in this more reflective process necessarily demands a shift in the role of the mentor. To facilitate this process mentors need to be able to move from being a model and instructor to being a co-enquirer. Those other aspects of their role may continue but in promoting critical reflection a more equal and open relationship is essential. As we implied earlier, thinking critically about teaching and learning demands open-mindedness and involves confronting beliefs and values. This is difficult and challenging work but we believe it is an essential element in what a true mentor must be.

Conclusion

From this preliminary examination of trainees' learning needs at different stages of development, we are then able to propose a fuller and more complete view of the role of the mentor. In the early stages of school experience, when trainees are still 'learning to see', mentors need to act as collaborative teachers, working alongside trainees, acting as interpreters and models. Once trainees have moved beyond that initial stage and started to take increased responsibility for the teaching process itself, mentors need to extend their role. While continuing some periods of collaborative teaching, they also need to develop a more systemic approach to training, acting as instructors by establishing routines of observation and feedback on agreed competences. Finally, once trainees have achieved basic competence, the role of the mentor needs to develop further. While other aspects of the role may continue, mentors in this final stage of development need to establish themselves as co-enquirers with the aim of promoting critical reflection on teaching and learning by the trainee.

Effective mentoring is therefore a difficult and demanding task and teachers performing the role need the time and inservice support appropriate to the increased responsibilities being placed on them. But in our enthusiasm for analysing the role of the mentor we should not lose sight of the point made clearly at the beginning of this chapter. The work of mentors, however effectively undertaken, can, by definition, be only one aspect of professional preparation. Trainee teachers continue to need preparation in other dimensions of professionality. They need a broad understanding of different styles of practice; an understanding of the practical principles underlying practice; and an appreciation of the moral, political and theoretical issues underlying educational practice. All of these other dimensions of professional knowledge are still best provided by those in higher education. Effective mentoring is a way of complementing and extending forms of training traditionally made available through higher education institutions. It is not intended to be, nor can it be, a substitute for them.

By way of conclusion we offer the following advice on how *not* to become an expert swimmer:

- Take plenty of lessons on the theoretical aspects of swimming before getting into the pool.
- Learn with an expert who has forgotten what it feels like to be a learner, eg, afraid of the water.
- Learn with an expert who feels that they have nothing left to learn, who maintains that there is only one right way (their way!!) to swim and who is more interested in displaying their skills than empowering you.
- Learn with an expert who believes in throwing you in at the deep end or who leaves you alone to play in the shallow end.
- Learn with an expert who expects you to refine your stroke while you are struggling to stay afloat.
- Best of all learn with two experts who have totally different views about swimming, make conflicting and contradictory demands on you, but in order to gain your swimming certificate you are required to please them both!

Acknowledgements

This paper is based upon research funded by the Paul Hamlyn Foundation. We gratefully acknowledge their support and the time given by teachers and trainees.

REFERENCES

Barrett, E, Whitty, G, Furlong, J, Galvin, C and Barton, L (1992) *Initial Teacher Education in England and Wales: A Topography,* Modes of Teacher Education Project, London: Goldsmiths College.

Ben-Peretz, M and Rumney, S (1991) 'Professional thinking in guided practice', *Teaching and Teacher Education,* 7, 5/6.

Berliner, DC (1987) 'Ways of thinking about students and classrooms by more and less experienced teachers', in Calderhead, J (ed.) *Exploring Teachers' Thinking,* London: Cassell.

Burn, C (1992) 'Collaborative teaching', in Wilkin, M (ed.) *Mentoring in Schools,* London: Kogan Page.

Calderhead, J (1984) *Teachers' Classroom Decision Making,* London: Holt, Rinehart and Winston.

Calderhead, J (1987) 'The quality of reflection in student teachers' professional learning', *European Journal of Teacher Education,* 10, 3.

Calderhead, J (1998a) 'Learning from introductory schools experience', *Journal of Education for Teaching*, 4, 1.

Calderhead, J (1988b) *Teachers' Professional Learning*, London: Falmer Press.

Calderhead, J (1989) 'Reflective teaching and teacher education', *Teacher and Teacher Education*, 5,1.

Calderhead, J (1991) 'The nature and growth of knowledge in student teaching', *Teaching and Teacher Education*, 7, 5/6.

Carter, K and Doyle, W (1987) 'Teachers' knowledge structure and comprehension processes', in Calderhead, J (ed.) *Exploring Teachers' Thinking*, London: Cassell.

Clandinin, DJ (1986) *Classroom Practice: Teachers' Images in Action*, London: Falmer Press.

Copeland, WD (1981) 'Clinical experiences in the education of teachers', *Journal of Education for Teaching*, 7,1.

DES (1989) *Initial Teacher Training: Approval of Courses (Circular 24/89)* London: HMSO.

DFE (1992) *Initial Teacher Training (Secondary Phase) (Circular 9/92)* London: DFE.

Eisenhart, M, Behm, L and Riomagnano, L (1991) 'Learning to teach: developing expertise or rite of passage?', *Journal of Education for Teaching*, 7,1.

Elbaz, F (1983) *Teacher Thinking: A Study of Practical Knowledge*, London: Croom Helm.

Feiman-Nemser, S and Buchmann, M (1987) 'When is student teaching teacher education?', *Teacher and Teacher Education*, 3, pp. 255–73.

Fish, D (1989) *Learning Through Practices in Initial Teacher Education*, London: Kogan Page.

Freeman, D (1991) 'To make the tacit explicit – teacher education, emerging discourse and conceptions of teaching', *Teacher and Teacher Education*, 7, 5/6.

Fuller, F and Bown, O (1975) 'Becoming a Teacher', in Ryan, K (ed.), *Teacher Education, 74th Year Book of the National Society for the Study of Education*, Chicago, IL: University of Chicago Press.

Furlong VJ (1992) 'Reconstructing professionalism: ideological struggle in initial teacher education', in Arnot, M and Barton, L (eds) *Voicing Concerns: Sociological Perspectives on Contemporary Educational Reforms*, London: Triangle.

Furlong, VJ, Hirst, PH, Pocklington, K and Miles, S (1988) *Initial Teacher Training and the Role of the School*, Buckingham: Open University Press.

Hillgate Group (1989) *Learning to Teach*, London: The Claridge Press.

Lacey, C (1977) *The Socialisation of Teachers*, London: Methuen.

Lortie, D (1975) *Schoolteacher: A Sociological Study*, Chicago, IL: University of Chicago Press.

McIntyre, D (1990) 'The Oxford Internship Scheme and the Cambridge analytical framework: models of partnership in initial teacher education', in Booth, M, Furlong, J and Wilkin, M (eds) *Partnership in Initial Teacher Training*, London: Cassell.

Nias, J (1989) *Primary Teachers' Talking*, London: Routledge.

O'Hear, A (1988) *Who Teaches the Teachers?*, London: Social Affairs Unit.

Russell, T (1988) 'From pre-service teacher education to first year of teaching: a study of theory and practice', in Calderhead, J (ed.) *Teachers' Professional Learning*, London: Falmer Press.

Schon, D (1991) *Educating the Reflective Practitioner*, San Francisco, CA: Jossey Bass.

Shulman, L (1986) 'Those who understand: knowledge growth in teaching', *Educational Researcher*, February.

Smyth, J (1991) *Teachers as Collaborative Learners*, Milton Keynes: Open University Press.

Squirrell, G, Gilroy, P, Jones, D and Ruddock, J (1990) 'Acquiring knowledge in initial teacher training', *Library and Information Research Report 79*, London: British Library Board.

Sternberg, R and Caruso, D (1985) 'Practical modes of knowing in learning and teaching the ways of knowing', in Eisner, E (ed.) *84th Yearbook of the National Society for the Study of Education*, Chicago: University of Chicago Press.

Tabachnick, B and Zeichner, K (1984) 'The impact of the student teaching experience on the development of teacher perspectives', *Journal of Teacher Education*, Nov–Dec.

Wilson, S, Shulman, L and Richert, A (1987) '150 different ways of knowing: representations of knowledge in teaching', in Calderhead, J (ed.) *Exploring Teachers' Thinking*, London: Cassell.

Yinger, RJ (1980) 'A study of teacher planning', *The Elementary School Journal*, **80**,3.

Zeichner, K and Liston, D (1987) 'Teaching student teachers to reflect', *Harvard Educational Review*, **57**,1.

5 Teachers' Expertise and Models of Mentoring

Donald McIntyre and Hazel Hagger

What can classroom teachers usefully contribute to the initial professional education of entrants to their profession? That there is a *need* for practising teachers to make a major contribution has been argued from several different perspectives:

> ideas about the kinds of knowledge which beginning teachers need and how these kinds of knowledge should relate to each other (eg, Benton, 1990; Booth *et al.*, 1990; Furlong *et. al.*, 1988*);*
> arguments based on research into the *processes* of learning to teach (eg, Elliott and Calderhead, and Maynard and Furlong, in this volume; McIntyre, 1988);
> ideologically-motivated arguments against the influence of educational 'theorists' in universities and colleges, and in favour of a more 'commonsense' approach to learning the very 'practical' job of teaching (eg, Hillgate Group, 1989; Lawlor, 1990; O'Hear, 1988).

In this chapter the emphasis will be on what teachers can most distinctively, appropriately and realistically offer in initial teacher education. Primary concerns will be with teachers' expertise, their conditions of work, and the implications for them of different conceptions of the mentoring role. A number of increasingly ambitious views of mentoring will be considered in terms of the extent to which they take advantage of the expertise which experienced teachers can offer to entrants to their profession and in terms of the feasibility of such roles being fulfilled effectively by practising teachers.

Zero Level

We start with conceptions of mentoring which owe nothing at all to teachers' expertise as teachers. Such conceptions seem to be common, perhaps understandably so, since they generally draw on models of mentoring quite fully developed in other contexts, and since they also have the appeal of being system-wide, covering a number of different purposes within a school staff. Most commonly, these kinds of imported and multi-purpose conceptions of mentoring are drawn by specialists in education management from the wider field of 'management' and are seen as contributing to the management of induction and staff development within schools. The popularity of such generic conceptions of mentoring makes it important that their strengths and weaknesses should be carefully considered.

A good example of this kind of view of mentoring is that articulated by Kelly et al., (1992). They start their paper with the sentence: 'The term "mentor" is being used to describe an increasing range of activities' (p.173), but characteristically, rather than differentiating these activities, they move on within a few lines to treat mentoring as a singular activity, 'a significant element in the staff development and target-setting process for all staff including trainees' (p.173), and they discuss mentoring under such sub-headings as 'The mentoring approach', 'Induction mentoring: the new head, the new teacher and the trainee teacher' and 'A mentoring system for staff development'. Characteristically, too, the references which they quote are from the journals *Industrial and Commercial Training* and *Management Education and Development*.

Kelly and his colleagues discuss mentoring in terms of the parts which mentors can play in facilitating different stages of experiential learning in general, and go on to suggest (pp. 177–8) general characteristics of good mentoring practice, eg:

When used as part of an organization's staff development programme, mentoring will provide protégés with

- opportunities for meaningful feedback on performance;
- opportunities for greater effectiveness in classroom/workplace;
- opportunities to observe others as role models in the classroom or in general management activities;
- personal support.

They recognize well enough the limits to possible generalization. For example, having discussed the role of the mentor in relation to head-teacher induction, they note that, 'For teachers in their first year, the mentor plays a very different role' (p.176), but, given their concern for the common elements of 'the mentoring approach', what they have to say about mentoring for newly qualified teachers or trainee teachers is understandably brief and superficial.

Such an imported, generalized, system-wide conception of mentoring has perhaps three potential advantages:

1. In so far as mentoring skills and strategies can be generic and context-free, the opportunity is used to learn from experience in other contexts.
2. It can help senior school management to construe initial teacher education not as something extra and different, stuck on to the work of the school, but as one element of an important, pervasive aspect of the school's work, to be planned as an integral component of that work.
3. It could be the starting-point for recognizing the importance and difficulty of developing what Kelly and his colleagues call 'the learning school'. Most British schools lack the conditions necessary to facilitate thoughtful reflection and learning by teachers – for example, the 'collegiality' necessary for teachers to share, analyse and collaboratively learn from their successes and their problems (cf. Cole, 1991; Little, 1990), or more basically the recognition that quiet places and times for reflection when one is not exhausted are necessary for teacher development. The absence of such conditions is a fundamental difficulty for school-based initial teacher education, as it is for teachers' professional development generally. It is a difficulty which certainly will not be overcome by anything so simple as the setting up of school-wide mentoring systems; but setting up such systems might possibly be a first step towards recognition of the need.

This kind of generalized conception of mentoring does however have major weaknesses:

1. Most obviously, it is *not very helpful* in offering guidance to, or in recognizing the needs of, the mentors of student-teachers or beginning teachers. The problems and possibilities of helping novice teachers to learn have (so far as anyone has yet discovered) so little in common with those of helping new headteachers to learn their jobs, or with those of helping people to learn jobs in industry and commerce, that guidance construed as being so widely relevant is certain to have very limited relevance to this distinctive context.
2. By emphasizing what is common to a wide variety of mentoring tasks, this approach inevitably presents a *distorted* picture of the expertise required for the mentoring of novice teachers. For exam-

ple, discussing 'the mentoring approach' in general, Kelly and his colleagues suggest that,

> The crucial starting point is concrete experience: a happening, or action. Development often starts with a surprise, puzzlement or shock when something has happened that was unexpected or didn't make sense. When this happens a mentor is someone to go to for help (Kelly *et al.*, op. cit., p.174).

This seems eminently sensible when discussing the learning of experienced teachers and the role of their mentor colleagues; but if school-based initial teacher education is not to be grossly irresponsible, much more initiative will be required from mentors in that context.

More generally, highly generalized conceptions of mentoring lead to those things which *are* generalizable across contexts, with emphasis on pastoral support, on counselling, on 'active listening', on developing appropriate climates for communication, on support in problem-solving, on encouraging reflection, and so on. These generic concerns, predominantly focusing on interpersonal skills, are clearly important for mentoring in initial teacher education as in other contexts, although the lack of context-specific elaboration can often lead to vagueness. What is omitted, however, is *everything that is distinctive* to the tasks of schoolteaching. If initial teacher education is to be school-based to any significant extent, then surely mentoring must to a very large degree be concerned with the distinctive tasks of helping novices to learn about classrooms and schools, about pupils, about teaching and learning, and to learn *how to teach*. It is not at all self-evident how that can best be done, and it is clearly something which mentors will have to learn deliberately. From the highly generalized conceptions of mentoring they will receive no help in this respect, but instead a view of mentoring in which the problems and the skills are overwhelmingly content-free and concerned with personal relations.

3. By neglecting aspects of mentoring expertise which derive from mentors' expertise as schoolteachers, and by emphasizing instead mentoring skills defined on the basis of mentoring activities in other contexts, this kind of conception of mentoring *deskills* teachers. It makes them heavily dependent on the 'expert' guidance of people from outside the school or, more dangerously, of those within the school's management hierarchy. It undermines mentor-teachers' confidence, probably already limited, in their own expertise and therefore their capacity to share that expertise self-

critically with beginning teachers. One further consequence of this would be the undermining of the enormous potential of school-based initial teacher education as a means of enhancing the status of classroom teaching and of enabling classroom teachers to recognize and develop their teaching expertise through articulating, sharing and reflecting on it. Another equally serious consequence could be to persuade people in schools that the tasks and skills of mentoring in initial teacher education are already well understood and so do not need to be developed through mentors' theorization and investigation of their own efforts.

On balance, then, such generic conceptions of mentoring are likely to be dangerously counter-productive if they are allowed a dominant influence. They may have some value, on the other hand, in offering insights which in a minor way complement conceptions of mentoring more firmly rooted in mentors' expertise as classroom teachers.

Minimal Mentoring: Support for Learning through Practice

Whatever other kinds of learning are involved in initial teacher education, few would question the necessary centrality of learning through practice. However clear, however thorough, however sophisticated or simple the learner-teacher's understandings of classroom teaching, it is only by putting these understandings into practice, by putting them to the test of practice, and by developing them through practice that he or she can become a competent classroom teacher. Beginning teachers tend seriously to underestimate the value and importance of other kinds of learning; but they are right to view their own practice as the *sine qua non* of learning to teach.

Learning through practice is generally much more effective if it is supported by a competent, experienced practitioner. Again, there are few who would question this. Even the pamphleteers of the extreme right tend to recognize in a simplistic way the need for such supervision. Lawlor (1990), for example, suggests that, 'the skills of teaching are essentially practical ones. They can be acquired only through experience, trial and error, and careful individual supervision', (p.8) and 'The mentor would attend the trainees' classes and guide their preparation and organization of lessons', (p.38).

Among conceptions of mentoring which depend on mentors' expertise as classroom teachers, supervision of beginning teachers' practice is thus the minimal consensual version. The case for such a mentoring role depends on the argument that practising teachers are better placed or better equipped to provide such supervision than are visiting specialist teacher educators based in universities or colleges.

The validity of this argument is not, it must be said, self-evident. As student-teachers quickly become aware, the quality of supervision they get from people who observe their teaching varies markedly; and many student-teachers find that the highest quality of advice and support comes from visiting tutors. The case for supervision by school-based mentors is therefore a strong one if and only if mentors

a. develop to a high level the kinds of supervisory skills which visiting tutors from colleges are in principle equally well placed to use;
b. capitalize on the distinctive opportunities available to them as school-based mentors; and
c. avoid the dangers distinctively associated with school-based mentoring.

Each of these three considerations is worthy of some discussion.

A. Supervision of practice teaching is a complex and difficult activity. Effective supervision depends on, among other things, achieving the following:

- ensuring that learner-teachers are helped to develop planning skills *as well as* skills of classroom practice;
- persuading learner-teachers to concern themselves not only with teaching satisfactory lessons *but also* with learning from their successes and failures in teaching;
- ensuring that learner-teachers direct their learning towards the attainment of teaching abilities which are agreed within the profession to be important *but also* providing genuine space for the learner-teachers' own individual preconceptions and agendas to reveal themselves and to be taken seriously;
- enabling learner-teachers to recognize and to learn from strengths in their teaching *but also* enabling them to face up to their problems;
- focusing on any particular occasion on an agreed small number of predetermined aspects of teaching *but also* being flexible enough to respond to other major concerns which arise;
- enabling learner-teachers to recognize successful strategies which they have learned *but also* persuading them of the need to learn other strategies for different purposes, for different contexts, or simply for variety;
- helping learner-teachers to test the adequacy of practices which they try and to make explicit to themselves the criteria they use *as well as* practising the use of various skills;
- helping learner-teachers not only to become better teachers *but*

also to develop skills, understandings and attitudes necessary to taking reponsibility for their own development;
- helping learner-teachers to learn *but also* explicitly assessing the strengths and weaknesses of their teaching and ultimately, if necessary, taking responsibility for judging them to be inadequate for entry to the profession.

The above list gives some indication of the complex and demanding nature of the task of supervising learner-teachers. All of the above requirements would seem to be as important for school-based mentors as they are for visiting tutors, but none of them would seem to be inherently easier.

B. It is also true, however, that the task of supervision can be transformed and be made much more valuable for learner-teachers if mentors can, *in addition,* take advantage of the distinctive strengths of their situation. These distinctive strengths may be grouped into three main categories, of information, continuity and validity.

Information: The quality of a mentor's support for learner-teachers both in their lesson-planning and in interpreting what happens in their classrooms can be greatly superior to that offered by a visiting tutor because of the mentor's knowledge of the situation. The behaviour patterns, the strengths and weaknesses, the problems and needs of individual pupils; the resources available in the school, where they are, and how to get access to them; the history of particular classes, what they have become accustomed to, what they have done, what their normal responses are – these are some of the kinds of information likely to be at a mentor's disposal and to be very useful in advising on the planning of particular lessons or in making sense of what happens. The skills of using such information selectively and appropriately are distinctive skills for mentors to develop.

Continuity: Mentors can provide in their supervision a much greater degree of continuity than is possible for the occasionally visiting tutor. The continuity relates both to the work of classes being taught and also to the developing skills and understandings of the learner-teachers and the problems which they inevitably experience. Simply being in the same school allows mentor and learner-teacher to converse on a daily basis, with successes, problems and new insights being reported, and reassurance or congratulation given, if only briefly. As a result, successes can be followed up, or problems confronted, in relation to the planning or teaching of lessons and to their supervision; and the mentor's experiences of dealing with the same classes and individual pupils, or using the same resources, can be brought quickly and directly to bear. The mentor's help for the learner-teacher can be much more available when needed and much more sensitive as a result of keeping track of the triumphs and vicissitudes experienced; and the learner-teacher can be enabled to feel part of an ongoing educational enterprise.

Validity. Diagnosis of a learner-teacher's developing strengths and emerging weaknesses should be possible with greater validity when it is the responsibility of a mentor. The mentor does not need to 'visit' the school or classroom and his or her observations of the learner-teacher should not therefore be experienced by the latter, or by pupils, as special occasions on which special efforts should be made to polish the truth. The potential frequency of such observation and of conversations about the learner's progress should allow assessments to be more reliable. The mentor's knowledge of the context, of what pupils are accustomed to and of how they normally behave should allow judgements to be made which take informed account of these factors. Of course, none of this is automatic: mentors need to learn to take advantage of the opportunities which are distinctively open to them.

C. It is possible that, as initial teacher education becomes more school-based, distinctive dangers associated with supervision by mentors will have to be guarded against. Two particular dangers are apparent.

The concentration into the hands of one person of the power to guide and assess the development of an individual learner-teacher's practice brings obvious dangers of *arbitrariness* and *idiosyncrasy*. Because the professional expertise of teachers is generally developed within the privacy of their own classrooms and therefore does tend to be idiosyncratic, mentors have to guard against judging or directing learner-teachers with emphasis on distinctive criteria or standards which would not be applied by other mentors. They can best do this by making their assessments in relation to carefully prepared consensual sets of criteria, and by using the services of moderators who work with several mentors.

The other obvious danger stems from the necessary closeness of the relationship between mentor and learner-teacher. If that relationship is one of mutual respect and of each recognizing the other's commitment to a high quality of professional teaching, the closeness of the relationship can facilitate learning and can increase the satisfaction which both can derive from it, even when there are marked differences in educational beliefs. A failure on either side to respect the other, especially a failure to recognize the legitimacy of the other's beliefs and commitments, or a lack of recognition by the mentor of the learner's adulthood, however naive and unskilled he or she may be, can interfere with learning opportunities in very damaging ways.

This minimal version of mentoring is thus very far from being a trivial undertaking. To take it seriously is a demanding commitment. Nonetheless, it is a conception of mentoring which does not take adequate advantage of teachers' expertise or of the school contexts in which mentors work.

Developed Mentoring: Making Effective Use of Teachers' Expertise

As is made clear by Maynard and Furlong, and also by Elliott and Calderhead, in other chapters of this book, learning to teach is a much more complex process than simply the practising of planning and teaching lessons, even when such practice is well supported. In particular, classroom practice involves using, and either assuming or trying out, *ideas* for and about teaching. Learner-teachers bring with them ideas which vary in their complexity, in the way they are mentally held, in the educational values they embody, in their intelligence, and in their practicality; and a major part of the process of learning to teach has to be that of clarifying, questioning, developing and testing these ideas, and complementing or replacing them with new ideas, which also need to be tested.

Furthermore, teachers acting as mentors have a great deal to contribute to these processes, in helping learner-teachers to become aware of, and to question their preconceptions, in offering them new ideas from their own experience and practices, and in guiding the learner-teachers in the use and development of ideas acquired from various sources. These kinds of contribution depend, however, on the use of a wider range of mentoring strategies than that of helping with the ordinary practice of teaching. In this section we briefly exemplify this wider range by outlining four further strategies which, in the context of the Oxford Internship Scheme, we have found to be feasible and powerful strategies for mentors to use.

Collaborative teaching

In the early stages of learning to teach, taking full responsibility for a class, even for half an hour, can be an awesome task. Commonly it is too complex a situation for learner-teachers to learn from, but instead one which obliges them to concentrate their energies on 'coping' and on finding strategies for preserving their self-esteem and for passing the course (cf. Lacey, 1977). If the task of learning to teach is to be approached rationally, learner-teachers need to try out their ideas and to develop their skills in simpler and less threatening contexts.

In the 1960s and 1970s, 'microteaching' was a widely used approach with just this purpose, student-teachers being given simple teaching tasks with small groups of pupils in order to practise particular aspects of their teaching. Microteaching was generally very effective, except that student-teachers found it difficult to generalize their learning from it to ordinary school classrooms. What is needed then is a similar kind of simplified, protected way of practising and trying out ideas, but within ordinary classroom contexts.

Collaborative teaching (cf. Burn, 1992) offers exactly these kinds of learning conditions. When a mentor and a learner-teacher take joint responsibility for a lesson, plan it together, and each play different parts in the teaching, with the parts played by the learner-teacher being selected to provide focused learning experiences, very nearly ideal conditions can be achieved for the practising of particular teaching skills or strategies. The learner-teacher can concentrate on given tasks without having to worry about other aspects of the lesson, and yet can see these tasks not as isolated exercises but as necessary integral components of the whole ongoing work of classroom teaching. The mentor, on the other hand, is also able to identify in a fully informed way with the total operation, including the parts played by the learner-teacher, and is thus ideally placed to offer constructive feedback. Collaborative teaching is of course a highly flexible approach: the tasks given to learner-teachers – exposition, story-telling, question-and-answer, giving instructions, managing transitions, chairing discussions, starting or finishing lessons, working with individuals, groups or whole classes, or whatever – can be carefully geared to their stage of development and their current learning needs.

As Burn (op.cit.) points out, a second major advantage of collaborative teaching stems from the joint planning which it involves. The discipline of having to explain to one's planning partner exactly what one's purposes are and the variety of considerations that lead one to choose particular ways of pursuing these purposes can help mentors to make explicit their own planning processes in a way that they would otherwise be most unlikely to do and which can be marvellously educative for learner-teachers. In extreme contrast to the common impression that 'experienced teachers don't plan lessons', the complexity and sophistication of experienced teachers' implicit planning can be made accessible to the learner.

For more advanced novices, collaborative teaching has other advantages, in that it enables and can encourage mentors to use more ambitious teaching strategies than they normally would, because of the availability of a second teacher in the classroom; and, of course, having two teachers can be a great asset to pupils.

Access to experienced teachers' craft knowledge

Collaborative teaching is a good way for learner-teachers to gain access to the thinking involved in experienced teachers' lesson planning. It is equally important, however, that they should gain access to the thinking which underlies experienced teachers' classroom practice, the sophistication of which is being increasingly documented by researchers (e.g. Brown and McIntyre, 1992; Louden, 1991). How can such access be attained?

It is important to recognize first that such access is not routinely or easily achieved. Teachers can often be persuaded to talk at great length about their schools, about resources, about curricula and especially about their pupils; it is much more difficult to get them to talk about their own teaching. Furthermore, when teachers do talk in generalized terms about their teaching, their generalizations frequently fail to measure up to the complexity and subtlety of the 'craft knowledge' which they can be shown to *use* in their teaching: teachers' expertise is understandably embedded in their practice and not necessarily easily articulated by them. Observation by student-teachers, as Calderhead (1988) for example has demonstrated, tends not to be helpful in giving them access to such craft knowledge. The very fluency with which experienced teachers achieve their purposes in classrooms hides from naive observers the sophistication of the knowledge being used; and teachers themselves tend to be very ready to assert that there is not much to be learned from observation of most of their lessons, which they see as 'routine' or 'ordinary'.

Gaining access to experienced teachers' craft knowledge is not only something that is highly desirable for learner-teachers to achieve but also something for which they need distinctive strategies and considerable help. It is necessary first that learner-teachers should be persuaded that the order, attention, interest and comprehension which experienced teachers generally achieve in their classrooms are the consequence not so much of their charismatic personalities, their general teaching styles, or the authority of their positions, but rather of the particular actions they take in the classroom and of the considerations which lead them to take these actions. Learner-teachers can be persuaded of this if, but only if, their mentors consistently discuss their own teaching, as well as that of the learner-teachers, in an analytical way which draws attention to the actions and considerations underlying their successes (and, no doubt, their occasional failures).

On the basis of such a general understanding, a learner-teacher can gain access to an experienced teacher's craft knowledge (or rather, a small part of it) through observing a lesson and then asking the teacher appropriate questions about that particular observed lesson. The effectiveness of the approach depends on there being time for reflective conversation, on the questions being firmly focused on the events of the observed lesson, on them being concerned with how the observed teacher achieved the good things he or she achieved, and on the learner-teacher's readiness not to think he or she knows the answers, but instead open-endedly to probe, to wait, and not to expect the understandings sought to trip off the experienced teacher's tongue. It also depends on the experienced teacher's understanding of what is sought and motivation to make his or her craft knowledge accessible.

For learner-teachers to learn about experienced teachers' craft knowledge, it is important that mentors should themselves take the lead in making their own craft knowledge accessible. Doing this has the triple value of not only fulfilling the immediate purpose but also of providing an opportunity to coach learner-teachers in appropriate interviewing procedures and providing the mentor with experience which can be used in briefing other teachers whose participation is sought. The mentor also has a key role in matching the learning needs of learner-teachers at various stages with the known strengths of colleagues, who can then be recruited on the basis of their distinctive expertise.

Discussing learner-teachers' ideas

From Lortie (1975) onwards, research has consistently emphasized the powerful influence which learner-teachers' preconceptions about teaching exert on their learning. One hopes that they will also acquire new ideas in the course of their learning, from conversation, observation, reading, university seminars, their own teaching and elsewhere. Whatever the source of their ideas, it is important that they should be helped to examine these ideas critically, because many of them are narrow, prejudiced, incoherent or unrealistic. Some of this critical examination can be done very effectively through the learner-teachers' attempts to put their ideas into practice in the classroom; but some things can 'work' in the classroom and be educationally undesirable; other ideas need a great deal of work on them before they are operational enough for classroom trial; and still others could not be tried out in the classroom because, in a particular school context, they would be impractical or unacceptable. Much of the critical examination of ideas therefore has to be done by reflecting on them, and especially by discussion of them. In this, mentors can play a key role.

Whatever other contexts a learner-teacher has available for the discussion of ideas, whether in university seminars or with peer-groups elsewhere, the mentor as the authoritative practitioner with whom the learner-teacher works has a crucial and distinctive contribution to make. It is the mentor as an experienced practitioner, within the context where the learner-teacher is practising, who is best placed to discuss with authority the practical implications of ideas within that context. What about time constraints? How would it work with a class of 30 pupils? Would it be compatible with the constraints of the National Curriculum? Where would one get the energy to sustain it? How much would the materials cost? How would the pupils react, or their parents, or the teacher next door? Without giving definitive verdicts, the mentor is uniquely well placed to explore with the learner-teacher the realistic implications and consequences of different ideas.

This is far from an easy part to play. One of the most difficult aspects of it is establishing relationships with learner-teachers which go beyond politeness, so that they feel able to raise their own most precious ideas for discussion and are not personally crushed by having their ideas critically and realistically considered. Another is avoiding the temptation to be pious, to pretend that the only considerations which do or should influence one are the pupils' best interests: mentors have as much right as anyone to theorize and to be idealists, but they have a distinctive obligation to help learner-teachers to come to terms with the practicalities of teaching.

Managing beginning teachers' learning opportunities

Mentors work in schools; in secondary schools they work in subject departments: one of their distinctive advantages as school-based teacher educators is that they can draw upon, and organize, the resources available in their school contexts in ways geared to the distinctive and changing needs of the learner-teachers for whom they are responsible. This complements the other advantage which comes with school-based teacher education: the opportunity to take stock of a learner-teacher's needs and, over an extended period, to cater for these needs, to monitor the ways they develop, and to respond to these developments.

It has already been suggested, in relation to gaining access to experienced teachers' craft knowledge, that an important task for the mentor is to recruit colleagues whose distinctive expertise can be especially helpful in addressing the needs, at different stages, of a learner-teacher. The expertise of their colleagues is, more generally, one of the major resources available to mentors who can draw on it to enable learner-teachers to, for example, observe different teaching strategies being used, to discuss different perspectives on, say, the teaching of their subject, and especially to enrich their planning and teaching repertoires through advice received when being supervised by different teachers or when teaching collaboratively with them. For mentors, the insights of colleagues into the developing strengths or persisting weaknesses of individual learner-teachers' planning, teaching and self-evaluation can contribute substantially to their own diagnostic and summative assessments.

Another major resource available to mentors is the range of classes taught in the school or the department. Within the constraints of timetabling practicalities and of their own and colleagues' concern for pupils' interests, mentors have to plan programmes for learner-teachers of observation and teaching of different classes, briefly or over extended periods, so as best to facilitate their learning at each stage. Heightening their awareness of particular kinds of problems, giving them tasks of appropriate difficulty, and ensuring that they gain sufficiently wide-ranging experience are likely to be major considerations at different stages of the training process.

In order to provide well-judged programmes of learning opportunities for learner-teachers, by drawing on colleagues' expertise and their classes, mentors are of course crucially dependent on the effective collaboration of their colleagues. The motivation and ability of colleagues to help in the work of initial teacher education depend heavily on the quality of their understanding of what is involved; and they are likely to develop the necessary understanding only if the mentor makes deliberate efforts to ensure that that happens. Engagement in initial teacher education can be a very enriching experience for a whole school or department (cf. McIntyre and Hagger, 1992); but it is very easy, in contrast, for mentors to fall into the trap of working in sophisticated, time-consuming ways with learner-teachers while the latter's presence is seen by colleagues merely as a way of reducing their own workload. Gaining the informed collaboration of colleagues is one of the most important tasks of mentoring.

In this account of what we have called 'developed mentoring' we have exemplified the kinds of strategies which on one hand are *necessary* if justice is to be done to the complexity of the processes of learning to teach and on the other hand are *possible* only in a context of largely school-based teacher education in which the key figure is a mentor who is a classroom teacher. The development and refinement of these and other strategies will depend upon the work of mentors themselves as they explore the possibilities open to them.

Extended Mentoring: Further Possibilities

There are at least three ways in which mentors' roles might be extended beyond that already indicated, to include responsibility for other necessary elements in initial teacher education. Here they can be considered only briefly.

Beyond competence

Until learner-teachers have demonstrated that they have developed the competence necessary for them to be deemed suitable entrants to the teaching profession, there is no way of escaping the need for mentors to be authority figures who, in teaching and assessing, may have to make unilateral judgements about what is satisfactory and what is needed. However, once such necessary competence has been established, a very different role is appropriate for the mentor and a very different relationship with the learner-teacher, since the primary responsibility for learner-teachers' further development lies with themselves. Help is still required, both because everyone benefits from a second perspective on their work, especially with such complex work as teaching, and also because learner-teachers need help in learning how to be effective self-developing teachers. The kind of help needed is, however, that which can best come from an experienced, but in important respects *equal,* partner: the concept of 'partnership supervision' discussed by Rudduck and Sigsworth (1985) is very helpful here. It is the learner-teacher who should be now taking the lead in setting agendas; and while his or her 'partner' may have more knowledge or information of various kinds to contribute, the judgements of the learner-teacher are now recognized as the important ones.

The transition to a new kind of relationship is not always easy. No doubt most mentors find one or other kind of relationship easier for them; and it is obviously more demanding to have to learn the skills and disciplines of working in the two different ways appropriate for the two stages. Nonetheless we believe that it is best for mentors to accept the responsibility of continuing to support learner-teachers, in this new kind of relationship, in this second major stage of their professional development. This is partly because, despite the importance of the change, the new stage of mentoring can build very usefully on understandings developed during the earlier stage; the focus of attention continues to be on the learner-teacher's classroom teaching. Also, relationships between mentors and learners can be most fruitful if the two stages are seen as complementary and if, from the very beginning, a clear understanding is negotiated that ways of working in the earlier stage will be complemented by the different approaches of this second stage.

In the context of the Oxford Internship Scheme, this change tends to occur around two-thirds of the way through the PGCE year.

The whole-school context of teaching

One of the great advantages of school-based initial teacher education is that it makes the wider life of the school, and the way it relates to parents, community and other organizations much more meaningful to learner-teachers. Issues of whole-school policies, of parent-teacher relationships, of relations with other schools or colleges can be understood as impinging significantly on the daily life of the classroom teacher. Similarly, the tasks of pastoral care and of personal and social education, especially in so far as these are the responsibilities of form tutors, can be experienced and practised by learner-teachers who are integrated into the life of the whole school.

There are some attractions in the idea that the mentor's role should be extended beyond a classroom teaching concern to these wider whole-school issues: clearly this would facilitate the learner-teacher's understandings of how classroom and whole-school concerns interact. Nonetheless, partly because of the importance we attach to these wider concerns, we believe that helping learner-teachers to learn about the school as a whole, and about the other tasks of teachers within schools, is best seen as a task for someone else, who might be called a 'professional tutor'. In each school, there is a role for a professional tutor who is a senior member of staff, who can coordinate learner-teachers' learning about different aspects of the school's work, and who has a key role in co-ordinating and facilitating the work of mentors within the school.

Drawing on sources of knowledge outside the school

In recent years there have been some (eg, Hillgate, 1989; Lawlor, 1990; O'Hear, 1988) who have argued that virtually the whole task of initial teacher education should be school-based, and that mentors should therefore have the total responsibility for introducing beginning teachers to the task of teaching in schools. It is important to recognize that these arguments are based not on a respect for school-teachers' capacity to undertake this whole complex task but rather on beliefs that teaching is a fairly simple practical activity, that teachers do not need to think about their work, and that thinking in an informed way about teaching would be confusing and very possibly corrupting for beginning teachers.

We hope that we have demonstrated in this chapter the complex and ambitious nature of the task of mentoring as we see it. It is because of our sense of the complexity of the task as we have described it, and because that task can only be done by mentors who are practising teachers in schools, that we believe that the *other* sources of learning which can be useful for beginning teachers should primarily be the responsibility of other people based in universities and working in very close partnership with mentors. Theoretical discussions of teaching, research evidence, information about practices used elsewhere are all practically relevant to classroom teaching, as is the unpicking of different ideological positions, and the consideration of educational values and of social implications of classroom practices. We believe that mentors can do their work much better and with much greater satisfaction if they do it in partnership with others who have these complementary responsibilities.

REFERENCES

Benton, P (ed.) (1990) *The Oxford Internship Scheme: Integration and Partnership in Initial Teacher Education,* London: Calouste Gulbenkian Foundation.

Booth, M, Furlong, J and Wilkin M (eds) (1990) *Partnership in Initial Teacher Training,* London: Cassell.

Brown, S and McIntyre, D (1992) *Making Sense of Teaching,* Buckingham: Open University Press.

Burn, K (1992) 'Collaborative teaching', in Wilkin, M (ed.) *Mentoring in Schools,* pp. 133–43, London: Kogan Page.

Calderhead, J (1988) 'The contribution of field experiences to student primary teachers' professional learning', *Research in Education,* 40, 34–49.

Cole, AL (1991) 'Relationships in the workplace: doing what comes naturally?', *Teaching and Teacher Education,* 7, 5/6, 415–26.

Furlong, J, Hirst, P, Pocklington, K and Miles, S (1988) *Initial Teacher Training and the Role of the School,* Buckingham: Open University Press.

Hillgate Group (1989) *Learning to Teach,* London: The Claridge Press.

Kelly, M, Beck, T and ap Thomas, J (1992) 'Mentoring as a staff development activity', in Wilkin, M (ed.) *Mentoring in Schools,* pp. 173-80, London: Kogan Page.

Lacey, C (1977) *The Socialization of Teachers,* London: Methuen.

Lawlor, S (1990) *Teachers Mistaught,* London: Centre for Policy Studies.

Little, JW (1990) 'Teachers as colleagues', in Lieberman, A (ed.) *Schools as Collaborative Cultures,* London: Falmer Press.

Lortie, D (1975) *Schoolteacher,* Chicago, IL: University of Chicago Press.

Louden, W (1991) *Understanding Teaching,* London: Cassell.

McIntyre, D (1988) 'Designing a teacher education curriculum from research and theory on teacher knowledge', in Calderhead, J (ed.) *Teachers' Professional Learning,* London: Falmer Press.

McIntyre D and Hagger, H (1992) 'Professional development through the Oxford internship model', *British Journal of Educational Studies,* 40, 3.

O'Hear, A (1988) *Who Teaches the Teachers?,* London: Social Affairs Unit.

Rudduck, J and Sigsworth, A (1985) 'Partnership supervision (or Goldhammer Revisited)' in Hopkins, D and Reid, K (eds) *Rethinking Teacher Education,* London: Croom Helm.

6 The Impersonation of Wisdom

Richard Smith and Geof Alred

Introduction

Our title comes from reflecting on the role of the original Mentor in Homer's *Odyssey*: 'To him, on departing with his ships, Odysseus had given all his house in charge, that it should obey the old man and that he should keep all things safe' (Book 2, p.226 ff.). Odysseus, who would have inducted his son into the skills of leadership, has gone away to fight at Troy and then, on his lengthy journey back, to undertake the learning that will make him fit to return home and re-establish order there. It is in the likeness of Mentor that Athene, goddess of wisdom, appears to Telemachus, Odysseus's son, giving advice, encouragement and spiritual insight. Thus Mentor is essentially a stand-in for Odysseus, and must personify the kingly quality of wisdom.

Why have we chosen to begin our chapter in this way, so remote from sensible, practical considerations such as whether or not the mentor should be a senior member of the school staff? The reader may like to be reassured that we are not under the impression that any solutions to the problems of initial teacher training[1] are to be found in literary etymology, nor do we suppose that the Homeric Mentor was particularly in the minds of those who chose this word to name schoolteachers with especial responsibility for the induction of new members of the profession.

We have begun in this way for a number of reasons. First, we feel it is necessary to insist that the question of 'mentoring' is far from straightforward. The sources of understanding that can and must be tapped to illuminate it go far beyond the thin and unsatisfying 'educational management' literature that usually forms the basis here. The idea of a 'mentor' has its origins, as our reference to Homer indicates and, we hope, makes memorable, in ways of thinking about the world that do not sit easily with the modern language of formal education.

There is, in general, a real problem here concerning how to write about education. Increasingly what is published about teaching seems to consist not of continuous, thoughtful prose but rather of lists, charts and diagrams. One has to work quite hard to avoid being drawn in to casual assumptions and ways of writing that now pass as unremarkable. So Homer stands here not as some cultural icon, intended to spread a reassuring, civilized patina across the proceedings, but as a reminder that there are other, powerful traditions of thinking about questions of leadership, power, authority and of what kind of knowledge gives someone the right to advise or instruct anybody else, and other ways of writing about them. At the very least, we should be less likely to fall into the poverty of thinking in which 'mentoring' becomes simply a label for a new bureaucracy of teacher-training.

Second, but arising from the first point, we want to highlight the issue of the kind of qualities that the mentor needs. It is a recurring theme of this chapter that there is a difference between being *wise* and having various kinds of knowledge or skills which can be passed on to another person. Until the last 20 or so years, perhaps, when it has been customary to reduce all kinds of quality, capacity, virtue, knowledge and understanding to 'skills', it was possible to speak without too much embarrassment of 'wisdom' as something like an enduring quality of certain kinds of human beings. For the Greeks it was *sophia*, for the Romans *sapientia*, as distinct from a range of words indicating various kinds of more specific ability, knowledge of facts or knowhow. We think it possible that recent usage is not necessarily an improvement on that of the preceding thousands of years, and argue that it is indeed a kind of wisdom that is needed for being a mentor. Thus this, too, is a reason for our title.

The Needs of the Beginning Teacher

It will be clear already that we question much of the accepted wisdom (so, ironically, it may be called) in this area. We do not accept a conception of learning to teach articulated purely in terms of the *competences* of the finished product, the qualified teacher. Our objection to 'competences' could be expressed along the same lines as the classic objection to reducing all abilities to 'skills': briefly, a teacher needs many virtues and capacities such as patience, integrity, a thought-out position on what he or she is doing as a professional, that is, a philosophy of education, as it used to be known; also an enjoyment of the company of the young, most of the time at least, intellectual acumen, a love of his or her subject, where appropriate, and so on. None of these is a *competence*, as it were something that could be worked up and then turned on when necessary. This is not to say that qualities such as patience cannot be learned; but if they can, it is clear that they are not learned in the same way as you learn to write on the blackboard.

The objection to 'competences' which we urge here is that competences start from a conception of the qualified teacher, of what he or she can do. Now it is clearly important in helping anyone to learn anything to have a sense of where they are going. However, it is also important to have a sense of where the learner is starting *from,* and it is that which excessive emphasis on competences tends to obscure. Trainee teachers start with manifest *needs,* manifest that is to anyone who has worked with them, if not to those captivated by the fascination of drawing up lists of competences. They are vicariously fulfilling parents' thwarted ambitions, for example, or they are caught helplessly on the scholastic, academic conveyor-belt, or they feel impelled to compensate for the deficiences of the education that was offered to them, or they nurse a sense of failure at not getting the extra couple of A-level points that would have set them *en route* for law or medicine. The importance of what young people of 18 bring with them to a B.Ed or BA Ed course, or graduates of anything from 21 to 45 to a PGCE course, simply cannot be overstated. Our own experience as tutors is echoed by Guy Claxton:[2]

> All students when they arrive at a teacher-training course have a personal theory about education, schools, children, teaching and learning; what is important and what is not, what is essential, what is normal, what is right. They have their own intuitive, largely tacit, largely unexamined set of beliefs, attitudes and values that are variously idiosyncratic, partial, simplistic, archaic and rigid....

We give examples below of some of the attitudes and opinions they bring with them. Other aspects of their past also constitute their needs, and these, one way or another, have to be dealt with. There is, of course, no universal, objective answer to be given to the question, 'well, what *do* trainee teachers need?' Our point is that the training of teachers has to proceed by attending to *whatever* needs they have and not only by considering what they ought to be able to do when they have finished their training.

Attending to the needs of the trainee teacher, properly listening, understanding how they have arrived at their beliefs, taking seriously the reasons they offer for those beliefs while at the same time knowing the whole person well enough to appreciate what the sources of their beliefs may be – all of this takes qualities of understanding, sympathy and humanity which, while they may involve certain skills, go well beyond consisting simply of skills. If this is what the mentor *does*, then what seems to be at stake here is the kind of *person* the mentor *is*, and this, although it goes against so many of our characteristic ways of thinking and talking about education, is not altogether surprising. For learning to teach is also a process in which people's whole sense of themselves is involved. As Phillida Salmon puts it:[3]

> As teachers, we do not just act as the gateway to knowledge. We ourselves represent, embody, our curriculum. And, in our teaching, we convey not just our explicit knowledge, but also our position towards it, the personal ramifications and implications which it has for us.

We are not denying that there are classroom skills that can be learned in order to deal with the problems which this poses: the point we are concerned to stress is that the experience of teaching, at all levels, is one in which our feelings, our sense of our identity, our vulnerability as human beings are all involved, and *necessarily* involved since it is from the way we handle these feelings that children stand to learn so much that is lastingly valuable.

If all this is so then the mentor must stand in the same relationship to the trainee as the trainee does to his or her pupils: as someone bringing their whole being as a person to bear rather than exercising certain skills. This, essentially, is what makes the business of learning to teach different from learning to be a gardener or a carpenter or a welder, and what makes the metaphor of apprenticeship so completely inappropriate for learning to teach.

Standing Back from Practice

Coping with feelings requires a degree of distance, of 'stepping back'. One of the functions of the training institution is precisely to provide this measure of distance: both a different perspective on events in classroom and staffroom, such as that found in theoretical and other writings, and the possibility of exploring feelings in a context sufficiently supportive for such feelings to be tolerated rather than treated as threats, denied and thus not learned from. (It has to be admitted that the latter possibility is not always as widely available in training institutions as it might be). Thus the feelings of vulnerability and the excitement of achievement of the beginning teacher are fully part of 'standing back', rather than merely being the material of casual and inconsequential chat.

Much has been said about the relationship between theory and practice in education; we want only to observe that the root notion of 'theory' is that of having a view, of enjoying a perspective. A sensible way to understand the role of theory in education is not as implying spectatorship rather than action, but as involving standing back and looking at the business of teaching and learning in a cooler and more reflective way than is possible in the middle of teaching itself. In that sense the mentor and trainee are 'doing theory' when they discuss the reasons why a particular part of a lesson went well or badly, why a particular child is failing to learn or the merits of a textbook or scheme of work.

Like everything else in education, the business of theorizing, of standing back, can be done well or badly. The first requirement for doing it well is to acknowledge that you are doing it, and not to imagine that you can set about teaching in a purely practical, atheoretical way. This, unless it means that you never think, talk or read about your professional practice, is simply impossible. As soon as you move from instinctive response to acting in the light of some perception of the world in front of you, one description of events rather than another, you are effectively choosing to interpret, to view from a particular perspective, to begin that process of standing back whose more familiar and more thoroughgoing manifestations occur in the seminar or lecture room, or in the careful reading of a book. This point needs emphasizing because of the widespread assumption, recently fostered with some care in high places,[4] that theory can seriously damage schooling and should be renounced by all right-thinking teachers. As soon as you allow yourself to think, as soon as you say to yourself, or to a colleague, '2x are lively this morning', or '2x are in one of their tiresome moods today'; or if you expect better things of Jane in English because you know she's an excellent mathematician; or if you adopt a particular sort of classroom organization because you want children to work 'independently'[5] – in all these cases you show that you have certain views (certain theories, that is) about what it is or is not reasonable to expect of the behaviour of 13-year-olds, or about the nature of intelligence (is it relevantly the same sort of thing in maths as in English?) or about how children, and perhaps people in general, relate helpfully to each other. It is simply colossal ignorance, as well as a kind of arrogance, to imagine that your particular theories are just common sense. As the literary critic Terry Eagleton remarks,[6] 'Hostility to theory usually means an opposition to other people's theories and an oblivion to one's own'.

As we indicated earlier, beginning teachers have *theories* of teaching lurking in their existing beliefs and attitudes. Theory is not something which they pick up from the training institution, as if they were hitherto entirely innocent of anything so useless, suspect and misleading. As part of our practice with trainee teachers on various kinds of programme we have, over the years, asked them at the very beginning of their courses to write about their own experience of education, at whatever level, and their reasons for wanting to become teachers. Thus, unlike if we required them to write down their views on teaching and how children learn, we have not, we think, forced them to 'come up with theories' that they did not really hold in order to satisfy us. We reproduce below a selection of remarks, which show very clearly that the writers held views or theories – in many cases very definite ones – which, so far from being uncontroversial or 'merely common sense', are open to challenge and which we saw it as part of our job to challenge, to help the writers to see that such views were not watertight but needed to be tested against experience, the evidence of research, the available literature (including imaginative and autobiographical literature where appropriate) and, not least, against the writer's other views or theories. (The writers, aged between 18 and 46, come variously from PGCE primary and secondary courses and a BA primary degree course in education).

> I think education's the most wonderful thing, schools should be full of colour and music and laughter, those are the conditions in which children can learn.
> No-one ever learns anything unless they're forced to. Being at school is hard work, and you wouldn't be there unless you had to be. None of us ever learns anything for pleasure, you've got to have a reason.
> I know I never learned anything unless I liked the teacher, if I didn't like him (or her) I'd make a point of doing badly. I could never see why I had to listen to someone I couldn't respect.
> Children learn at their own speed. You can't force them. If you try it ends up like Dr Blimber's[7] with vegetables forced in the greenhouse, children over-developed in their heads at the expense of their being allowed to grow up properly.
> The teacher's job is to stretch them. Otherwise there would be no point in going to school, would there?
> You have to start from your own experience. That's why I'm primary and not secondary. If you can't relate what you're taught to what you already know or think it's just pointless, it means nothing to you.
> I'm glad to see this new emphasis on proper subjects, even in the infant school. We've been messing around with sand and water for too long. Tell me, what's the point of that?
> Children only learn when they're quiet.

As these remarks make clear, there is much work to be done with those who embark on a teaching career. Equally clearly, such matters as these – rooted in people's whole outlook on the world, in many cases – cannot be addressed casually while one class files out of the room and another prepares to come in, nor in the exhausted half-hour at the end of the teaching day.

The Wisdom of the Mentor

We began this chapter with allusion to the original Mentor, partly as a way of marking that we wanted to take seriously the idea that being a mentor is rooted in a way of thinking and being that is in danger of being increasingly alien and unfamiliar in the educational world of National Curriculum ring-binders and a curriculum that can be 'delivered'. In this world, where educationalists are being encouraged to use the language of business and the marketplace, the idea of being a 'mentor' risks becoming little more than a label to cover a new model of teacher training in which higher education is notable, like Odysseus, for its absence – a kind of humane gloss, reassuring in its classical origins, for a profoundly unhumane conception of what is involved in learning to be a member of one of the most complex and demanding professions.

By contrast, we want to take seriously the idea of a mentor as one who fulfils a highly humane, civilized and civilizing function. First of all, the mentor offers a model of what the trainee may some day become. We do not say 'a model of the professional teacher'; this kind of trite phrase, carrying its own overtones of brisk, slightly detached superiority, is a good example of the influence of management-speak. Compare the reflex by which in certain sorts of writing teachers are invariably called 'busy teachers'. There are other sorts of teacher to become; the 'busy teacher' is unlikely to make a good mentor. It takes *time* to listen. One of us, entering the profession untrained at a time when it was still possible to do so (and reckoning pretty quickly that he had better do a PGCE course since there was an awful lot to learn) remembers with gratitude and affection those teachers at whom it was possible to look and think that this was no bad sort of person to grow up to be. These were not particularly 'professional' teachers. They were warm, amusing, ironic, in love with their subject, respectful of their pupils. One of our students, reflecting on a head of department under whom she had worked very happily on teaching practice, wrote:

> When I brought him a problem, something that I couldn't do, usually he said he couldn't do it either, and we started from there. He was a bit of a shambles, the kids loved him. He was great.

One of the things a mentor can do is show not just how to do certain sorts of things, but how to live with uncertainty and the awareness that teaching is an unscientific and generally untidy business.[8] There are few things more undermining for a beginning teacher than the sort of experienced practitioner who appears to be able to get everything right, even if he or she can also pass on some of the techniques for doing so. This 'negative capability', as it is sometimes called, after the poet Keats' remark in a letter about the importance of the ability to live with doubts and uncertainties, without the irritable need to reach for fact and reason, is connected with the ability to support others, to convey the sense that their doubts can be borne since you, for your part, appear able to bear yours.

When we look at those who have been our mentors, often we perceive that they have had what might be called a philosophy of their job, a well worked-out sense of what their professional duties meant to them and what part they played in their lives as a whole. We see that they *stood for* a certain conception of teaching and of education, and often were able to articulate it, perhaps in anecdote and reminiscence if not in any more explicit way. At any rate their sense of what they were about went well beyond the typical folk-wisdom of the staff-room; 'You have to love children, you know', or 'In the end it's about helping each child to fulfil its own potential'. Worthy and to some extent true though these remarks may be, they do not amount to a coherent vision, an over-arching idea of what the whole business amounts to, on a level that could be defended against rival conceptions.

That is to say that the mentor's knowledge extends beyond the instrumental. He or she knows well enough about means – about how to pitch work at the right level for the class, how to organize an integrated day, even how to gain access to the photocopier. But the mentor has also some understanding of ends: of what education is for, and that understanding is of a different quality from instrumental expertise, for it continually questions, dwells on the object of understanding, attempts to see it from different angles. It is more like understanding (or knowing) a poem, or a person, than understanding the internal combustion engine or photosynthesis, and it is this understanding that has become increasingly marginalized in modern education. The sense that education, and good teaching, are something of a mystery, rather than something that can conveniently and readily be contained in lists of competences and criteria; that education consists at least sometimes in the 'induced, shared, contemplation of a work, an object, an artefact',[9] with no particular sense of what outcome is to be expected from the contemplation, no preordained target met, was readily enough understood from the earliest times and has only recently seemed in danger of disappearing altogether. So too the teacher who has a proper philosophy of teaching and of education does not have something which he or she *knows*, as if it could be passed on in propositional form; nor is this an irrational attitude, as if it were of a piece with one's feelings about oysters. To have a philosophy is to find education, in all its richness, a fit object for reflecting upon in itself, apart from any outcome or payoff. The teacher who treats education as worthy of contemplation, of what would once have been called spiritual devotion, of a kind of sustained attention and seriousness, is the sort of person whom the beginner would be glad to have as a mentor. This is not the sort of thing nowadays to be found in serious books on education. But is it not so? When we read, in the obituary of a great musician, perhaps, or a politician or painter, that so-and-so was their mentor, this is what we find: that that person was a source of inspiration and support to them, that the mentor embodied for them an ideal of what it meant to be a musician or politician or painter. It does not mean that the mentor simply gave them advice in their early ideas on how to sustain their vibrato or fix the committee or mix the colours. We must be clear that if the notion of a mentor in teaching is allowed to become purely instrumental then the notion has changed, has become debased.

Bound up in this sense of contemplation is the further idea that the mentor too is a learner, for contemplation is a continual re-examining and re-appraising. This does not mean, of course, that the mentor must necessarily be in the process of acquiring further professional qualifications, such as an MA in mentoring. Indeed, such training[10] risks developing the essentially instrumental and bureaucratic cast of thinking (though it need not necessarily do so) which is antithetical to being a good mentor. The continual learning is rather that of one who finds the world endlessly rich and surprising, and welcomes other people as fellow-learners rather than as pupils or apprentices.

Thus an important aspect of the mentor's knowledge is self-knowledge. To know what you stand for, not in a finished and self-satisfied way but as a matter of having certain commitments, certain principles and ideals; to be aware of your own shortcomings and be able to treat them with a degree of irony rather than complacency on the one hand or bitterness on the other; to see yourself as one continuing to travel rather than one who, unlike the trainee, has arrived – these are features of self-knowledge as it has traditionally been conceived. To this might be added that to have self-knowledge is to have access to what might be called sources of energy and renewal, the capacity to return to teaching not with manic bursts of enthusiasm and 'commitment' but with the restoration that comes from being able to rise above the detail and the trivia and see the process as interesting and potentially absorbing. This is connected again with the ability to develop a philosophy of teaching, a sense of what you are about strong enough to sustain you through the inevitable periods of weariness and staleness.

In a world that, as we have noted, tends to reduce all forms of thinking to the glib formula of 'knowledge, skills and attitudes' there is a clear need for a term to pick out the range of qualities that we have described – non-instrumental understanding, contemplation and self-knowledge. That word is 'wisdom' and we use it, in full awareness and defiance of what would now be considered its otherworldly air (for why do we call everything a 'skill', if not to reassure ourselves how very down-to-earth and democratic it is?[11]) to insist that the qualities that the mentor needs are distinct and unusual, complex and rooted in the kind of person he or she is, not simply the abilities that they have.

Mentor, Nestor and Other Pitfalls

All roles and positions have their characteristic flaws, ways in which they can typically be corrupted and marred, and this is as true of the role of the mentor as of any other. If we spell out some of the ways we think the activity of the mentor is vulnerable to being twisted and turned into something damaging this must be taken not as implying some characteristic weakness in the teaching profession just waiting to emerge when it finds a suitable opportunity, but as a warning of the shoals that need to be negotiated. Reader, as tutors and supervisors we have run aground on some of them.

First, as will be clear from the foregoing, there is the fantasy of expertise. This is the mistake of believing that there are certain discrete skills which can be acquired, without too much difficulty, by pretty well any teacher dispatched to acquire them. We believe that people can be helped to be mentors, and to be better mentors, and the ways in which we think that can be done are implicit in much of this chapter. To deny that this is a matter of *expertise*, however, is to insist that being a good mentor cannot be separated from the kind of person you characteristically in general are. People do change, though sometimes slowly and often only in small ways. There is no body of knowledge, skills or competences waiting to be picked up which will turn any teacher who comes on a course or reads the right books into a good mentor.

Second, there is the fantasy of experience. This is the mistake of believing that pretty well any *experienced* teacher will make a good mentor, and the mistake is so widespread and so obviously tempting that it deserves a special label. In Nestor, king of Pylos, Homer created a wordy veteran of many campaigns, ready to inflict an account of them on his listeners at any opportunity. To put it politely, he is not a listener. The educational equivalent is the teacher as 'old sweat', who has seen it all and thus can pass it all on to the next generation.

But Nestoring, to coin a barbaric verb (and 'mentoring' ought to be seen as no less barbaric), will not do. Experience cannot be poured from one person into another, any more than expertise; and if pure experience made good teachers then schools would be full of teachers steadily growing more and more excellent. It is no slur on the profession to point out that this is not so. Where people develop professionally it is because they have the *right* experience and learn how to acknowledge it, reflect on it and use it.

Third, there seems little doubt that acting as a mentor is destined to become a career move, attracting incentive allowances and other perks. There is a paradox here in that the mentor in school needs to carry a certain amount of influence over colleagues and to be in a position to ensure that the requirements of trainees are in general met. But a mentor is not essentially a figure of authority, in a formal sense at any rate. It is rather the case that he or she derives their standing, as we have argued, from the sort of person that they are. This important, indeed vital, point risks becoming lost where the mentor takes tone and colouring, as it were, from a position in the school hierarchy. Connected to this is the further point that there is no necessary reason why the mentor should be a particularly senior teacher. Younger teachers, with the advantage of being closer in outlook to the trainee, and more in touch with the feelings they bring with them to their new career, may well make better mentors. It all depends, as we have emphasized, on the kind of person. Nothing should be allowed to obscure this central and vital point.

Fourth, there is a world of difference between being a mentor, a supervisor and an assessor. It is extremely difficult to fulfil the role of mentor, encouraging a trainee to talk honestly about their feelings and failings, if you are responsible in the end for passing them into the profession or failing them. The roles do become confused; many of us turn to our mentors for references, for example, and they do not cease thereby to be our mentors. The roles seem inevitably destined to overlap, given institutional constraints, as they do in current forms of initial training. All involved need to maintain the liveliest sense of the problems this can cause.

Conclusion

We have tried to take seriously the idea that being the *mentor* of a student teacher in a school is a very particular role, distinct and quite separate from being, for example, supervisor, tutor or assessor, and we have argued that there are great benefits for students in having mentors as well as those other professionals around them whose job is to instruct, supervise or evaluate their 'performance'. The mentor has a different part to play, and it is a mistake to expect the mentor to do everything. Indeed, as we have indicated, it is part of the original sense of a *mentor* that he or she steps into a gap, answers a particular need created by an absence. In the context of the trainee teacher in school, that absence might come from the diminishing part played by higher education, with its opportunities for reflection, for finding support and intellectual stimulus; or it might come from the sense that even where an institution of higher education is fully involved, even where the student teacher is surrounded by tutors, supervisors, assessors, lists of competencies, aims, objectives, exit criteria and all the rest of the apparatus, still there seems to be a void at the heart of things.

What we have tried to sketch is an alternative *vision* to the one of being a mentor that seems destined to trundle into schools on bureaucratic wheels. In the end the reader can only be asked to examine the different visions on offer in the different accounts of 'mentoring', and consider just which catches the flavour of the kind of school he or she would like to be involved with, or like their children to be taught in. There is a difficulty here, as we noted at the beginning of the chapter. Requiring the reader to examine and consider already begins to shape one substantive vision rather than another. Increasingly the 'busy teacher' becomes reluctant to do more than scan lists and glance at diagrams. But there are some things which just cannot be said in that way. Thus the issue of 'mentoring' is one more field on which the battle will be fought for the soul of the profession. Will teachers properly *reflect* about mentoring, will they *read* books on the subject, or will they simply raid their lists, tables and conclusions to construct the next agenda, working paper or policy document?

As this implies, the kind of 'mentoring' that a school goes in for has implications for the tone of the whole institution and not just for the experience of the trainees that pass through it. A school can become further dominated by documentation, driven a little madder by more pro-formas to fill in and more boxes to tick. It can become an envious sort of place in which only certain teachers, risen to the appropriate level of the hierarchy, are deemed worthy to induct new members of the profession, with a consequent sense on the part of the rest of the staff that they have become 'de-professionalized', 'de-skilled'. Alternatively, a school might become a 'mentoring' sort of place as a whole: one where it was customary to observe a kind of ironic wisdom *about* the business of teaching rather than a place that imagined it could simply communicate the wisdom *of* the profession. This would be a school – and such schools do exist – where it was quite normal to acknowledge your imperfections, your failures, even your outright disasters. This is an institution that would acknowledge what a difficult, uncertain, inexact and *painful* business teaching often is.

> It is difficult to stay put and stay open to the experience of not being liked; of making constant errors of judgement; of not knowing what to do; of being observed and criticised by teachers and tutors as well as the kids; of being harassed and tired and sometimes downright miserable. It *is* a tough job to learn, for most people, and it is easy to retreat into bitching and blaming and not really telling the truth to anyone, perhaps not even to oneself, about how it is going. Yet understandable though they are, these retreats and evasions prolong the agony. The more one can acknowledge one's incompetence, the quicker competence comes (Claxton, op. cit., p.173).

Thus there is a world of difference between the school whose staff acknowledge their incompetences – and not merely to indicate how they can, with suitable brisk professionalism, be overcome – and the school which allows itself to be drawn into the fantasy of 'competency-based training', whether these are the competences of the mentor or those of the trainee teacher. One personifies wisdom, the other merely impersonates it. Of course it takes a great deal of confidence to acknowledge your incompetences, and this will take increasing courage as schools are forced to compete with each other and display their glossiest image, as teachers are subjected to appraisal and as their job security is diminished. But there is no escaping the paradox that unless we can be open about our failures, about the essentially unscientific and uncertain nature of teaching and learning, such courage and confidence will not be found in the world of schools, not for established teachers and certainly not for the trainees to whom many of them will be mentors.

NOTES

1. We use this phrase, for convenience, to label the continuum that stretches from 'training' to 'education'.
2. 'The psychology of teacher training: inaccuracies and improvements', *Educational Psychologist*, **4**, 2, 1984.
3. *Psychology for Teachers*, Hutchinson, 1988, p.42.
4. For example, by Secretary of State Kenneth Clarke in 'Primary education: a statement', DES, 3 December 1991.
5. Examples of how teachers hold theories of 'independence' in M Griffiths and R Smith, 'Standing alone', *Journal of Philosophy of Education*, **23**, 2, 1989.
6. *Literary Theory: an Introduction*, Blackwell, 1983, p. vii.
7. In Dicken's *Dombey and Son*.
8. cp. Isca Salzberger-Wittenberg *et al.*, *The Emotional Experience of Teaching and Learning*, Routledge, 1983.
9. AS Byatt, *The Virgin in the Garden*, Penguin, 1978, p.76.

10. This is one essential difference between training and education: training is instrumental, while education is not.
11. cp. R Smith, 'Skills: the middle way', *Journal of Philosophy of Education*, **21**, 2, 1987.

7 A Model of Teaching and its Implications for Mentoring

Richard Dunne and Gareth Harvard

It is undoubtedly instructive for student-teachers to work alongside experienced teachers and to undertake teaching tasks for themselves. It is not difficult to find people to testify to this; on the contrary, it is rather difficult to find anyone to deny it. What is more, such testimony is not necessary: it is clearly the case that these are powerful learning experiences. It is a mistake to assume that classroom experience automatically provides the most appropriate learning. This seems to be assumed in recent proposals to locate more of initial training in schools, but is equally apparent in the structure of existing teacher education courses. There is a need for closer attention to be given to the purposes of classroom experience and the deliberate work that can meet these purposes. We do not argue that general classroom work is always of negative value; it is often neutral and can be useful. But it is seriously counter-productive when unprincipled experience is legitimized as a major component of teacher training courses: it is not unproblematically the case that more experience is better experience. It may be that more experience yields more learning (on some definition into which it is not necessary to enquire), yet more learning is not in itself better learning.

There is, of course, an apparent convergence of opinion about what transforms experience into professional action, summarized in the almost universal aspiration to produce 'reflective practitioners'. Even if we were to allow that there is some consensus as to the meaning of this, and some agreement about the relationship between this quality and improved performance, it would still be necessary to show what the novice must do in the preparatory stages. Although we wish to avoid the word 'reflection' because it has become so devalued by careless use, there is undoubtedly some attraction in Lucas' (1991) assertion that it involves 'systematic enquiry into personal practice ... in order to improve that practice ... and to deepen one's understanding of it'. However, our studies confirm what McIntyre (1991) has elegantly and convincingly argued: that enquiry into one's own practice, on the one hand, is so difficult that it is to be aspired to rather than employed as a learning strategy by the novice; and, on the other hand, is, in any case, more appropriate to the experienced professional whose skills are largely routinized. It is this position which is our starting point: that the understandable and legitimate concern of the novice is performance; that there is something other than performance, needing careful definition, that crucially characterizes professional activity in teaching; and that the gradual development of this quality, initiated during initial training, must be sustained and nurtured during professional life.

A Model of Teaching

Our model of teaching has as its major thrust what Ryle (1949) has called 'intelligent practice':

> It is the essence of merely habitual practices that one performance is a replica of its predecessors. It is of the essence of intelligent practices that one performance is modified by its predecessors. The agent is still learning (p.42).

In order to be specific about what comprises the 'practice' for teachers, we have nominated three factors: *performance*; *intellectual processes*; professionally relevant *schema*. This is summarized in Figure 7.1.

Our analyses of teachers' work suggest that this initial model can be further described without loss of generality. We recognize that the teacher's performance is largely, and the student's most significantly, in the classroom; but there are other situations in which professionals and beginning teachers perform, including staff meetings, interviews with parents, lectures, seminars, in-service courses, action-research projects, governors' meetings, assemblies, committees. Conse-

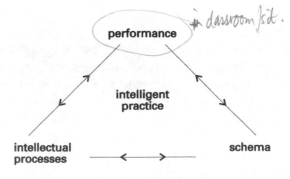

Figure 7.1 *A model of teaching*

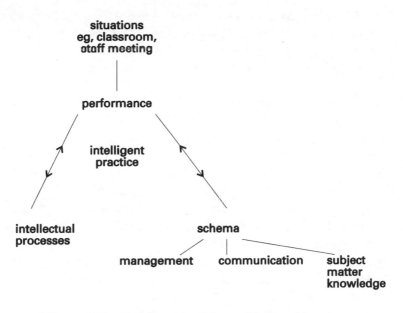

Figure 7.2 *Development of the model of teaching*

quently, we recognize that performance can be located in each of a number of different *situations*.

Our emphasis on developing schema with beginning teachers represents an aspiration for a shared vocabulary and value system which establishes a paradigm for professional development. It is because these schema are to be relevant in the variety of situations outlined above that we have nominated the generic competences of *management, communication* and *subject matter knowledge* for deliberate attention. Figure 7.2 summarizes these related points.

The following discussion shows how the model of teaching in Figure 7.2 can inform course development for the initial training of teachers.

Three Complementary Models of Student Learning

The model of teaching outlined above illustrates how professional activity is conceived over a variety of situations in which certain acts of cognition, incorporating the three factors of performance, intellectual processes and schema, are exercised and evidenced. It is necessary now to examine the implications of this for the *development* of intelligent practice, that is, to describe a model of student learning. In considering this, we have given attention to a methodological model, a pedagogical model and a psychological model. An important aspect of these deliberations is how this organic system can preserve the integrity of the psychological model whilst being realistic about the methodological constraints; we will show how it is the crucial concept of mentoring in the preparation of a professional portfolio that offers the pedagogical solution. The three models are described below.

The methodological model

Throughout initial training the student is assisted in the acquisition of professional activity by a supervisor, a university tutor, who periodically conducts conferences with the student. These attend to the generic competences of management, communication and subject matter knowledge. These conferences focus on evidence in the form of an 'object' which is a systemically valid assessment item; the objects are generated in and brought from the currently appropriate situation of, perhaps, school-based work, a lecture course or self-directed learning. The production of each of these objects may involve other people, for example, lecturers, school-based staff, industry-based staff, experts in a given field, and it is the combined impact of these contributions which we characterize as 'mentoring'. This will be developed in later sections, but the attention given to these contributions is best illustrated by a discussion of the techniques and conditions which are evident in generating appropriate objects during school-based work. Furthermore, it will be seen that additional 'conferences' appear at different stages in this work.

Teaching is a complex activity. To help student-teachers learn how to teach we have identified the nine dimensions of teaching listed in Figure 7.3. We have described elsewhere (Dunne, 1992; Dunne and Harvard, 1992; Harvard and Dunne, 1992a, 1992b) how each dimension is summarized in (usually) eight criterial levels. This category system of the nine dimensions, together with their associated criterial statements, are known as the 'teaching practice criteria'. There are a number of important points about this category and criterial system. First, the nine dimensions provide a mode of analysis which is designed to promote learning; they are not intended as a mutually exclusive set of teaching behaviours. Second, the language of the criterial statements is deliberately problematic because, as will be discussed later, it provides the basis for negotiated understanding of classroom events. Third, although the criteria can be (and are) used for making assessments of student-teachers' classroom work (Dunne and Harvard, 1992; Harvard and Dunne, 1992a), it is our view that they are adequate for this purpose only when used in the context of our deliberate approach to learning.

Our scheme involves the student-teacher in working with three tutors during school-based work: the class-teacher; the teacher-tutor

8 critical levels

dimension 0 – Ethos
dimension 1 – Direct instruction
dimension 2 – Management of materials
dimension 3 – Guided practice
dimension 4 – Structured conversation
dimension 5 – Monitoring
dimension 6 – Management of order
dimension 7 – Planning and preparation
dimension 8 – Written evaluation

Figure 7.3 *The nine dimensions of teaching*

(a member of the school's teaching staff trained to undertake supervisory work different from that of the class-teacher); the university supervisor. We will show that the division of roles is planned as a central feature of the development of intelligent practice.

Novices are faced with the problem of making sense of a complex activity. Observation and experimentation alone do not enable them to perceive which aspects of the teacher's performance are essential and which are idiosyncratic; and nor is the teacher typically able to represent this information in a way that promotes intelligent practice. We have designed certain techniques which facilitate this process. In our scheme, this entry to craft knowledge is gained by modelling the class-teacher: the student-teacher observes the class-teacher at work during a short episode (say, distributing materials, assigning tasks, supervising group work or telling a story) and attempts a similar episode. The class-teacher observes the student practising a variety of similar episodes and discusses each one soon afterwards; in this way both participants refine their perceptions of the pivotal events. When they are confident that the student-teacher can produce a good performance of this type, they nominate a time when this will be undertaken and closely observed. However, this more formal episode is preceded by the student and class-teacher, in a supervisory conference, collaborating on producing a written outline of the content and sequence of the proposed episode. This item, on one side of a sheet of paper, is known as the *agenda* for that teaching episode. Its importance lies in being a representation of a complex event which is already well-known in performance terms by both people. There is one further aspect of the agenda: during this conference, when the content and sequence are agreed, a note is made of a dimension (see figure 7.3) to which the class-teacher will attend during the observation.

The class-teacher's purpose during the observation is to annotate the agenda with points, relevant to the selected dimension, about the student-teacher's and the pupils' actions and responses. The emphasis is on observable features, including both those that are present and those that are absent. The annotated agenda is known as the *validated account* of that episode, 'validated' in the sense that it is valid as the basis for further learning, and as such is an object that is taken from the classroom to a conference with the teacher-tutor.

The validated account is an accessible representation of a classroom episode containing craft knowledge that the student, in terms of performance, has appropriated from the class-teacher; it is also an assessment of how the student has performed. The manner of its preparation (from shared experiential knowledge) and the style of its presentation (requiring further interpretation) confirm it as a systemically valid assessment item. Later conference work (with other mentors) will raise to consciousness certain aspects of this craft knowledge and thereby render it available for modification and deployment in related circumstances. Consequently, the validated account is an important feature of the deliberate approach to learning to teach. Modelling is employed for each new aspect of classroom work which for that student is distant from current personal practice. However, the production of validated accounts does not always proceed on the basis of modelling. Three methods are used: modelling; inductive planning; and theoretical planning.

There will be certain aspects of the classroom work which, although different in, say, sequence, subject matter and duration from the modelled episodes, are nonetheless sufficiently similar for the student to construct an agenda by working inductively from current accomplishments. These episodes can be practised and treated in the same way as previously, with the class-teacher making annotations during a closely-observed session. These, with appropriate conferences, generate the validated accounts which derive from inductive planning.

However, the accounts which are produced from theoretical planning derive specifically from conferences with the teacher-tutor, and it is necessary to describe some aspects of such conferences to illustrate how these validated accounts are developed.

The student-teacher's work with the class-teacher, represented in the validated accounts, comprises the evidence which is used in a conference with the teacher-tutor. Working from a particular representation (the validated account) the student-teacher has the responsibility of describing the purposes and detail for the teacher-tutor who has not observed the episode. It is the outcome of this which enables the student-teacher to engage in theoretical planning and later, with the class-teacher, to generate validated accounts on the basis of such planning.

Although the conduct of the conference deserves detailed discussion (Harvard, 1992), we can summarize it here in three phases: (i) What? (ii) So what? (iii) Now what? This short-hand reflects the requirement for the student: (i) to describe, by reference to the validated account, what happened in the episode; (ii) to locate the several events during the episode in the criterial statements of the nominated dimension; and then to explore how the same event can be located in other dimensions; (iii) to suggest, describe and agree what kinds of performance would be necessary to justify description in a higher-level criterial statement, or in yet another dimension. The outcome of the conference is an agreed, written statement that outlines the student's intentions in future, observed episodes. This statement is known as the 'zone of development'. It is the zone of development, with its requirement to plan on the basis of as yet unrehearsed criterial statements, that is the basis of the theoretical planning for further validated accounts.

There is a further purpose for the zones of development: they are used, together with the contributory evidence of the validated accounts, as the objects for the supervisory conferences conducted by the university supervisor. This mentoring role has the specific function of promoting the student-teacher's consciousness of how learning is taking place by further consideration of the appropriate objects in relation to the generic competences of management, communication and subject-matter knowledge (see Figure 7.2). It is in these conferences, however, that the objects brought from school-based work are discussed, not in isolation, but with reference to and with the same status as objects generated during the variety of other situations in which the student has worked. One particular aspect that we are developing is the vicarious experience of students' work with videodisc sequences accessed with a bar-code facility (Harvard, 1990; Harvard, Day and Dunne, 1991a, 1991b; Harvard, Day and Dunne, 1992). There is not the space here to describe the ways in which assessment items are designed for and generated from other situations; suffice it to say that these objects may be validated by an intermediate conference (similar to that of the teacher-tutor) but most often it is the marking of an assessment item (whether the item itself is written, audio-recorded or video-recorded) which validates it for use in the conference.

The conference work, focusing on the three generic competences, uses the same approach as outlined for the teacher-tutor conference; consequently, we have developed additional criteria that have wider application than the class-room-focused competences (Harvard and Dunne, 1992b).

Selected aspects of the student's evidenced work are systematically examined in the conference in relation to the criterial statements for the generic competences.

Science of teaching

The pedagogical model

The methodological model described above has been developed in recognition of a number of practical realities. For instance, the identification of a teacher-tutor in each participating school means that, as each cohort of students enters the school to work with a succession of class-teachers, it is the enduring contact of the teacher-tutor with the university and the fact of the teacher-tutor working on the school site which enables the class-teacher to be inducted into the scheme without lengthy training. But each decision of this type is not based solely on methodological considerations: in each case, the pedagogical and psychological models have been examined for the implications of a structural change from existing practice. In this case, the separation of roles which enables the teacher-tutor to undertake some work (conferencing) which might easily have been assigned to the class-teacher has been adopted for clear pedagogical and psychological reasons. This section outlines some of the pedagogical reasoning which underpins the design of the scheme.

Ryle (1949) has made the important point that 'the knowledge that is required for understanding intelligent performances of a specific kind is some degree of competence in performances of that kind' (p. 53). A major pedagogical decision is derived from this: that each part of our work with students involves modelling in order to provide that 'degree of competence' which affords access to 'understanding' (although it is not assumed that this easily happens: this also is given specific attention). In the classroom, the performance which is to be modelled is the typical classroom practice of the teacher. It is not assumed that this practice is ideal, nor that it is to be the subject of critical appraisal; it is modelled because the practice of teachers is the material outcome of reasoning about specific children in a particular situation, and students need some degree of competence in performances of that kind. It is very difficult for its originator (the class-teacher) to stand outside this performance and to analyse and reconstruct it: it is not impossible, but to be asked continually to do so for the benefit of the student is to be asked to work constantly in a state of awareness which does not sit comfortably with the normal practice that provides the learning material for this aspect of the students' work. The teacher-tutor, still working from a close knowledge of the organizational and cultural limitations of the school as an institution but being outside this specific episode, explicitly models this process by overtly working with the visible and shared criteria.

Further, the university supervisor models the process of thinking and planning beyond the current constraints, assisted by the generally applicable competence categories of management, communication and subject-matter knowledge.

There is a further crucial aspect of the pedagogical model: the learner undertakes preparatory work for the several conferences. For the conference with the class-teacher, this preparatory work consists of the student using modelling, inductive planning or theoretical planning (see above) and selecting a time formally to demonstrate a specific performance. For the teacher-tutor conference, there is a need to make a selection of validated accounts which best represent the student's current performance. For the conference with the university supervisor, the selection of zones of development and their contributory validated accounts focuses on what best represents the student's current thinking. This progression is extended beyond the conference with the university supervisor into a written evaluation which, intended as a representation of current understanding, characterizes and becomes part of the professional portfolio.

It is this pedagogical model which most clearly illustrates the way in which we conceptualize 'mentoring' rather than 'a mentor', preferring to summarize the complementary work of a number of actors in assisting students in the acquisition of professional activity. The pedagogical model also insists that mentoring takes place in relation to the overt evidence of the objects brought forward from previous work. Mentoring resides in the organic relationship of the pedagogic work of the several actors attending to the various objects. The professional portfolio, consisting of a selection of objects to represent the subject's current understanding, is itself a pedagogic object. Some implications of this will be discussed in the concluding section.

The psychological model

The specific ways of working outlined in the two sections above have been developed in response to a central problem of experiential learning: how performance, intellectual processes and schema are related. Our use of the idea of intelligent practice, suggested by Ryle (1949), represents only an aspiration; the selection of a set of techniques to achieve this is guided by a specific psychological model developed from the work of Vygotsky, who established the central principles of Soviet psychology as: (i) the integral unity of external activities and the psyche; (ii) an approach to the psyche as a phenomenon which by its nature is social. These principles, which have been extensively developed by Leontiev and Galperin (see Talyzina, 1981), deny the dualism of 'doing' and 'thinking' and, in insisting that human mental acts are socially determined, locate their origins in the process of adult-child interaction. We have shown elsewhere (Dunne, 1992; Harvard, 1992) how we have utilized this work in planning courses for student teachers, but will summarize the main features here.

One significant feature has been prompted by Arievich (1988) who has shown how the essential features of the post-Vygotsky development can be appreciated by reference to a mental act's 'outsidedness', meaning its reference to the outer world, its object-relatedness. He emphasizes that 'those forms of activity which later on become the forms of human consciousness primarily have an objective or object-directed (as opposed to inward-directed) character'. This is an important idea because it suggests that Vygotsky's view of the social nature of cognition can result in an over-emphasis on verbal interaction to the detriment of specifically developing its role in the context of purposeful activity. This, then, is why, for the purposes of learning, we have focused attention on the use of specific objects: the performance of the class-teacher; the annotated agenda; the written evaluations; the teaching practice criteria. But these have not been randomly selected. Galperin's work (see Talyzina, 1981) has been significant in the framing of a stage-by-stage process for the development of mental action, and it is this which has motivated our selection.

There is a further problem which has received attention in the post-Vygotskian psychology discussed by Talyzina (1981): this refers to the predicates of complex learning. It is a mistake to assume that the complexity of acquiring professional activity can adequately be addressed by arbitrarily dividing that activity into manageable portions and attending to each separately. Although this is widely recognized, the solution to this problem is too often assumed to lie in induction into the 'authentic' activity which appears in the professional life of practitioners, without appreciating that the social organization of professional life does not necessarily reflect professional knowledge and the way it is utilized. In the case of the professional activity of teaching, classroom work draws on curriculum design, test technology and detailed planning as well as specifically interactive aspects, representing the contributions of a variety of different agencies and individuals on a series of different occasions. All this is not understood by the novice; in order to render it understandable 'some degree of competence in performances of that kind' (Ryle 1949, p.53; and see the discussion above) is required by the learner – yet 'performances of that kind' are not available except in this very context in which it is so difficult to recognize them.

What is required is to design courses that deliberately engage students in learning episodes which capture the essence of the professional activity yet do not assume that engagement with the full activity is unproblematic. But, in order to relate this to the full professional work of the teacher, the psychological model requires that each piece of learning persistently orients the student to the nature of the activity by attending to an outline of the basis for orientation. Since our analyses of the work of experienced professionals show that they are constantly involved in management, communication and subject matter knowledge, exercising deliberation and judgement on the basis of uncertain evidence, it is these which underpin the ways of working with students. It is for this reason that we have provided a map (the various dimensions and their associated criteria) of what it means to acquire professional activity; but they have been made deliberately problematic. They represent not a clear recipe for success, but an outline which makes sense only through giving them the kind of attention that characterizes the professional activity of which they are an outline; this requires that the conferences are conducted in ways which promote such attention. Again, the psychological model indicates (Dunne, 1992) that it is important to avoid the premature routinization of any stage in the development of mental action; if the conference were conducted by a tutor who already knows in the same terms as the student what has contributed to the production of the object under discussion, there would be an inevitable use of the condensed terms that have already featured in its construction. However, the involvement of a tutor who is distant from the event provides the necessity of locating the nature of the work in more abstract terms and to provide justificatory examples from practice. Our separation of the tutoring roles and our conceptualization of mentoring residing in the relationship among these is based on such considerations.

Conclusion

Existing teacher-education courses place considerable emphasis on the role of school-based work. Recent advocacy for locating training in schools might be seen as a logical development of that emphasis, although the motives of some of its advocates (Hillgate Group, 1989; Lawlor, 1990; O'Hear, 1988) may be rather different from those of the professional teacher-trainers who have developed a variety of schemes over the years (Dunne and Harvard, 1992; Lacey and Lamont, 1976; McIntyre, 1990). There have always been difficult organizational problems in placing students for school-based work, especially in making the experience a coherent part of their course, and this has often resulted in an undue emphasis on methodological considerations at the expense of a well-developed view of what is involved in acquiring professional activity. There is the potential in the new arrangements for solving methodological problems in a principled way, but there is also the danger that organizational considerations will dominate: for instance, the assumption that the notion of 'partnership', in itself, will improve the quality of preparation for teaching is somewhat dubious, yet there is every sign that the organizational features of this will dominate thinking.

Our model of teaching, with its emphasis on the continuing development of performance, intellectual processes and schema, has pointed to some clearly defined complementary roles in mentoring and the need for this to be directed towards the compilation of a professional portfolio. The above discussion of the three models is a contribution to course planning in initial training.

Each of the techniques and methods described here has been used by us and brought together in a coherent approach to whole-course planning, although no course yet includes all of these as an enduring feature.

The mentoring role of the university supervisors, in our analysis, is crucially important in enabling students to go beyond their current practice, but does not require them to observe the student in the classroom. We advocate that judgements be made about the students' classroom performances by school-based staff but 'In judging that someone's performance is or is not intelligent, we have ... in a certain manner to look beyond the performance itself' so that we consider 'abilities and propensities of which this performance was an actualization' (Ryle, 1949, pp 44–45). The university supervisor should be engaged in precisely this. The students' work in the preparation of a portfolio is evidence of this aspect, but it is not a finished product. It is designed to be used in future situations, for instance, in an application for employment (whether in school-teaching or outside it) or in professional life. Faced with a new situation, the student would be expected to make a selection from objects in the portfolio in order to express how previous experience relates to the envisaged work. Clearly, this has implications for the prospective employer, who would need to characterize the new situation in ways that are amenable to the professional activity which we expect of the student. Furthermore, our conception of a portfolio, as an expression of professional activity rather than merely as a record of achievement (Harvard and Dunne, 1992b), has implications for the accreditation of prior learning. We would not expect evidence of earlier achievement, in itself, to be examined as a possible contribution to a collection of professionally relevant items. We would expect, rather, that the student would have to analyse and reconstruct that earlier learning in the light of a developing understanding of the envisaged situation, and it is the collected evidence and the written justification that would be examined.

REFERENCES

Arievich, I (1988) 'From Vygotsky to Galperin: development of an idea of a mental act's "outsidedness"', paper presented at the IV Cheiron Conference, Budapest.

Dunne, R (1992) 'The acquisition of professional activity in teaching, in Harvard, G and Hodkinson, P (eds) *Action and reflection in teacher education*. New Jersey: Ablex Publishing Co.

Dunne, R and Harvard, G (1992) 'Competence as the meaningful acquisition of professional activity in teaching', in Saunders, D and Race, P (eds) *Developing and Measuring Competence*. London: Kogan Page.

Harvard, G (1990) 'Some exploratory uses of interactive video in teacher education: designing and presenting interactive video sequences to primary student teachers', *Educational and Training Technology International*, 7, 2, 155–173.

Harvard, G (1992) 'A model of how students learn how to teach and its implications for mentoring', in Harvard, G and Hodkinson, P (eds) *Action and reflection in teacher education*. New Jersey: Ablex Publishing Co.

Harvard, G and Dunne, R (1992a) 'The role of the mentor in developing teacher competence', *Westminster Studies in Education*, 15.

Harvard, G and Dunne, R (1992b) The use of portfolios in the meaningful acquisition of professional activity in teaching', paper presented at the RSA (Higher Education for Capability) Conference : Using records of achievement in higher education, Wakefield, UK, July.

Harvard, G, Day, M and Dunne, R (1991a) 'Some exploratory uses of a videodisc system in teacher education', paper presented at the International Symposium on Information Technology in Support of Learning, University of Lancaster, 8–11 April.

Harvard, G, Day, M and Dunne, R (1991b) 'Studying students' schemas of typical classroom practice using interactive learning techniques and videodisc materials prior to beginning a teacher education course', *Interactive Learning International*, 7, 101–118.

Harvard, G, Day, M and Dunne, R (1992) 'Eliciting and developing students' schema of classroom practices using a videodisc system', awaiting publication.

Hillgate Group (1989) *Learning to Teach*, London: Claridge Press/Educational Research Centre.

Lacey, C and Lamont, W (1976) 'Partnership with schools: an experiment in teacher education', University of Sussex Education Area Occasional Paper 5, Brighton: University of Sussex.

Lawlor, S (1990) *Teachers Mistaught*, London: Centre for Policy Studies.

Lucas, P (1991) 'Reflection, new practices and the need for flexibility in supervising student-teachers', *Journal of Further and Higher Education*, 15, 2, 84–93.

McIntyre, D (1990) 'The Oxford Internship Scheme and the Cambridge Analytical Framework', in Booth, M, Furlong, J and Wilkin, M (eds.) *Partnership in Initial Teacher Education*, London: Cassell.

McIntyre, D (1991) 'Theory, theorising and reflection in teacher education', paper presented at the Conference on Conceptualising Reflection in Teacher Development, University of Bath, UK, 20–22 March.

O'Hear, A (1988) *Who Teaches the Teachers?*, London: The Social Affairs Unit.

Ryle, G (1949) *The Concept of Mind*, Harmondsworth: Penguin.

Talyzina, N (1981) *The Psychology of Learning*, Moscow: Progress Publishers.

8 Reflective Mentoring and the New Partnership

David Frost

The headlong dash towards school-based teacher training seems to be the cause of a great deal of anxiety in schools at the moment and, not surprisingly, I find that teachers who have been hastily designated as mentors are anxious to know how to cope. As a tutor in a college of higher education I am privileged to work with teachers who are being asked, amongst other things, to take more active roles in the supervision of articled teachers and PGCE students. In addition, they are being asked to take on the role of mentor in relation to licensed teachers, newly qualified teachers, returning teachers, and, in some cases, colleagues who are engaged in certain kinds of school-based in-service programmes. Recent moves by the Secretary of State to give schools a leading role in ITT present us with an urgent need to consider the development of the art of mentoring and the question of what kind of roles mentors will play in relation to the new more school-based PGCE programmes. So far, these roles seem very often to have been thrust upon individuals who see themselves as having insufficient time, expertise, experience and, perhaps most crucially, confidence to carry them out. The responsibility for playing such a pivotal role as 'gatekeepers' for the profession weighs heavily on some shoulders.

So far, resourcing for licensed and articled teacher schemes has allowed very little time for mentor support beyond what can only be described as token training courses. These have amounted to no more than a few days with insufficient ongoing support for reflection and evaluation. A number of such 'training days' have been provided by my own college as part of the package agreed with the LEA.

My colleagues and I are inhabitants of what Elliott (1991a) has described as 'the contemplative academic culture' of higher education in which the discourse of reflective practice is now dominant and so it is not surprising that, when asked to provide mentor training, we tend to want to adopt an approach which seeks, for example, to encourage mentors to examine their experience of professional problems; to conduct empirical investigations and to reflect on the worthwhileness of their professional practice. This encouragement to engage in reflective practice is often characterized rather inaccurately as 'theorizing' and we find ourselves under pressure to provide 'practical solutions' to what seem to be obvious and urgent problems. This was illustrated for me at a recent training day for mentors of licensed teachers where the protests were particularly strident and angry. A significant number of the mentors, impatient with what were perceived as indulgent discussions about reflective practice, demanded unequivocal answers to questions such as:

- How often should we observe the licensed teacher?
- What are the observation criteria?
- What instrument should we use to record the competence demonstrated in the classroom?
- What are the classroom competences expected?
- What are the performance indicators which will enable us to make clear and unambiguous judgements?
- How can we be sure that we are working to the same standard as colleagues in other schools?

It was clear that answers about 'professional artistry' or the mentor as 'critical friend' were not going to wash. The mentors wanted an off-the-peg, tried and tested, out-and-out system and preferably one which had been validated by a superior body. Clearly, the responsibility for the assessment of student-teachers seemed both novel and onerous.

In the traditional teaching practice context, teachers have often seemed reluctant to take part in the observation and assessment of student-teachers. They have tended instead to adopt a sort of pastoral, 'agony aunt' role in which general support and encouragement is offered. Some have also taken on a 'coaching' role where a certain amount of instruction is given, particularly in relation to subject-specific craft knowledge, but in many cases the unenviable task of assessing is left to the college supervisor. Where the school/college partnership works well, of course, the responsibility for assessment is shared and there is evidence that college supervisors' roles have involved elements of pastoral and coaching roles (see Lucas, 1989). In any case it seems inevitable that, as teachers begin to find themselves more accountable for their part in the process of 'gatekeeping' for the profession, they will be forced increasingly to take on responsibility for the assessment of student-teachers. It would seem that the lack of time, expertise and confidence referred to earlier will lead to a perceived need for a systematic approach which specifies the nature and frequency of observations, the procedures for recording the outcomes and so forth.

Can it be assessed?

So what might such an approach involve? A basic element of the approach would be the drawing up of an agreed competence specification which would be used as a basis for a profiling system. The profiling system would require that regular lesson observations are conducted and a standard instrument is used to record statements about the competence observed. The instrument would almost certainly consist of a pro-forma marked out with the competence headings but it may go further and include performance indicators which could be ticked off. The profiling system would require a set number of observations and regular summative review sessions so that a cumulative picture of the student-teacher's professional competence is built up. Such a system seems to offer an efficient solution to an urgent problem but there is a real danger that it will militate against genuine reflection and consequently have the effect of marginalizing theory and the central question of values in education.

Within the context of the evolution of PGCE or B Ed programmes, dependent as they are on a partnership with schools, the development of more systematic and standardized approaches to the supervision of student-teachers may make good sense, of course. There has been a clear need to provide criteria in the form of competence specifications and procedural guidance in the form of observation schedules in order to ensure that supervisors, students and the teachers in the schools collaborate in the pursuit of a broadly similar set of classroom skills. However, this approach has to be seen in the context of the traditional 'teaching practice' which is just one element within a programme which has many other opportunities for analysis and critical debate about educational issues. It is assumed, in this context, that the critical debate about theory and the exploration of values will take place, for the most part, in the seminar room and the lecture theatre. For this reason the system of assessment and reflection on competence cannot easily be translated across to the more school-based programmes where the lion's share of the professional learning has to take place in the occupational setting. Despite the rhetoric about reflective practice, I suspect that many licensed and articled teachers' schemes have done no more than build on and systematize the traditional division of labour in which the school teacher/mentors are concerned with observable classroom competence while the college tutors are left to deal with questions of theory and values. If we are to contemplate a general shift towards school-based ITT I would suggest that we need to question this division of labour rather than continue to push anxious and overstretched teacher/mentors into using profiling systems which may be narrowly behaviourist and limited in scope.

In order to consider the full significance of this issue we need to examine it in its wider ideological and political context. It has already been suggested that the need for standardization within school/college partnerships has been influential, but these developments can be understood as part of a more fundamental drift in society. Adler (1991) draws on Kliebard to argue that the teacher education programmes can be located within the 'social efficiency' curriculum tradition – reflecting the dominant values of the industrial society. This approach arises, for example, from the need to break down the task of the factory worker into behavioural units in order to maximize efficiency and provide instruction in relevant skills. It is based on a set of dominant values which permeate Western industrial society and underpin such developments as the NVQ model of occupational assessment. A full and coherent account of the development of competency-based teacher education can be found in Elliott's recent book, *Action Research for Educational Change* (1991a).

An approach which seems to be typical begins by conducting some kind of occupational analysis which makes it possible to draw up a competence specification. In some professional contexts this is limited to a list of 'can-do' statements although some of these may imply something more complex than routine behaviours. Take, for example, the matter of a trainee radiographer 'putting the patient at their ease' in the context of taking an x-ray: the competence element is expressed in the same kind of language as 'placing the patient's arm in the correct position for the x-ray', but the activity demands that the trainee has a high degree of situational understanding, a degree of empathy, a range of interpersonal skills and the confidence to act appropriately in social situations. Nevertheless, the model used tends to rely on a fairly closed specification of competence which includes knowledge as well as skills but which can be used in a routine 'box-ticking' way. That is to say that the question is whether the observer can observe the sort of behaviour which suggests that the trainee has acquired the relevant knowledge or developed the relevant skill. The role of the mentor in these kinds of contexts has two basic dimensions: first, to carry out observations and make assessments of the trainees' developing competence; and second, to provide support for reflection on the development of competence. Mentorship here tends not to be connected with what is characterized as the 'theoretical input' of the training programme. In other words, the supervised experience is organized for the purposes of putting into practice the behaviours which have been the subject of instruction. Consideration of the theoretical underpinnings of these practices is done in the seminar room. This is the approach which is currently used in the context of nurse education programmes where there has been a recent retreat from a training system based on clinical supervision and towards a more academic, college-based programme which draws upon the social science disciplines.

It is interesting that this development in nurse education occurs at a time when the 'new right' has successfully attacked the disciplines approach in ITT. The political climate in recent years can be seen to have given impetus to the growth of technicist approaches in teacher education and this can be seen as part of a more general hegemony manifest in educational discourse. In post-Thatcher, post-Education Reform Act Britain, a progressivist approach to classroom practice, for example, can be seen to be somewhat of an embarrassment in institutions of higher education. As the Secretary of State has predicted, the teacher training institutions are finding amongst their new recruits individuals who are quick to spot, amongst their tutors, the idealist brought up on a diet of Postman and Weingartner and Ivan Illich. Indeed, one has the impression that the profession is trying to distance itself from the overtly progressivist ideology. In higher education these days there seems to be a tendency to try to avoid arguing for student-centred learning on philosophical grounds; since the publication of the National Curriculum we are more inclined to allow the rubric of the statutory orders to suggest the need for a wider range of teaching strategies – the appeal here is on technicist grounds which aspires to neutrality. We justify proposals for this or that teaching approach on the grounds that it is effective in bringing about children's learning or, better still, that it clearly satisfies a requirement laid down in law. Effectiveness is the watchword, so we would rather ask the question 'Does it work?' than 'Is it right-on?' This non-ideological approach is, of course, of itself ideological as Inglis (1974) has pointed out. However, there can be no doubt that a more systematic approach to the assessment of professional competence finds increasingly widespread support.

It is ironic, I think, that more systematic approaches to the assessment of student-teachers have tended to develop in the context of PGCE and B Ed courses operated by institutions which tend to be dominated by what Andy Hargreaves has called 'the critical-humanist discourse of professional development' (see Hartley, 1991). It is interesting to consider how such developments are eased into place by an accompanying rhetoric about 'professional artistry' and 'the teacher as researcher'. It turns out that the pragmatism of partnership which drives the development of such systems coincides rather neatly with the development of the bureaucratic machinery aimed at the imposition of a centralized system of control and standardization. It would be a tragedy indeed if all the effort and ingenuity aimed at developing the reflective practitioner approach to professional development merely served to legitimize the imposition of a narrow, behaviourist systems approach.

I would like to argue here, therefore, that we should now fully embrace the notion of the school-based PGCE with mentors playing a central role in the planning and delivery of comprehensive and coherent programmes; that is to say, programmes which include the consideration of theory and questions of value. Mentorship, in this scenario, is much more than an extension of the college-directed assessment process.

Such developments appear to threaten the interests of the institutions of higher education and some will try to fight a rearguard action to defend the idea of the college-based reflective process but I believe that we need to face up to the arrival of the new approach and make sure that it develops in such a way that the critical and theoretical dimensions are not only preserved but actually enhanced. As Elliott (1991b) has argued, it is too late to develop a critique once policy has begun to be translated into organizational changes and the re-allocation of resources. Once this process is underway the negotiations and consultations are inevitably reactive but, given this limitation, it is essential that we act quickly to colonize the development of school-based initial teacher education and in particular the concept of mentoring as it is emerging in schools and transform it into a radical and dynamic force for the development of an enhanced, critical professionalism. We should do this not simply because we are faced with a *fait accompli*, but because, ultimately, it is the only way to overcome the theory and practice gap and to prevent the persistent tendency in ITT for new recruits to become cynical and to develop a dangerously atheoretical approach to their own professional development. Recent research in New Zealand indicates that MacDonald was right to suppose that student-teachers tend to identify with the occupational culture of schools very early on and are therefore resistant to a deeper consideration of educational issues (MacDonald, 1984; Munro, 1989).

So, it is vital that mentorship in schools is allowed to develop in a way which goes beyond narrow behaviourist approaches. In order to do this we need to be clear about the nature of reflective practice and to examine the lessons learned so far. One of the key ideas within the rhetoric of reflective practice is the notion of theory arising from, and rooted in, practice. The action-research movement has brought the concept of reflection-in-action increasingly to our attention and there is now a reasonable level of acceptance of the idea that the classroom practitioner can be encouraged to go beyond self-evaluation in terms of chosen strategies and skills and to engage in a consideration of the adequacy of explanations of educational phenomena and curriculum proposals. It has been noted, however, that this tends to happen only in the context of award-bearing in-service programmes.

Adler (1991) has conveniently set out what she sees as being three distinct meanings which can be ascribed to the term 'reflective practice'. The first and most basic way to talk about reflective practice might also be described as 'reflective teaching', where teachers are encouraged to reflect on the effectiveness of their own classroom skills. This is basically an act of classroom self-evaluation. The second approach is that usually associated with Schon (1983) and is characterized by the term 'reflection-in-action'. Central to Schon's view of the development of professional artistry is the idea of tacit professional knowledge which is refined through action and reflection but which is not necessarily made explicit verbally. This seems to correspond to McIntyre's (1990) view that, in teacher education programmes, we need to tap into teachers' 'craft knowledge' and make it accessible to the novice. According to Adler, this view of reflective practice is limited in that it does not allow for the practitioner to bring into question the social and political contexts of educational practice. She suggests a third view of reflective practice which seems to be based on the work of Kenneth Zeichner in the United States. Zeichner's view extends the concerns of the practitioner beyond classroom techniques and situational understanding and is characterized by the term 'reflection as critical inquiry'. This approach to reflection takes in the ethical and moral dimensions and it is this aspect of reflective practice which I believe is already under threat and could be extinguished completely in the context of school-based ITT. Zeichner's research, using discourse analysis in teacher education programmes, is very interesting and has important implications for mentorship.

Zeichner and his colleagues have shed some light on the nature of the discourse which takes place between tutor and trainee in the context of initial teacher training programmes, and the analysis of this discourse demonstrates well the way in which theorizing can take place within the process of supervision. Four types of discourse were identified (Zeichner et al., 1988):

- factual discourse – this is concerned with the description of events and relationships between observed phenomena;
- prudential discourse – this is concerned with evaluation of practice and the giving of instruction or advice;
- justificatory discourse – this is concerned with the rationale for given practices;
- critical discourse – this is concerned with discussion about the adequacy of explanations about pedagogical phenomena.

It is interesting to note first of all that this research finds that only approximately 2 per cent of discourse falls within the heading of critical discourse and that when the subject matter of the discourse is analysed it appears that a similarly tiny proportion of any discourse is concerned with the aims or goals of the lesson or the curriculum in general. This paints a rather depressing picture and suggests that precious little discussion of moral and political issues may be going on in the context of supervision. This is of crucial concern as we consider the shift towards school-based teacher education; as classroom experience and mentorship become the dominant contexts for professional development this may mean that a consideration of educational theory and questions of value will become completely overlooked.

It must be noted that Zeichner's view of reflective practice is not set in opposition to one which holds 'effectiveness' as central. Indeed, there is no reason to see 'reflective teaching', 'reflection in action' and 'critical inquiry' as being in any sense at odds with each other. One might argue that basic classroom effectiveness is best served by an approach to professional development which seeks to promote critical inquiry. I am concerned, however, about the limited way in which Zeichner considers the question of values. It is argued that critical discourse involves the assessment of the 'values embedded in the form and content of curriculum materials and instructional practices' (Zeichner et al., 1988, p.353). I would want to argue that, although it is clear that values are embedded in the practices adopted in the classroom, it is important to be aware of the fact that the individual student-teacher acts according to personal value positions and that these taken-for-granted actions transcend the particular teaching strategies or curriculum materials chosen for use within a particular lesson. Adler (1991) draws upon the work of a number of writers to make the point that the critical discourse which is an essential element of teacher education has to begin with the pre-existing beliefs of student-teachers. The teacher education programme must render problematic the taken-for-granted assumptions and explanations and challenge the student-teacher to 'examine moral and professional ambiguities' (Adler, 1991, p.143). It is evident that individuals come to the teaching profession with differing value positions and ideological predispositions and it is essential, therefore, that a training course such as a PGCE is designed to challenge individuals and to encourage them to undergo a process of values clarification. However, I would contend that this is unlikely to be done effectively without consideration of particular instances of practice. In Zeichner's terms this means examining the materials and strategies chosen to reveal the values embedded in them, but I would want to take this further and say that we need to engage the student-teachers in the analysis of their own actions in the classroom in order to reveal their personal values and call them into question. This view of discourse fits well with Elliott's (1991a) view of professional competence which holds the question of values as central: '...to act competently is to demonstrate abilities to realize the values – obligations and responsibilities to others – which are intrinsic to good practice'. The values manifest in the classroom are an essential part of the make-up of the individual student-teacher and so the discourse will have to be concerned with the individual's values and not just the values which are embedded in the off-the-peg strategies and materials.

Arguably, PGCE courses have always addressed these dimensions in one way or another. I take it that a successful seminar on the aims of education will certainly have enabled individuals to consider the value positions embedded in educational policies and practices and might also have encouraged some to re-examine their own cherished beliefs. This traditional academic approach has been called into question in recent years and, in many institutions, has been supplemented, at least, with a series of active learning workshops and so it is more likely that current PGCE students will be provided with experiences which focus more deliberately on the question of personal values. The induction week of the PGCE course on which I am a tutor, for example, features a number of workshops aimed at values clarification and there is no doubt that PGCE students and articled teachers are increasingly provided with contexts which enable them to explore their educational values as they proceed through their course. I recall one PGCE student who made the following comment in the context of a course evaluation: 'This course is the hardest thing I have ever done. Every day I have to put my values on the table and let everybody push them about'.

Another device which enables student-teachers to engage in ongoing reflection is the professional development portfolio. These are now in widespread use in one form or another and they usually feature narrative writing and reports on empirical tasks. I have some reservations, however, about the authenticity of such reflective writing when it is tied into a college-dominated assessment process which separates out the 'professional knowledge' component of the professional competence specification. The professional development portfolio may be the key device for encouraging reflection but we need to give urgent consideration to the role of the mentor in relation to it. The mentor is the individual who will have first-hand knowledge of the context of the student-teacher's experience and will be in the best position to enter into a focused dialogue based on the reflections contained within it. It is arrogant in the extreme for higher education tutors to suppose that they must retain control over the knowledge aspect of the student-teacher's professional development. It can be argued that the most fruitful reflection arises in the post-observation dialogue between mentor and mentee. Here again there have been developments towards what is generally called 'clinical supervision' (see Lucas, 1989) although it is clear from evaluations of our own PGCE course as well as those from the licensed teacher schemes that student-teachers actually experience a wide range of different supervision techniques. The model illustrated in Figure 8.1 indicates how the process of supervision is tied into the assessment process. It is important to note that the stages in this process need to be kept separate in order to maximize the extent to which the student-teacher can learn from the experience.

It seems to me to be inevitable that, as we move towards a more school-based approach to ITT, the mentors will be asked to operate some kind of observation and assessment system based on a model such as the one shown in Figure 8.1. But there is a danger, because of the pressure of accountability, that the crucial stage of 'analysis'

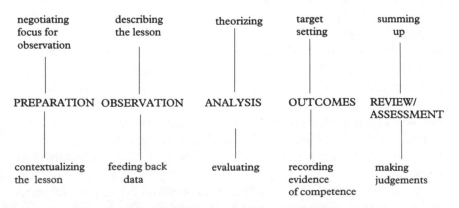

Figure 8.1 *The process of supervision*

may become neglected and this would mean that the opportunity for effective critical discourse would be severely reduced. The analysis of observed classroom practice provides an ideal opportunity to engage in high-level reflection which might begin with the evaluation of teaching skills and the curriculum but can be extended to encompass the development of a critical pedagogy and the clarification of personal values.

It might be helpful at this stage to try to summarize what I believe to be the purposes of reflection:

- to enable the teacher to assess his or her own skills and to improve them;
- to enable the teacher to evaluate the chosen teaching strategies and materials in terms of their appropriateness;
- to enable the teacher to question the values embedded in those practices and proceed to challenge the aims and goals of education;
- to enable the teacher to continue to examine and clarify their personal values and beliefs about society and pedagogy;
- to enable the teacher to theorize about the context of their pedagogical practice – that is, to try to develop explanations about the pupils, the interactions in the classroom and about the processes of teaching and learning;
- to enable the teacher to examine the adequacy of theories about pedagogical contexts and processes and develop a critique of them.

It may seem, of course, to be rather a tall order to ask mentors in schools to become responsible for facilitating this kind of reflection. It was made clear at the outset that mentors are struggling with insufficient time and without the necessary experience, expertise and confidence. In addition to this, mentors may not have quite the same ability to stand back from the particular institutional imperatives and prevailing ethos of their own schools as might visiting tutors from the colleges. It must be remembered that a PGCE programme is an induction into the profession as a whole rather than an induction into a particular school. If mentors are going to be able to facilitate the sort of critical reflection which has been described above, they need to be highly reflective practitioners themselves and they need also to be committed to the self-conscious development and enhancement of that reflective capacity. The difficulty is that not all schools are blessed with a culture which is conducive to reflection. There has been some glib talk about designating schools as 'teaching schools' but the government's proposals so far have been concerned with locating teacher training in 'the best schools' as defined by very narrow indicators such as examination passes and truancy rates. There must be some doubt as to whether schools as they are at the present time are suitable sites for teacher education, initial or otherwise. Indeed some commentators are quite pessimistic: 'More school-based training will foster more rapid socialization into a redundant occupational culture and the obsolete practices it sustains' (Elliot, 1991b, p.315). Elliott is referring here to a culture which embodies what he calls the 'infallible expert' model of professionalism as opposed to one based on reflective practice.

It may not be part of this government's plan to encourage a reflective climate in schools but I believe that it is up to head teachers to consider carefully what kind of school cultures they want to build and to take steps to ensure that they build the sort of cultures which are conducive to reflective practice. If head teachers want to create self-managing, self-generating, self-evaluating, 'empowered' (Hargreaves and Hopkins, 1991) schools, they will have to take steps to avoid the slide towards an apprenticeship model of professional development and this means the active pursuit of the climate for reflection. Fortunately, the government's determination to strengthen the schools' part in the planning and delivery of ITT provides head teachers with a window of opportunity both to initiate developments in their own schools and to influence the nature of ITT in the future through their negotiations with the higher education institutions.

So, what can head teachers do to create reflective schools?

1. They can subscribe to and defend a view of mentoring which is centrally concerned with support for the sort of critical reflective practice described above.
2. They can insist that mentors play a full part in future school-based teacher education programmes. That is to say that mentors should not be limited to the assessment of classroom skills but should be concerned with the facilitation of the kind of reflection which is concerned with the theoretical dimension and questions of values.
3. They can designate as mentors teachers who are themselves highly reflective professionals.
4. They can ensure that mentors have an adequate time allocation and realistic job descriptions so that they are able both to work with student-teachers and pursue their own professional development.
5. They can ensure that mentors are provided with substantial and extended support.

This latter point about support for mentors is perhaps the most crucial and challenging because of the resource implications and it needs, therefore, to be thought through very carefully.

I believe that individuals need to learn about reflective practice experientially. That is to say that, in order to develop the necessary understanding and skills, mentors must engage in critical reflection themselves and this needs to take place within a collaborative and supportive framework. I would therefore propose, first, that mentors belong to a support group which may be convened within a single school, within a consortium or within a geographical area. The purpose of the group would be to provide a forum for discussion and the sharing of common concerns, but such a group would also provide a context for collaborative action research focusing on the problem of initial teacher education and, perhaps, on professional development in general. Second, I would propose that mentors are provided with a framework to guide their own reflection in the form of a professional development portfolio. The portfolio would help the individual mentor to carry out investigative and reflective tasks but, because it entails the keeping of evidence about the process of mentoring and the individual's development as a mentor, it would also provide a basis for review with appropriate colleagues. My third proposal concerns the link with the institutions of higher education. It is assumed that there remains a need for specific training in relation to the generic mentoring skills but beyond this I believe that the college tutor has a key role to play in providing the ongoing support and challenge which will enhance the mentors' own reflection. I believe that it is essential for mentors to be engaged in accredited action research at Masters level. This is essential partly because of the need to counter the natural subjectivity and narrowness of perspective arising from the specific institutional context and also because of the complexity of the professional task facing mentors. In order to be able to facilitate critical reflection on the part of student-teachers, the mentors must revisit for themselves the fundamental questions about the nature of the learning process, the nature of knowledge and the nature of learners both young and adult. Perhaps even more fundamental than this, however, is the need to explore the values which underpin reflective practice and to develop an enhanced commitment to the sort of goals which tend to be shared within the educational research community. All of the above proposals might be summed up by saying that mentors should adopt an action research perspective as spelt out recently by Elliott:

Action research improves practice by developing the practitioner's capacity for discrimination and judgement in particular, complex human situations. It unifies inquiry, the improvement of performance and the development of persons in their professional role (1991a, p.52).

By adopting a very positive view of mentoring, head teachers can transform the culture of the school and this will lead to an increased capacity to cope with innovation and change. There are management implications of course: mentors in secondary schools would need to be organized as part of a professional development team led by a professional tutor – a role recommended by the James Report 20 years ago. The professional development team could then work together to build the kind of culture which can create what Holly and Southworth (1989) called 'the learning school'. Such schools depend on the development, over time, of collaborative cultures which consist of:

pervasive qualities, attitudes and behaviours which run through staff relationships on a moment-by-moment, day-by-day basis. Help, support, trust and openness are at the heart of these relationships (Fullan and Hargreaves, 1992, p.65).

All this may be flying in the face of the thrust of government policy of course and it may well be true to say, as Hartley (1991) does, that:

In the current political climate...policy at the national or state level, in the grip of the monetarists and their mandarins, is expressly at odds with inquiry-based modes of learning (p.88).

But the setting up of joint planning arrangements for the design of the new PGCE provides a real opportunity for heads to pursue goals which are genuinely educative. The resource implications are challenging of course, but it is significant that the government has not specified what kind of financial arrangements might be put in place in relation to future, more school-based PGCE courses. These circumstances present us with a major opportunity to rethink the relationship between schools and the institutions of higher education. For their part, schools need to see the costs of mentoring as just one element of a general provision for professional development. The professional development team would be responsible for a range of related budget items such as appraisal and the organization of development days. The team would need to negotiate with an institution of higher education an appropriate set of financially sensible arrangements which encompassed ITT, in-service training and mentor support. It may be quite difficult to arrive at a workable formula in the first instance, but experience in my own institution suggests that it will be possible to strike bargains which are mutually advantageous. It does mean, of course, that tutors in higher education will have to rethink their traditional roles in relation to ITT and turn their attention to the empowerment of teacher/mentors and professional tutors in schools through award-bearing action research.

At the present time, schools and the higher education sector are being asked even more vigorously than ever before to enter into partnership over training. The opportunity is before us and the choice has to be made: either we can fall into a pattern which seems to be in some sense predetermined, or we can make a positive choice for enhanced professionalism. The first option entails the traditional division of labour along theory and practice lines with mentors being asked to carry out the assessment of classroom skills according to a narrow, behaviourist model while college tutors fight a losing battle to engender critical reflection through tokenistic theoretical input in college-based seminars. The second option would be to raise our expectations of mentorship so that it becomes pivotal in the development of a critical pedagogy for both student-teachers and serving staff; to establish in schools expert professional development teams to pursue the goals of reflective practice and to build school cultures which are conducive to reflection; and to foster comprehensive relationships between schools and institutions of higher education so that schools can not only draw upon the considerable experience and expertise built up in the colleges and universities over the years, but also so that the efforts and creative talents of mentors can be fully recognized and accredited through award-bearing action research programmes. I believe that the second option – for reflective mentorship – is the profession's best hope.

REFERENCES

Adler, S (1991) 'The reflective practitioner and the curriculum of teacher education', *Journal of Education for Teaching*, 17, 2.

Elliott, J (1991a) *Action Research for Educational Change*, Buckingham: Open University Press.

Elliott, J (1991b) 'A model of professionalism and its implications for teacher education, *British Educational Research Journal*, 17, 4, 309–19.

Fullan, M and Hargreaves, A (1992) *What's Worth Fighting for in your School?*, Buckingham: Open University Press.

Hargreaves, D, Beardon, T, Booth, M and Reiss, M (1992) *School-led Initial Teacher Training: The Way Forward*, Cambridge: Department of Education, University of Cambridge.

Hargreaves, D and Hopkins, D (1991) *The Empowered School*, London: Cassell.

Hartley, D (1991) 'Democracy, capitalism and the reform of teacher education', *Journal of Education for Teaching*, 17, 1.

Holly, P and Southworth, G (1989) *The Developing School*, London: Falmer Press.

Inglis, F (1974) 'Ideology and the curriculum: the value assumptions of systems builders', *Journal of Curriculum Studies*, May.

Lucas, P (1989) 'Clinical methods of supervision: a note of caution and challenge', *New Era in Education*, 70, 2.

MacDonald, B (1984) 'Teacher education and curriculum reform; some English errors', address to Spanish teacher educators, Valencia (CARE University of East Anglia, mimeo).

McIntyre, D (1990) 'The Oxford Internship Scheme and the Cambridge Analytical Framework: models of partnership in initial teacher education', in Booth, M, Furlong, J and Wilkin, M (eds) *Partnership in Initial Teacher Training*, London: Cassell.

Munro, R (1989) 'A case study of school-based innovation in secondary teacher training', unpublished PhD thesis, University of Auckland, New Zealand.

Schon, D (1983) *The Reflective Practitioner*, San Francisco, CA: Jossey Bass.

Zeichner K, Liston, D, Mahlios, M and Gomez, M (1988) 'The structure and goals of a student teaching program and the character and quality of supervisory discourse', *Teaching and Teacher Education*, 4, 4, 349–63.

Part III
Realities of Mentoring

9 Are Mentor Teachers Teacher Educators?

Sharon Feiman-Nemser, Michelle B Parker and Kenneth Zeichner

Introduction

Created by the same omnibus piece of education legislation, the Teacher Trainee Program[1] and the Mentor Teacher Program in the state of California have developed within the broader national debate in the United States about enhancing the teaching profession. The Teacher Trainee Program in California addresses a chronic teacher shortage problem by allowing school districts to hire college graduates who lack a teaching certificate. It is an alternative to issuing emergency teaching credentials to individuals who lack any formal teacher education. Supporters argue that the Program helps upgrade the quality of the field by attracting talented candidates with strong academic credentials and relevant work experience.

If the Teacher Trainee Program, like other 'alternate route' programmes in the United States,[2] is designed to help *recruit* capable people into teaching, the Mentor Teacher Program is designed to help *retain* capable teachers by expanding their rewards and opportunities. In the rationale for the Mentor Program, the California legislature declares its intent to 'provide incentives to teachers of demonstrated ability and expertise to remain in the public school'.

The requirements of the Teacher Trainee Program intersect with the inducements of the Mentor Teacher Program to form a structure of support for beginning teachers. The legislation requires school districts implementing a teacher training programme (ie, an alternate route programme) to assign a mentor teacher to each trainee. The legislation also allocates funds to school districts participating in the

Mentor Teacher Program; $4000 stipends for district-designated mentors, and an additional $2000 per mentor to cover the costs of implementing the Program (eg substitutes, released time, travel). The mentors' primary responsibility is to guide and assist new teachers.

An improvement over 'sink or swim'

While concerns about recruitment and retention provide a large part of the motivation for the Teacher Trainee and Mentor Teacher Programs, they also reflect a growing recognition that new teachers have two jobs when they enter teaching – carrying out the job they have been hired to do and learning to do that job (Wildman *et al.*, 1989). If this is true for those who have already completed a pre-service programme, including a stint of student teaching, it is certainly true for those with no previous professional preparation, such as candidates enrolled in the Teacher Trainee Program.

The idea of assigning mentor teachers to work with beginning teachers is gaining acceptance, even in a profession where norms of autonomy and non-interference protect the right of beginners to 'sink or swim' in the privacy of their own classroom (Devaney, 1987). Providing support and assistance to new teachers is seen by many as a clear improvement over the more typical pattern of isolation, survival and trial-and-error learning that characterizes the entry of most beginning teachers into teaching (Feiman-Nemser, 1983). But what form should that support and assistance take? To what extent do the expectations, approaches and content of the assistance vary with the background of the candidates and the contexts where they work? As programmes for beginning teachers proliferate, it becomes increasingly important to conceptualize the 'curriculum' of teacher induction and to consider the role of mentor teachers in helping novices learn to teach.

This chapter grew out of our efforts to learn more about the contribution of mentor teachers to the learning of beginning teachers in the Teacher Trainee Program of a large urban school district in California. In this school district, teacher trainees teach full-time in junior or senior high schools while participating in a two-year, district-sponsored training programme leading to a teaching credential. Mentors work with one to four trainees while continuing to teach 60 per cent of the time. We wanted to know what the face-to-face, close-to-the-classroom work between mentor teachers and teacher trainees was really like and how that work added up as preparation for teaching and professional socialization.

Limited help from extant research

What do we know about the role of experienced teachers in the preparation of beginning teachers in alternate route programmes? What forms of 'guidance' and 'support' do mentor teachers offer novice teachers? Studies of alternate route programmes generally cite the contribution of mentor teachers as a key to the programme's success, but say little about the specific nature of that contribution.[3] Even studies which claim to look 'beneath the surface...to the heart of what programs...actually do and to whom' (Adelman, 1988, p. 55) report limited data. For example, on the basis of interviews with administrators and programme participants in an exploratory study of seven alternate route programmes, Adelman (1988) concludes that alternate route programmes provide more field experience and more intense supervision than traditional teacher education programmes. She also notes that clinical supervision is the preferred supervisory model.

Even when researchers focus on a single programme, they rarely provide more than surface information about what mentor teachers do. An evaluation of the California Teacher Training Program (McKibben, Walton and Wright, 1987) reports how many times each teacher was observed, the length of the observation, the frequency of conferences and the most frequently discussed topics. Based on such findings, the researchers conclude:

> The law requires that teacher trainees be guided and assisted by mentor teachers.... This formal support system for teacher trainees is one of the strengths of the program.... The trainees have also sought and received help from other persons who have not been formally assigned to guide and assist them, and have engaged in collegial dialogue with other teachers in their schools. *As a group, the trainees speak very highly of these formal and informal support networks. Guidance and assistance from experienced teachers added to their own effectiveness as teachers, according to many of the trainees* (p. 29, emphasis added)

None of these studies tells us very much about the character and quality of the *practice* of mentoring, especially as it is carried out with novice teachers who lack formal teacher preparation. Neither do they help us understand what the labels 'assistance', 'support', 'guidance', 'clinical supervision,' etc. stand for in particular situations.[4] What do such novice teachers need to learn? How do their mentors help them to learn to teach while teaching? How do mentor teachers enact a new role for which no real precedents exist? This chapter was motivated by these questions.

Sources of data

To learn more about what mentor teachers do when they work with beginning teachers, we examined three sources of data: 1) a training manual (Little and Nelson, 1990) assembled by the Far West Laboratory out of materials developed by the school district for the core training of new mentors; and 2) transcripts of conferences between mentor teachers and teacher trainees; and 3) interviews with mentors about those sessions. These data were collected by researchers from the National Center for Research on Teacher Learning at Michigan State as part of a larger study of teacher education and learning to teach. In this chapter, we look at each source of data for information and insights about the work of mentors and teacher trainees.[5]

What are Mentors Taught to Do?

A 30-hour, required training course for mentors in this urban school district introduces mentors to their new role and provides skills and strategies they can use in their work. The training connects views about teaching and learning to teach with specific procedures and techniques that can be used in face-to-face, close-to-the-classroom work. Created by the district's professional development staff, the training stresses the idea that research presents valid knowledge about teaching which can be passed on to novices along with the accumulated wisdom of practice.

Because the work of mentoring differs from the work of classroom teaching, it is thought to require new and different skills. Mentors need preparation in ways to help novices handle their typical problems: 'classroom management, basic lesson design and delivery, evaluating student progress' (Little and Nelson, 1990, p. 2). Since mentoring is more than passing on a 'bag of tricks', mentors must be able to 'describe and demonstrate underlying principles of teaching and learning'. They also need to learn how to 'talk clearly and straightforwardly about teaching without offending the teacher' (Little and Nelson, 1990, p. 4).

Elements of the training correspond to the six sections of Little and Nelson's *Leader's Guide*: orientation to the mentor role; assisting the beginning teacher; classroom organization and management for new teachers; classroom consultation, observation, and coaching; mentor as staff developer; cooperation between the administrator and mentor. Each section is broken down into specific training segments with activities, handouts and directions for how teachers can practise particular skills in their school. We concentrate in this chapter on the first four sections of the *Leader's Guide* because they bear more directly on close-to-the-classroom work between mentors and novice teachers.

Mentor training

In 'Orientation to the mentor role', mentors are welcomed to their new responsibilities and assured that they are taking on a very important job. Testimonials from veteran mentors provide descriptions of the 'wonders and traumas' of the work. Presentations by state and local officials clarify the procedures and guidelines to which they must adhere. There are workshops on leadership styles and 'survival skills' such as how to balance classroom teaching and mentoring responsibilities, and a review of the 'elements of good teaching' as identified by teacher effectiveness research. The training design assumes that mentors bring with them a grasp of recent research on effective classroom teaching because of their previous participation in district skill-building workshops.

In the section called 'Assisting the beginning teachers', mentors learn about typical problems beginning teachers face. They hear suggestions about ways to be helpful (eg, develop a resource file of materials for beginners to use; hold an orientation to explain procedures such as filling out grade reports) and they discuss the issue of developing relationships with novices.

The section on 'Classroom organization and management for new teachers' introduces mentors to 'well-tested, practical programs' derived from classroom-based research on effective management. Planning checklists for separate areas of management (eg, organizing the room, developing a workable set of rules and procedures, monitoring student responsibility, planning activities for the first week, maintaining management systems, organizing instruction) are distributed.

In 'Classroom consultation, observation and coaching', mentors learn about 'tested techniques of classroom observation and feedback'. This section rests on the view that, since teaching and learning take place in classrooms, teachers must see each other working in classrooms with students in order to be helpful. Much of the material in this section comes from the literature on coaching (eg, Joyce and Showers, 1988) and clinical supervision (eg, Acheson and Gall, 1987).

One workshop offers a general framework for talking about teaching regardless of grade level or subject. The framework combines the common features of 'effective' lessons with six levels of thinking derived from Bloom's taxonomy of cognitive objectives. The framework could be used to structure observations and conferences and to help novices learn how to plan 'effective' lessons.

Mentors also hear about the value of 'scripting' lessons when they observe. Besides preserving the sequence and context of the lesson, a 'script' is seen in this training programme as easier for teachers to accept because it provides an objective, non-evaluative record of class-room transactions.

Since observation is only useful if it leads to thoughtful discussion of actual teaching, mentors hear about ways to structure conferences. Numerous handouts accompany this part of the training. They include a list of coaching skills (eg, active listening, passive listening), a list of feedback techniques (eg, elicit feelings, avoid giving direct advice, provide specific praise), a list of 'opening' questions (eg, 'How do you feel about my coming to observe the lesson?', 'Did the students respond to you as expected?') and 'focusing' questions (eg, 'Why do you think so many students came up to you when you were at the reading table?', 'How could you make your directions a little more clear?'). Pointing to the importance of these skills for mentors, the *Guide* states:

> Asking mentors to observe and be observed, we are asking them to do something that is at one and the same time important and *difficult*. Getting close to the classroom means getting 'close-to-the-bone' – talking to people in detail about their ideas and performance. (Emphasis in the original.)

comm.

Commentary

As seen through the *Leader's Guide*, the training for new mentors promotes a view of mentoring as a technical activity that can be controlled by applying specific strategies and techniques. The training downplays the 'wisdom of practice' in favour of procedural knowledge derived from research. Presumably these procedures can be applied to generic problems experienced by generic beginning teachers.

The picture of effective mentoring parallels the image of effective teaching as embodied in direct instruction. Teachers must learn to manage instruction; mentors must learn to manage conferences. Organized around a non-evaluative anecdotal record or 'script', the effective conference is one in which the mentor sets the agenda, directs the conversation, provides most of the data, and determines the outcome.

Reading the *Leader's Guide*, one gets little sense of teaching as an intellectual or moral activity. Issues of student learning, diversity, curriculum or assessment rarely come up. Nor do questions about purposes – the teacher's or the mentor's. The training gives the impression that goals are unproblematic and given, whether in teaching or mentoring. Finally, it is curious that a programme premised on the valued contribution of experienced teachers pays so little attention to mentors' own ideas about teaching and learning to teach. The training runs the risk of de-skilling mentor teachers by substituting neutral procedures for collective practical intelligence in the solution of practical problems.

Three Examples of Mentors At Work

We wanted to go beyond this glimpse of how mentors were prepared for their work and examine the character and quality of mentoring as it was enacted by some of the participants in this particular teacher education programme. For one day, researchers followed mentors as they observed and conferred with secondary English teacher trainees. We interviewed both mentor and teacher after the conference, probing their reasons for actions and statements. We will now briefly examine three different cases of mentoring in this school-based urban teacher education programme.

Case 1 – Candace (mentor) and Kevin (teacher)

Before the observation, Candace tells the researcher that she has been helping Kevin develop a 'weekly programme' and think about where to find materials. When she observes, Candace says, she looks for 'teacher direction' rather than independent seat-work because 'remedial students' need the teacher to model oral language. Candace thinks that Kevin has changed a lot since the beginning of the year. 'He has more of a class routine and he doesn't base his lessons as much as he used to on personal opinion'. Candace sees her role as helping Kevin move away from basing lessons on personal opinion. She makes suggestions and tries 'to question him so that he defines for himself what it is that he's basing his approaches on'.

The observation

While Kevin teaches his eighth grade remedial class, Candace 'scripts' the lesson. Kevin begins by telling students to write a story about a train wreck, making it up or drawing on something they had seen. While he takes roll, fills out tardy slips and distributes books, students write.

After 20 minutes, Kevin reads a list of 10 study questions which go with the next story they will read. 'The questions should give some background for the story and give some reasons why we should read it...and should care about this story', he explains. Students quiet down as Kevin writes the questions on the board. Some require factual recall (eg, 'Tell how Ivanov saved the train from being wrecked'), interpretation (eg, 'Why is Ivanov's job important?') and imagination (eg, 'Think of another way Ivanov might have saved the train'). Kevin explains what each question is getting at, then students copy the questions into their notebooks. The explanations and copying take the rest of the class period.

The conference

Candace starts the conference by complimenting Kevin for displaying a list of classroom rules. Then she turns to the opening activity, asking whether students had read about or had any recent experiences with train wrecks. Kevin responds that the assignment was 'just an introductory thing'. Trying to place the exercise in the larger context of writing, Candace asks whether students ever do brainstorming or the clustering of ideas and whether they ever work in small groups and pairs to revise their work. Again Kevin says they do so with longer assignments, but that this was 'just an introductory thing'.

Although Candace seems unhappy with Kevin's response, she moves on. Complimenting Kevin on his study questions, she reminds him that the school has a copy machine which would save students from having to write the questions down. Kevin explains that he didn't have the questions ready in time.

Next Candace asks Kevin whether he has students read aloud or silently. Kevin explains that he generally has students read the story silently, answer questions, then read the story and their answers aloud. 'Which way do you think students get more out of the story?' Candace asks. 'All three', Kevin replies. The students are 'very visual and kinesthetic. They like to do copy work but reading is much more difficult'. Candace does not probe this statement or open up a discussion about student learning. Instead she compliments Kevin for showing sensitivity to the attention span of 'these young people' by varying the activities.

Candace brings up several more topics, finding something to praise, then asking Kevin about his practice. Then she gets him to consider how well his lesson fits with the components of effective lessons endorsed by the district:

> Candace: ...I was thinking about your lesson today. Um, our writing, your little, well, the thing that, how would that fit in here? Where would you think it would fit best?
>
> Kevin: That's an introductory thing. That's before the, um (looking at the sheet which details the steps of the teacher-directed lesson plan).
>
> Candace: So, it'd be somewhere up here at the beginning?
>
> Kevin: Yeah, it's before the, um, right before the initial instruction.
>
> Candace: Okay. And then the guided group practice would be?
>
> Kevin: The guided group practice is gonna be doing the study questions.... The independent practice will probably be questions nine and ten on the guide. We'll finish off tomorrow, then they'll do their

homework. The remediation or alternative activity will probably be the game on Thursday.

Candace mentions that the students are 'nicely behaved,' then asks Kevin about his seating arrangement. 'Do you assign seats?' (No.) 'Does it work well letting students choose their own seats?' (Yes, because if students misbehave they know they will be moved away from a friend.) Candace comments that the girls and boys sit separately and asks Kevin whether he ever puts 'an on-task girl with a couple of off-task boys?' Kevin agrees that mixing up the boys and girls would work but that, for now, students are behaving. The conference ends without any sense of closure.

Comments to the researcher

After the conference Candace tells the researcher that she would like to have seen 'a lot more teacher involvement [in the lesson] than I saw today. I felt that there needed to be more student-teacher interaction'. Still, overall she is pleased with the conference and the lesson. She senses that Kevin is beginning to think about his teaching in more detail and follow a sequence. She is pleased with his lesson planning, especially the use of an introductory activity. She is glad that Kevin is teaching vocabulary and using pre-writing activities for longer assignments.

Commentary

It is hard to tell what Candace is trying to accomplish in this conference. One senses her discomfort with some of Kevin's practices, but each time she seems to accept his explanation. Kevin is unlikely to think critically about the bases for his approaches without more discussion of the issues raised by what he does and does not do. The whole conference has an artificial quality. Candace and Kevin seem to be going through the motions without taking the content seriously. Does it matter that Kevin has an introductory activity, if the activity itself has limited educational value? Is it important that the lesson provides guided practice, if that means copying down questions which the teacher could photocopy? By her silence on these matters, Candace seems to be endorsing these activities as acceptable ways for students to spend time in school. While Candace uses some of the specific strategies introduced in the mentor training – scripting the lesson, asking focusing questions, offering praise – it is hard to connect them with an educative purpose.

Case 2 – Rita (the mentor) and Chad (the teacher)
The observation

Rita watches as Chad's eighth grade remedial English students, composed mostly of Latino males, file in. Chad divides the students into two groups, keeping one and sending the other to work with an aide. For most of the period, both groups read aloud a play, with each student taking a part. Since the activity ends before the class is over and Chad has nothing else planned, students visit until the bell rings.

The conference

After class Rita and Chad sit down to discuss the lesson. Rita opens the conference by asking Chad how he felt about what had happened. 'It was comfortable', Chad replies, adding that the lesson fitted the looser structure characteristic of his Friday classes. Chad then comments on differences in the two groups:

Chad:	I was very disappointed to find out from my aide that when she gave directions to the second reading group, two students refused to read and one of them is a very bright student.
Rita:	Maybe they were a little disappointed that you were not with the group, you know – that it was little less important perhaps. You can't worry about that–maybe not breakfast, maybe too much breakfast, you know, you don't know what is going to happen.
Chad:	But I felt good in my own group with the fact that (name of student) whose reading ability is the weakest of all ten members of the group was the one most anxious to read.
Rita:	That's great.
Chad:	He asked to be the narrator and he also read two parts.

Consulting her notes, Rita begins her commentary on the lesson. She tells Chad that dividing students into groups is good as long as there is an aide. Alternatively, Chad could put two students in charge of assigning parts and directing the reading so that he could circulate.

Rita praises Chad's new room arrangement, saying she likes where he put the overhead and podium, and how he darkens the classroom when students enter. That helps students calm down and focus on the activity. She says she plans to try that in her own classroom.

Since the play is part of a unit on winning and losing, Rita says somewhat tentatively that Chad might have made the connection explicit. 'If there had been a moment maybe just to say, "Now this story ties into this unit, we're talking about winning. Is this man losing because he can't read?"' Before Chad can respond, Rita retracts the suggestion on the grounds that it does not fit with the 'loose' Friday structure. Chad agrees, then wonders how much this story about an adult learning to read fits with the family backgrounds of his students. Rita and Chad agree that many of the students are probably the first generation to be literate (in English). Rita points out that students probably hear at home the same kinds of speeches – 'of laying down the law' – delivered by the father in the play. Chad is excited that one student, probably the first reader in his family, has 'picked up that it's important to be able to read'. Chad mentions that one student corrected another's reading and Rita comments, it's nice to let students correct each other instead of having the teacher make all the corrections.

Turning again to her notes, Rita says, 'I just have odds and ends I wrote down'. She likes the fact that Chad took the parts of the women in the play to show male students that it was 'an ok thing to do.' She confesses that she wondered whether the activity would take the whole period. She thought Chad could have stopped before the last act and asked students to do some writing. 'You could even ask, "How do you think the story will come out?" or, "What is this character going to do through the story?" '

Chad likes the idea and laments the fact that he and the aide had not agreed to that. Rita elaborates on the idea, suggesting that he could have put students in pairs and asked them to create some dialogue between characters and then had students study punctuation and grammar from what they write.

> I don't think in a group like that you can expect too much. They're not going to write another act; they're not going to be able to do that, I don't think. But you could say, 'The story up until now talks about', or 'Find an adjective as you're going back over it that describes each of the characters'...and that's an easy way to get a little bit of grammar in without having to teach grammar. They accept it differently. Sometimes I think we have to play their game.

Rita praises Chad for selecting an 'up-to-date' play and using a different format on Fridays. Then she comments that Chad probably felt 'uncomfortable' about running out of things to do. She has brought a folder of 'sponge activities', things that teachers can use to fill up time. Chad admits his discomfort, saying he probably should have had the students read for half the period and then do some writing. Pursuing the idea of writing, Rita asks if Chad uses 'clustering' or brainstorming, pre-writing activities in which students gather their ideas with the help of peers before starting to write. Chad says he does.

Rita compliments Chad on his calm manner with students. 'At home someone is always yelling at them all the time...' She suggests that they work on lesson planning next time. Chad admits he has trouble with planning and budgeting time. Even though he teaches the same grade level, the students differ so much in terms of their abilities that he has to plan different lessons. Rita acknowledges the problem and suggests he look at some new anthologies of short stories and new grammar books that the school recently received.

Afterwards, Rita tells the researcher that she thought the conference went well though she wishes Chad would bring up problems. Perhaps, she reflects, 'I'm in there too soon that I don't give him a chance'. Overall, she is pleased with Chad's progress.

> I think that he now accepts we all have problems and it's not an easy job and the more we can work together and share materials and share ideas...and we have talked at one of our last sessions about working through a lesson, a unit plan, on 'educational decisions'...he seems more eager now to say, 'Fine. Let's get together and talk about whatever problem it is'.

Commentary

Because Rita dominates this conference, we learn very little about Chad's thinking. Nor do we learn the reasons behind Rita's praise, questions or suggestions. What ideas about the relationship between writing and reading or about student learning lie behind Rita's suggestion that Chad stop the reading so that students can do some writing? Rita tends to link students' actions and feelings to external factors (eg a darkened room, an overhead projector) rather than to issues of curriculum and student learning. She misses a chance for such a discussion when Chad comments on how students in the two groups responded to the play-reading activity.

Most disturbing is the way Rita reinforces a deficit view of the students' families and home backgrounds and promotes low expectations about what they can be expected to learn in school. She tells Chad not to expect too much from the students and supports his assumption that their parents are illiterate. Neither Rita nor Chad express any appreciation for the knowledge and cultures that students bring to school or consider how they can use these perspectives to enhance learning. The conference reinforces the view that the main task in educating eighth grade remedial students is to keep them happily occupied in activities that give the appearance of learning.

Case 3 – Lila (the mentor) and Clark (the teacher)

Leaving her own class with a substitute, Lila comes over to Clark's school to observe his fifth period class and talk to him during sixth period. As he teaches his eighth grade class of ESL students, described by Lila as 'medium low and low', she takes notes.

I just put it down very dispassionately [she explains to the researcher] nothing with a lot of adjectives, just statements of things that were occurring, comments about the material, comments about the way he presented it, comments about the students and their reactions, comments about the whole period and how it went.

The observation

As students enter, Clark directs them to copy the sentences on the board and correct the punctuation and capitalization while he takes roll. After reviewing the sentences orally, Clark turns to the main activity of the period – reading aloud from 'Will Stutely's Rescue', a Robin Hood tale in an anthology of American literature. Every few paragraphs, Clark stops, asks some recall questions and then ends up paraphrasing the passage. As the period progresses, students become restless and fidgety, and most stop paying attention to the story. With 10 minutes to go, Clark give students 10 words from the story to define and use in sentences.

The conference

Lila begins the conference by telling Clark 'some positive things I saw', but quickly raises her first concern. She praises Clark for using a 'dispatch' activity at the beginning of class, then observes that students took too long to settle down. When Clark tries to explain that his students are 'hyper', especially after lunch, Lila suggests that he have students read a novel of their choosing as a different 'dispatch' activity. Lila later tells the researcher that she has been trying to get Clark to do this since the beginning of the year.

Next Lila warns Clark not to let students get out of class so easily. One boy had entered the classroom with his shirt half off, and Clark had sent him to the bathroom to fix it. That kind of incident will give students the idea that they can get away with doing silly, distracting things, Lila tells Clark. She also tells him not to talk over students or recognize anyone who calls out answers, both behaviours Lila noted in the lesson. Rather, Clark should get students to listen before he speaks and encourage them to raise their hands.

Turning to the main activity of the lesson, Lila compliments Clark for reading the story aloud 'because the language is very difficult', but asks whether a more accessible version of the story is available. Lila tells Clark that the students, not the teacher, should do the paraphrasing. She also thinks that the reading went on too long, resulting in a 'one-dimensional lesson'.

Lila believes that every English lesson should have a balance of reading, writing and speaking. 'They (students) should be writing every day about what they are reading', Lila tells Clark. If Clark stopped the reading sooner, students would have had more time to write, and not just sentences with vocabulary words. Lila suggests pairing students to work on the discussion questions.

Next Lila focuses on the questions Clark posed at the end of the reading: 'Should Robin Hood be taking from the rich to give to the poor?' She thinks it would make a good journal entry, but Clark plans to use it as the basis for a discussion because 'it will help students connect the reading to their own lives'. He wants students to think about what would happen if Robin Hood were living in America today, taking from the rich to give to the poor. Lila worries that students will not see the moral dimension. 'In reality', she tells Clark, 'some people are richer than others and students need to realize that reality even though they may not like it'.

Lila returns to the question of finding suitable materials, suggesting that the next story might come from a different anthology. As a former reading coordinator, Lila knows what books are available and has made frequent suggestions to Clark about using alternative texts. Today she tells him to use an anthology called *Literature Scope* which has stories that are 'high interest and low level' without being watered down. Clark interrupts to say that he is planning to use *Wise and Weak*, a story about a gang. He assumes that students will be interested because of their familiarity with gangs.

Comments to the researcher
After the conference Lila reiterates her concerns to the researcher. She wishes Clark would use texts that the students could comprehend. She thinks he should rely less on whole-group discussions and have students work in pairs or small groups to answer discussion questions. Finally, she worries that the students missed the moral dilemma posed by Robin Hood's actions.

> 'Is it okay [she asks] if somebody is rich to take his money just because he's rich? These kids can relate to that because many of them do come from low income homes. Might they think it is okay to knock on their neighbor's door or barge in and take something just because the neighbor has more? [Sighing, Lila sums up her sentiments] I try to reinforce the good things, but I'm getting a little weary because a lot of (my) suggestions are not implemented. I mean a lot.'

Commentary
Drawing on her own knowledge and experience, Lila tries to influence Clark's practice by suggesting more appropriate activities and materials. We know that Lila has made similar suggestions before. We

don't know whether she has linked them to ideas about curriculum and learning. Lila says that every English class should have a balance of reading, writing and speaking activities. Why does she think that? Where does this idea come from? Is Lila expressing her own personal views, the position of the district or the collective wisdom of the field? By not connecting her suggestion to 'best practice', Lila may inadvertently reinforce the belief that what teachers do is a matter of personal preference.

Lila's concerns for the lesson run the gamut from 'classroom management to materials to methods to time allotment'. She seems frustrated that Clark has not taken full advantage of her expertise. Uninterested in Clark's explanation, she offers her opinions on everything without delving into anything. Rather than treating her notes as something she and Clark can study together, Lila uses them to remind her of all the points she wants to make. Though Clark has access to her accumulated wisdom, one wonders whether he is learning to think critically about his own teaching.

Comparative Analysis of the Examples

Common topics

In terms of content, the three conferences reflect some common views about good English classes. All three mentors believe that students should do some reading, writing and speaking in every English class. They also seem to share a general orientation to writing which comes through in their questions about pre-writing activities and suggestions about journals and other assignments that reinforce the reading-writing connection.

All three mentors emphasized issues of classroom organization and management, stressing the importance of having an opening activity, filling up the time and getting students' attention before proceeding with the lesson. Usually they treated these matters separately from considerations of curriculum or student learning. One exception is the implication from Lila that students would settle down more quickly if they had novels of their own choosing to read.

The value of small-group work is a third common thread. All three mentors suggest some form of small-group work for writing and discussion. We can also see common patterns in the way mentors structured the conferences and used particular strategies and techniques. All three mentors scripted the lessons they observed, then used the script as an agenda. Rather than identifying a basic question or issue to discuss in some depth, they all walked through the lesson, commenting or questioning the trainee on each part. By talking about so many things, they never probed anything.

Mentors structured the conferences and dominated talk. They asked all the questions, made most of the statements and offered all of the suggestions. Not only did they begin the conference with a compliment, they sought opportunities to offer praise.

The influence of training

We can clearly trace some of these commonalities to the content of mentor training. If the point of the training was to get mentors to treat particular topics or use particular strategies, then these examples offer evidence that the training was a success.

But the examples also document how the procedural orientation of the training narrowed thinking about the value of particular strategies and limited the treatment of certain issues. For example, all the mentors used praise without explaining the bases for their assessments. All the mentors scripted the lessons but did not analyse the scripts to identify patterns or underlying issues. All the mentors suggested strategies for managing students but they rarely connected the issues of student attention and involvement with the nature of the academic tasks provided to students.

Missed opportunities

The conferences reveal little about what the beginning teachers are thinking. That is because the mentors seem relatively uninterested in probing their ideas. Mentors do not find out what their trainees know about their subjects, their students or the curriculum.

Nor do mentors share their own *thinking* about the lesson. What do they think about the value of the content, the appropriateness of the teaching, or the likelihood of learning? Though they give suggestions and materials, they do not provide a rationale or make explicit the connections they see.

In this way, beginning teachers in these three cases miss opportunities to develop sound reasons for what they do, to learn principles of teaching and to think about ways to represent knowledge to learners. By not learning about the rationale and sources of mentors' ideas, they may also continue to regard their suggestions as expressions of personal preferences rather than collective wisdom about good practice.

Conclusion

This study has raised many questions in our minds about how to

regard the support and guidance that mentor teachers in this particular urban school district give teacher trainees. Clearly the teacher
trainees are learning to teach. What they appear to be learning about
teaching, though, makes us question whether it is appropriate to regard these mentor teachers as field-based teacher educators and their
work as a form of 'clinical teacher *education*'. The focus in these three
cases of mentoring on performance and not on the ideas behind a
teaching performance, and the lack of connection to helping pupils
learn worthwhile things makes it difficult to consider this mentoring
as legitimate instances of teacher education.

When we began this inquiry, we wanted to describe the character
and quality of mentoring by providing a grounded picture of what
mentor teachers do and what they talk about with teacher trainees in
a particular alternate route context. This was the first step in comparing the work of mentor teachers in this school district with the work
of university supervisors in a standard teacher education programme.
Along the way, and before we got to our comparative case study
analysis, we uncovered some intriguing similarities between mentoring in this alternative route programme and the supervision of student
teachers as it is described in the literature. For one thing, the Mentor
Teacher Program is organizationally separate from the Teacher
Trainee Program, making it difficult for mentors to know what
teacher trainees are learning in the formal components of their programme. The same condition exists in many pre-service programmes
where cooperating teachers know little if anything about what student
teachers learn on campus.

Second, studies of student teaching supervision (eg Zeichner *et al.*,
1987) point to the lack of attention to student teachers' purpose and
goals, to the content of what is being taught and to what pupils are in
fact learning. Our discussion of mentor training and our examples of
mentors' practices suggest some of these same characteristics of
'guided practice' in this one alternate route programme. While we
cannot draw any firm conclusions from such a limited number of
examples, the hypothesis that the traditional supervision of student
teachers is more similar to than different from the 'mentoring' of
alternate route candidates is worthy of consideration.

The assumption that the activity of mentoring necessarily facilitates
the ability of beginning teachers to understand the central tasks of
teaching and to engage in pedagogical thinking (Feiman-Nemser and
Buchmann, 1987) is problematic given our analysis of these three
cases of mentoring in this one urban school district. Mentoring as it
is currently carried out in some school districts may not offer any
improvement over the more traditional methods of teacher supervi-

sion that it is intended to replace. More attention needs to be given to the specific ways in which mentors are prepared for their work and to making the reality of mentoring more in tune with the rhetoric of mentoring (Little, 1990) than it appears to be in these cases.

NOTES

1. Later legislation changed the name of the Teacher Trainee Program to the District Intern Program. This chapter is based on data gathered in 1987–89 when the original name was used.
2. These alternative route programmes are widespread across the US and are somewhat similar to the Licensed Teacher Scheme in the UK (Wilkin, 1992). In both cases, the teacher's formal education for teaching takes place almost entirely in the schools.
3. For an exception see Stoddart (1990).
4. This study is part of a larger comparison of supervision or 'guided practice' in alternative route and induction programmes. In this chapter, we concentrate on how mentor teachers in this one urban school district guide the practice of teacher trainees. Elsewhere we compare the character and quality of the guidance trainees receive with the character and quality of guidance received by beginning teachers in a university and school district-sponsored induction programme (Feiman-Nemser and Parker, 1922).
5. For a list of publications from this larger study, contact the NCRTL at Michigan State University, College of Education, 116 Erickson Hall, East Lansing, MI 48824-1034.

REFERENCES

Acheson, K and Gall, M (1987) *Techniques in the Clinical Supervision of Teachers* (2nd edn), New York: Longman.

Adelman, NE (1988) *An Exploratory Study of Teacher Alternative Certification and Retraining Programs*, Policy Studies Associates, Inc., US Department of Education, Contract No. 300-85-0103.

Devaney, K (1987) *The Lead Teacher: Ways to begin*, New York: Carnegie Forum on Education and the Economy.

Feiman-Nemser, S (1983) 'Learning to teach', in Shulman, L and Sykes, G (eds), *Handbook of teaching and policy*, New York: Longman.

Feiman-Nemser, S and Buchmann, M (1987) 'When is student teaching teacher education?', *Teaching and Teacher Education*, 3, 4, 255–273.

Feiman-Nemser, S and Parker, MB (1992) *Mentoring in Context: A comparison of two U.S. programs for beginning teachers*, East Lansing, MI: National Center for Research on Teacher Learning (Special Report, Spring).

Joyce, B and Showers, J (1988) *Student Achievement through Staff Development*, New York: Longman.

Little, JW (1990) 'The mentor phenomenon', in Cazden, C (ed.) *Review of Research in Education*, Volume 16, pp. 297–352, Washington, DC: American Educational Research Association.

Little, JW and Nelson, L (eds) (1990) *A Leader's Guide to Mentor Training*, San Francisco: Far West Laboratory for Educational Research and Development.

McKibben, M, Walton, P and Wright, D (1987) 'An evaluation of an alternate route into teaching in California', paper presented at the annual meetings of the American Educational Research Association, Washington, DC.

Stoddart, T (ed) (1990) *Perspectives on Guided Practice*, East Lansing, MI: National Center for Research on Teacher Learning, Technical Report 90–1.

Wildman, TM *et al* (1989) 'Teaching and learning to teach: the two roles of beginning teachers', *Elementary School Journal*, **89,** 4, 471–493.

Wilkin, M (ed) (1992) *Mentoring in Schools*, London: Kogan Page.

Zeichner, K, Liston, D, Mahlios, M and Gomez, M (1987) 'The structure and goals of a student teaching program and the character and quality of supervisory discourse', *Teaching and Teacher Education*, **3,** 4, 349–62.

10 Mentoring for Teacher Development: Possibilities and Caveats

Bob Elliott and James Calderhead

Introduction

This chapter is concerned with how growth in teaching can be fostered in student teachers through mentoring. It begins with an analysis of the growth process by drawing upon recent research on student teachers' learning. It then compares and contrasts this with the conceptions of mentoring and student teachers' learning held by a sample of mentors involved in an articled teacher training scheme. This comparison of the two is used to raise issues concerning the roles and responsibilities of mentors, their potential contribution to student teachers' professional development and obstacles that may have to be overcome to reach this potential.

The Nature of Professional Growth

Attempts to understand teacher development have recently drawn upon research on teachers' beliefs and mental processes (eg, Richardson, 1990). Such research suggests that the professional growth in neophyte professionals is influenced by a range of factors with particular emphasis on the following.

- the expectations for professional development that the neophytes bring with them to their training (Calderhead, 1988; Elliott and Lange, 1991);
- the structure, style and content of the formal curriculum of teacher education (Blum and Labasco, 1984; Doyle, 1986; Eraut, 1985; Teich, 1986);
- the learning strategies employed by trainees (Brown, 1978; Calderhead, 1988; Calderhead, 1990; Kober, 1980);
- the nature of the work environment into which graduates will move (Mitchell and Marland, 1989; Zeichner and Gore, 1990).

While it might be argued that research on beginning teachers should provide the basis for the design of initial teacher education programmes (Floden and Klinzing, 1990), policy directions tend to be shaped more by political forces than research initiatives. For example, in Britain there are clear moves from central government that 'schools should play a much larger part in initial teacher training' and that 'higher education institutions...focus on the competencies of teaching' (DES, 1992, p.1). At the same time, research findings point towards the difficulties of cultivating the professional knowledge and thinking of the teacher and the complexities of teachers' work that take it beyond conceptualization in terms of a list of competencies (eg, McGaghie, 1991).

While there is acceptance by politicians, researchers and teachers that development programmes for student teachers should be more 'school-based', there appears to be little agreement about what that entails or even why it is desirable. For example, the move may appeal to politicians for both ideological and financial reasons. They appear to believe that such a move would not only reduce the costs of pre-service education but would produce teachers who were more able to perform the practical classroom tasks which they feel are at the heart of education. On the other hand, the move may appeal to teacher educators because it increases the opportunity student teachers may have for gaining access to more experienced teachers' craft knowledge (Brown and McIntyre, 1988) and interrelating classroom practices with campus-based tuition.

Within such a climate, institutions concerned with teacher education need to take considerable care in how they conceptualize teacher development and how they structure training programmes to foster this. Simply placing students in schools may not always result in students learning how to teach (Edwards and Mercer, 1987) and school-based programmes, depending on how they are structured and developed, may produce at best teachers who have demonstrated behaviours listed in sets of predefined competencies. At worst they may produce para-professionals who are able to reproduce little more than what they have observed in other teachers.

This is not to deny the real possibilities and potential that exist in such programmes but they need to be well thought through and founded on appropriate principles of professional learning. This chapter synthesizes what we currently know about teacher development from research initiatives and uses these ideas, together with some findings from the authors' research on mentoring, to highlight issues concerning how development might be best fostered in beginning teachers by school-based mentors.

Professional Growth

The following analysis describes the nature of professional growth in teachers in terms of a series of significant dimensions.

Growth is multidimensional

Research highlighting the differences between experienced and novice teachers (Berliner, 1987) and the changes reported by students during their training (Calderhead and Robson, 1991) implies that teachers undergo a growth process which is complex and multidimensional in nature. For example, learning to teach involves changes in knowledge and beliefs and not simply changes in skills suggested by much of the earlier process-product research (Brophy and Good, 1986). In a review of contemporary research on teacher learning, Kagan (in press) concludes that growth occurs within a number of domains:

1. there is an increase in the knowledge that novices have about pupils, how they learn and the importance of their backgrounds;
2. the focus of the beginners' concerns moves away from themselves as actors in the classroom to those learners to whom their teaching is directed;
3. routines for teaching become automated and the need to think through each minute step is diminished;
4. novices become more aware of their own thinking about what they are doing and its impact on pupils – there is an increase in metacognition;
5. there is an increase in instructional problem-solving on behalf of the beginning teacher which is 'more differentiated, multidimensional, and context-specific'.

It follows that not only is growth complex but, given that knowledge associated with teaching assumes a range of forms (Shulman, 1986a), development programmes for teachers may need to incorporate a range of experiences, learning tasks and environments to develop these different forms of knowledge.

Growth is based on prior learning

Research also indicates the importance of students' previously acquired images of teaching. Experience during their own school days appears to shape how novices see themselves as beginning teachers (Leinhardt, 1988). Images of teaching formed during this period appear to be not only stable across time (Calderhead and Robson, 1991) but 'powerful influences' on how novices develop (Calderhead, 1988, p.54).

Research illuminating the imagery in teacher knowledge is useful in highlighting a number of aspects of professional growth in teaching. Growth in knowledge about teaching begins prior to formal teacher preparation courses. The difficulty here, however, is that knowledge formed during these very early times creates images of teaching from the perspective of the pupil. Such images are often not helpful to the novice teacher because they are based on what teachers can be seen to be doing rather than what they are thinking in order to achieve these states. For this reason, student teachers have been found to think about teaching as telling and learning as memorizing (Calderhead, 1991). In this sense these images are immature and inflexible in nature. They are not able to be used readily as the basis of teacher planning and action.

Such conclusions contrast with what we know about the nature of more experienced teachers' thinking and action. For example, Shulman's research (1987) with teachers in the early stages of their careers has led him to conclude that teachers engage in progressing cycles of thought involving comprehension, transforming, instructing, evaluating, reflecting and forming new comprehensions of teaching. This conclusion suggests a constructivist perspective on teachers' work which intimately relates thought and action. In a similar vein, Schon (1983) concludes that, in the professions, knowledge and action are inextricably linked and teacher knowledge is often embedded in the very act of teaching.

The theorizing of Shulman and Schon points out the contrast between the images of growth and teaching that underpin the work of more experienced teachers and the images of teaching that novices bring with them to their initial training. Such a contrast illustrates one of the central tenets of professional growth for beginning teachers, namely that growth requires novices to confront previously constructed images of teaching, acknowledge them and their sources and subsequently adapt them.

Growth in teaching involves different forms of learning

One of the difficulties of language is that we often use the same word for different referents. When we refer to the outcome of an educational experience, irrespective of the nature of that experience, we claim that learning has occurred. We then conclude that, irrespective of the experience, learning has an invariant quality about it and, for example, that learning to ride a bicycle, learning to count and learning to teach are similar phenomena.

Much learning in schools is often linguistically oriented involving 'book knowledge' (Calderhead, 1991). The assumption here is that if we are able to talk about a phenomenon or practice then we have learned it and consequently are able to engage in associated practices. Teacher preparation courses have sometimes been developed on such a premise. Such courses assume that learning to teach and learning about teaching are either one and the same or that the latter is a prerequisite for the former. Such assumptions are questionable and often cause difficulties for student teachers during their courses (Russell, 1991).

Students come from school with not only images of teaching but, perhaps more importantly, images of development and learning (Elliott, 1992) which influence how they think about their own development. Professional growth probably requires novices to recognize the existence of such images and accommodate them in their learning to teach. In this sense growth in teaching involves an increase in metacognition.

Shulman's (1986a) analysis of forms of knowledge has encouraged debate about the importance of case knowledge in fostering professional development. Since that time there has been increasing interest in the possible use of case knowledge in teacher development in the same manner that it is employed in the professional development of doctors and lawyers. However, it may be argued that the powerful cases that student teachers bring to the profession are those which they have developed across their extended apprenticeship period (Lortie, 1975) and such cases have emotional and personal components attached to them, making them quite different from those employed in legal or medical education.

The individually created case knowledge *of teaching* is different from the case knowledge *about teaching* that is often created by researchers. It is the latter which is often the basis of the claim that learning to teach could use case knowledge in the same manner as medical and legal education. Cases about teaching may be useful in assisting the growth process of student teachers in that they may assist the novices to develop generalizable analytical skills. On a broader frame they may also assist in establishing the situated knowledge of the teacher as a central component of teacher education. However, notwithstanding these points, it seems to be the novices' personally developed cases that are powerful influences on their learning. Learning to teach appears to be quite distinctive and does not find ready parallels with other professions.

Growth implies cognitive and affective changes

One of the difficulties concerning checklists of competencies, such as those published by accrediting authorities, is that they list only the behaviours expected of teachers. There are, however, obvious cognitive and affective elements of teaching. The assumption is often made that if novices have particular knowledge about teaching they will be able to exhibit these behaviours. What the lists do not recognize is that growth in teaching requires interrelated changes in cognition, beliefs attitudes and behaviours. To focus on one in the absence of others is unlikely to bring about significant changes in beginning teachers. Affective components of learning to teach, including attitudes towards children, parents and other teachers, as well as attitudes about subject matter, are often developed during periods of stressful academic study in teacher preparation courses.

There is the danger that little attention may be paid to affective components of learning to teach during traditional preparation programmes because of the focus on academic work. Kagan (in press) has argued that interacting at length with school pupils may provide novices with the opportunity to reflect on their own value systems and hence address these affective components.

Growth occurs in a range of contexts

Student teachers claim that there is a range of contexts in which they develop their ideas about teaching. These range from formally structured learning environments, through semi-structured environments that the students organize amongst themselves, to being alone (Elliott, 1992). Being alone is important for students, so that they can work through the complexities of their task, but the need to learn in a school context is also important. In such contexts it is probably more than the individual teachers that are important in assisting the novice to develop appropriately. Just as a supportive environment is an important prerequisite for reflection amongst teachers (Calderhead and Gates, in press) so also an appropriately supportive school environment may be necessary to foster cognitive and affective orientations to teaching amongst novices. A total school environment, including leadership from the head, an acceptance of professional debate and challenge as well as encouragement amongst the staff, may be essential characteristics of a school if a student is to develop those essential orientations to practice.

Growth requires both support and challenge

Daloz (1986, p.214) has argued that a two-dimensional model such as that indicated in Figure 10.1 is a useful device for discussing different approaches to fostering professional growth.

In the quadrant where challenge and support are both low the *status quo* is likely to be maintained but when challenge is increased without

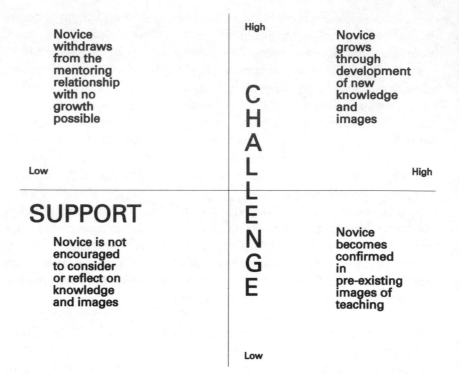

Figure 10.1 *Two-dimensional model of mentoring relationships (adapted from Daloz, 1986).*

comparative changes in support there is likely to be no growth. In this case the student is likely to withdraw physically from the development programme or, at best, resort to using previously formed ideas. In other words, there will be little increase in problem-solving characteristics and the student will sternly defend practice in terms of images from the past.

There is evidence to suggest that challenge is a necessary component for professional growth to occur. For example, Hollingsworth (1988; 1989) has argued that where there is a mismatch between the beliefs of student teachers and their supervisors in schools, the student is more likely to reflect on their own belief systems. In discussing findings such as these, which suggest that student teachers may be more satisfied with supervisors who are warm, Kagan (in press) concludes that although students experience cognitive dissonance when challenge is high, it is often uncomfortable.

Conclusions

A number of factors emerge from the above analysis. First, growth in teaching is a process that occurs across a considerable period of time and needs to be fostered in ways that are unique to the profession. Such fostering needs to attend to both the affective and cognitive aspects of teaching. It means, for instance, that 'throwing students in at the deep end' will probably, at best, produce teachers whose prime aim is the development of survival skills.

Second, because growth is complex and multidimensional in nature, learning to teach will probably occur at different rates for different students. The stage models of growth proposed by Fuller (1969), and more recently by Berliner (1987), suggest an invariant developmental pattern. Given the different profiles that students bring with them, it is likely that some will be quite advanced in some dimensions and novices in others. Such differentiation probably continues throughout their career where teachers move to expertise in different areas at different rates. Thus, it is unlikely that there would be a uniform linear progression in all domains of development as suggested by the stage models. Rather, what is more likely is development across a range of dimensions at different times for different students. Learning to teach, in this sense, is idiosyncratic and personal.

Third, growth can be fostered or hindered by the knowledge, values and ideas that the beginning teacher brings to teaching as well as the contexts in which such growth is developed. Further, given the unique combinations of support and challenge required to address these prior orientations, growth needs to be fostered in a range of contexts. While the histories of the student teachers are all-important, perhaps more important is the relationship between these histories and the formally structured teacher education curriculum through which the novices are expected to progress.

Fourth, those who foster growth in novices require a distinctive and comprehensive language to assist them in the process. Such language would not only enable a diversity of classroom experiences to be incorporated into the novice's images of teaching but it would enable developers to adequately reflect on their complex task.

Finally, there is need for considerable individual support, in both emotional and cognitive spheres, for beginning teachers if they are to develop and grow as teachers. While current demands for a reflective profession suggest that student teachers study and develop in traditional university academic environments, such environments may not provide the necessary support for the students to grapple with previously constructed and reinforced images of pupils and teachers which are at the heart of their learning to teach.

Such conclusions beg the question of how such growth can be fostered within teacher education courses through processes of mentoring. For example Shulman (1986b) has argued that the most substantial contribution that a mentor can make is to help other teachers extend their thinking about their educational practices but what it means to 'extend their thinking' and how such initiatives are conceived by practitioners are not clear.

The above review of the research also points to some implications for mentoring. In order to facilitate growth, mentors need to have well formulated ideas about how teachers develop professionally. Also, they need to be able to recognize the images of teaching that novices bring with them to their training, the diversity of possible teaching styles and how the latter can be constructed from the former. They require not only skills for counselling but also a language of practice which incorporates the complexities of training and teaching.

Contemporary initiatives in which beginning teachers are placed for a considerable time during their preparation course in a school with a mentor, attempt to grapple with the twin needs of traditional academic education and an individually supported programme to assist the novice with the complexities of learning to teach. While analyses such as the above can provide advice about what is required to assist students in their development, there is little research about the practices of mentoring from the perspective of the mentor. In Little's (1990, p.297) words, 'rhetoric and action have nonetheless outpaced both conceptual development and empirical warrant'. Advice about 'core skills which all mentors in education need' (Shaw, 1992, p.85), or conditions which are conducive to good mentoring, has enabled mentoring programmes to become established in schools. However, as Wilkin (1992, p.18) notes, 'the profession is feeling its way' and there is a commitment that mentoring should be the best that can be devised.

As a way of moving forward to identify how mentoring can best facilitate professional growth, as identified in the research literature, these issues are examined here in the light of how a sample of mentors perceive their role and the contexts in which they undertake the task.

Mentoring: A Research Project

The research discussed here is related to an articled teacher training scheme for primary teaching in which student teachers spend four days per week in schools under the guidance of a mentor. In the scheme, a tutor from the higher education institution organizing the programme was attached to the mentor-articled teacher pair and nine such mentor-articled teacher pairs were studied. The mentors spanned a full range of teaching experience and tended to be teaching in lower primary or infants grades.

The findings relate to interviews conducted towards the end of the first year of the two-year course. Each mentor was interviewed for about an hour with questions focusing on:

- perceptions of mentoring roles;
- specific approaches the mentor was adopting;
- the rationale for these approaches;
- the mentors' perceptions of how the articled teacher was learning to teach.

Each interview was transcribed and analysed by examining similarities and differences across the range of mentors' responses to the four questions noted above.

Perceptions of mentoring roles

Each of the mentors in this study recounted the variety of mentoring roles in different ways. They clearly referred to it in terms of fostering the student's learning to teach but they characterized this in different ways. For example, some mentors discussed their role in terms of being a 'guide' or a 'leader'. These mentors appeared to believe that the role required them to open up the context of the school for the articled teacher so that she could encounter what was to be learned and be ready to assist if the articled teacher strayed into difficult territory.

Such perceptions may imply that these mentors felt that they had a good grasp of the terrain to be traversed by the student and a view of where the journey should end. It may also imply that the mentors believed that there was only one way to teach and that they were guiding or leading the novice to that viewpoint.

The mentors often discussed their roles in terms of being a 'good listener', 'being a friend', or 'enabling'. On occasions, some of the mentors implied that there was a dependency relationship between themselves and the novice which shaped the way they viewed the role. This was most apparent when one mentor described herself and her articled teacher as a 'mother hen and her chick'.

It was quite common for the mentors to refer to the role in terms of being an organizer of experiences for the novice throughout the school. Such experiences enabled the novice to complete a range of tasks set by the higher education institution.

Most of the mentors referred to the organizational aspect of their role where they organized activities for the articled teacher to enable her to complete various tasks for her campus learning. Also, many mentioned a collaborative aspect of the role such as planning of the timetable, 'narrowing it down with the week and the daily programme'.

In some cases, although only rarely, there was reference to the articulation of craft knowledge to the articled teacher. Such articulation was either in response to questions from the novices or as a result of watching the novices teach and comparing it with their own teaching. These mentors often interrelated their own development with that of their students. They linked the articulation of their personal knowledge with reflection on their teaching.

On only a very limited number of occasions were there references to the role of '*agent provocateur*' with the novice. In fact, only one mentor specifically focused on the importance of such a role. She commented on how she 'continually challenged the student with new things, to develop (her) learning and experience'. This mentor appeared to believe that learning to teach required her articled teacher to demonstrate more than teaching strategies. In terms of the earlier review of research she appeared to understand the multidimensional aspect of learning to teach.

Thus, across and within each of the mentors' elaborations of their roles there is a diversity of perceptions. On balance, the mentors appeared to perceive the mentoring role more in terms of nurturing or supporting the novices so that they can learn 'by whatever works' in their school or their classroom. In this sense there appears to be a conforming rather than critical orientation to the role.

Specific approaches to mentoring

Given the different views that mentors had of their roles, it is not surprising that they reported a wide range of mentoring strategies. For example, some reported approaches which built on the nature of the personal relationship that had developed between them and the student. Generally, these mentors arranged for the novices to be located in their classrooms for almost all of the time, although some did indicate that they had arranged for the novice to visit other teachers' classrooms. Their views appeared to stem from the fact that, in teaching, the 'relationship is central'. In one case, this view was extended to the point that 'relationships are essential to everything really. Life!'. Such a pervasive view about growth and development is likely to influence a mentor's overall approach with her articled teacher.

One of the most frequently reported approaches that mentors claimed to be using was that of 'active listening'. Using such an approach, articled teachers reported on their experiences in the school and classroom context and, subsequently, mentors became sounding-boards for the novices' ideas. Many argued that such an approach not only encouraged students to think of creative solutions to problems but encouraged a level of independence in problem-solving. It could be argued that such an approach not only encourages such problem-solving but also empowers novices by placing the learning and development agenda directly in the hands of the articled teacher.

While most of the mentors were able to discuss particular strategies, such as active listening, a small number were unable to discuss their approaches in any detail. For example, one mentor indicated that mentoring was 'a very personal thing' and that 'you have to be born for it'. This mentor's approach was primarily an organizational one, making sure that teaching tasks were set and the formalities of record-keeping were completed.

A significant point of note with regard to the approaches adopted by the mentors, is that very few of them appeared to adopt an approach whereby they openly challenged their novices' ideas and images of teaching, particularly those which they brought with them to their training. In nearly all cases, when asked directly whether they challenged the students' ideas and beliefs, most replied that either there was no need to do so or that such an approach was inappropriate for novice teachers. Further, some mentors talked about the need to protect and defend their articled teacher at times when their ideas may be challenged.

Some of the mentors, however, did indicate that during discussion sessions they encouraged the novices to 'discuss' their views about teaching. There was a range of positions about when students should be encouraged to discuss their views of teaching, which types of incidents should be used to provoke thought and how often the discussions should occur.

With regard to the issue of when the novice should be encouraged to reflect on practice and beliefs, most of the mentors indicated that it was 'when things go wrong' that they encouraged the novice to think about an incident. It was as if breakdown in class management or other teaching routines were needed in order to generate reflection. Mentors did not appear to adopt approaches in which they deliberately provoked students to reflect on their previously developed images of teaching by setting puzzles for the students to resolve, by deliberately adopting contrary positions to the student or asking the student to justify particular teaching events in terms of what the student believes or knows.

While contrasts between theoretical positions, developed as part of campus learning, and school practices might be thought of as one source of debate and provocation, there was little evidence that the mentors used these opportunities. In fact, one mentor noted that she had decided 'to manipulate a little bit what the institution asked her (the articled teacher) to do'. Such 'manipulation' involved prioritizing the novice's tasks to be completed and identifying which were more relevant, in terms of the mentor's perspective. While it was undoubtedly undertaken to eliminate undue stress on the novice, it points to the importance of all parties working together, because such 'manipulation' may unwittingly circumvent planned dissonance for the novice, by having *her* identify priorities and importance.

A final point concerns views about the scope of experiences and the breadth of the environment in which the novice should learn about teaching. Some mentors felt that it was appropriate, during the first year of development, to keep the student primarily in the single classroom. Others felt it more appropriate to begin with a wider scope. These latter mentors saw the school and other local institutions as the environment in which development should occur. Obviously, factors such as the security of the novice in different environments play a role in determining the scope of experiences selected by the mentor, but further studies are required to relate more fully different growth patterns to learning environments.

In conclusion, while a diversity of approaches was reported by the mentors in this study, the particular approaches that were adopted by any particular mentor appeared to be compatible with the way the mentor perceived her role. Those who perceived 'the relationship' as central to the role advocated a series of interpersonal counselling encounters as most effective in developing understandings about teaching. Others, for example, who perceived the role more in terms of revealing personal knowledge of teaching, highlighted the importance of personal reflection and discussion of the outcomes of this process. How do I perceive my role?

Rationale for mentoring approaches

Most of the mentors were able to provide rationales for their approaches to mentoring. In many cases mentors indicated that they began to think about mentoring in the same terms as they thought about their own teaching. In fact, the first image of mentoring that they formed was often based on their images of teaching. Others indicated how they formed subsequent images based on relationships with other teachers on the staff, relationships with family members and, in some cases, based on other career roles. For example, one mentor referred to her role as a counsellor and another to her role as a trainer in the retail business.

Some mentors indicated that their rationale for mentoring was based on how *they* would have liked to have been trained. In other words they were reflecting back to their own student days in order to assist them with ideas about mentoring. It appears that, just as novice teachers begin with images of teaching and development based on their own career as a student in a classroom, novice mentors may begin with images of mentoring based on experiences in other contexts which may or may not be appropriate.

In some cases, the mentors indicated that they adopted particular strategies because of the way they thought about their teaching. For example, some mentors appeared to believe that teaching is a set of behavioural routines and so knowledge of teaching was simply information about when to enact these routines. They further seemed to indicate that this is learned through trial and error. However, such trial and error learning probably requires novices to hold well developed problem-solving skills and the mentors often seemed to assume that novices possessed these skills prior to their course.

Other mentors believed that differences amongst teachers are accountable for in terms of individual personalities. In such cases it seemed to be the resourcefulness of the articled teacher which often determined the learning agenda. She was expected to 'find things out', although the mentor would provide the 'shoulder to cry on, someone to talk to and with, and to set her on her guidelines'.

Another point of interest here is how a small number of the mentors sought to interrelate the learning which the novice experiences in the school context with that which occurs in the higher education institution. In order to achieve this interrelationship, one mentor indicated that 'we analyse the theory in terms of what the reality is'. In indicating how this interrelationship actually influenced the direction of the novice's development, the mentor said that she was 'adjusting the goalposts every week'.

The conclusion from this section is that mentors' assumptions about the mentoring task are often embedded in a network of other assumptions and values. For example, it appears that assumptions about the very nature of teaching and how learning occurs provide part of the rationale for the mentors' approaches. These are supplemented by the values that are attached to learning which the articled teachers undertake outside the mentors' control and direction.

Perceptions of how novices learn to teach

Often, amongst the mentors, there was a view that learning to teach required students to experience a range of teaching environments from which they could select specific teaching events and 'absorb' them. From the mentor herself, other teachers, or the whole school environment, the articled teacher would obtain 'anecdotes...experience and knowledge'. Such information sometimes concerned 'mistakes' that the mentor said she had made in her own teaching and 'passed to the articled teacher so that she would not have to make the same mistakes'. On other occasions it concerned specific children to be taught. These mentors believed that absorption of information should preferably take place after discussion of the information or personal trialing of suggested strategies. It was a common view amongst the mentors that such experiences would assist the novice to learn the 'nitty-gritty' of teaching.

In some cases the mentors seemed to imply that the growth which occurs in the mentoring relationship is a mirror of the growth process in learning to teach. Confidence in teaching follows confidence in the mentor. In order to encourage novices' growth, these mentors indicated that they needed to be extremely supportive and positive so that mistakes can be made and learning occur. In this sense learning was seen to progress through three stages: gaining confidence in the relationship, gradually doing things with less support and, finally, being independent of the support.

Other mentors referred to different stage models of growth. For example, it was common for mentors to claim that because the novice had progressed from teaching a small group to teaching the whole class or progressed from teaching a half-hour to teaching a half-day that growth in teaching had occurred. These mentors seemed to have a uni-dimensional model of growth where teaching behaviours are extended to a greater number of children or for longer periods of time. This position contrasts with the research evidence outlined in the beginning of this chapter indicating that growth was complex and multidimensional.

In most instances there appeared to be only lukewarm support from the mentor for growth attributable to learning in the higher education institution, although most pleaded ignorance of what was undertaken at the institution. For example, one mentor observed that she was 'not a tutor and I don't know exactly what they do in college', and 'it's distanced enough for me to do my own thing and take what I see written down with a pinch of salt'. At the other extreme, one mentor recounted how she spent a considerable amount of her spare time reading the papers associated with the novice's courses in order to 'marry the two together – the theory and the practice'.

Finally, it is also interesting to note the different ways that mentors thought about the outcomes of their mentoring. Some mentors indicated that the focus of their novices' learning had been on specific teaching techniques embedded in experience. Growth in teaching, in these terms, is identified with being able to take the class for larger periods of time. It is as if these mentors held a definition of growth expressed in quantifiable terms, equating competence with sustainability in teaching. For example, one mentor noted that growth involved 'experience and absorbing different things from courses', while another indicated that the novice was 'taking over lessons and preparing them for herself...so she's developed that far...from just observing to taking small groups and then taking whole classes'. In contrast, there were scant references to any changes in novices' beliefs about teaching, their perspectives on children or how they thought about subject knowledge.

One conclusion from this analysis is that mentors had views about learning to teach which were more simplistic than those implied in the research literature. Such a conclusion is perhaps not surprising given the limited opportunities that the mentors had to reflect on their new role and develop a language to discuss and reflect on a process which is both distinctive and complex.

Conceptions of Mentoring: A Discussion

A number of themes run through the above analysis and interrelate how mentors perceive their role and tasks, how they justify their ideas and actions and how they believe teachers learn to teach. These highlight a number of issues for school-based teacher training and the development of beginning teachers.

A question of responsibility

All the mentors stressed the high levels of responsibility that they felt for the articled teacher. In traditional preparation courses, where students are located in schools for practice teaching experiences, the students are only passing visitors and school supervisors generally regard the higher education institution as being responsible for the students' development. In the case of mentoring in articled teacher schemes, the role of school personnel is entirely different. One mentor explained the responsibility associated with this change in these terms:

> It's more of an intimate responsibility rather than general because you are responsible for a particular person for two whole years, which is really quite a commitment. You are, I suppose, in overall charge of her. The college do their bit but ultimately it is us who are responsible for their development.

Inherent in this description is the realization of what it means to care for an articled teacher and to facilitate her growth for the greater part of her training, often with little outside support.

Due to obvious financial restrictions, there is little ongoing support and assistance for mentors from higher education institutions. In such a climate, this sole responsibility and, in some cases, the feeling of being alone in the task of fostering a novice's professional growth, may be a difficult issue to address.

The importance of interpersonal relationships

Many of the mentors talked about the importance of the personal relationship between themselves and their students. In many cases mentoring was seen as a direct function of an extremely intense personal relationship which the mentor developed with the articled teacher. Such a relationship often spanned the boundaries between personal and professional issues where, according to the mentors, no problems of either nature are 'hidden'. Often such mentors discussed the nature of this relationship between themselves and the student as an extension of other relationships in the school. For example, one of the mentors indicated that the school in which she worked was a place where 'we work on a very friendly basis. We've all got a relationship with everyone...'.

In thinking about their role as mentors in these terms, they often referred to the similarity between the mentor-articled teacher relationship and their own family relationships. Where the age and gender factors were appropriate, the relationship was referred to as 'mother-daughter' by some mentors and a 'sister' relationship by another. Friendship, with honesty and mutual respect, were key words used by the mentors in describing these relationships.

In contrast, a couple of mentors saw their role more in terms of simply being available when needed. For these mentors, the focus seems to be simply on 'being there' for discussions and guidance. Such a conception of the mentor role is rather informal and less intense than that previously outlined.

In one case, the mentor noted that her role was 'quite an informal sort of job I would think. I have the responsibility (for the novice) but I don't think it's a formal role as such'. This case illustrates the complexity of issues involved in mentors' role conceptions. On the one hand she indicated that 'it was better that she (the student) spent time away from me to start with and it's worked very well that way – we're not under each other's feet', and her task was to 'arrange timetables (for the novice)...and to be there if she needs me'. On the other hand, while she 'made an effort as far as possible to make sure she's (the articled teacher) ok each day', this mentor also outlined how 'the relationship has deepened quite a lot...and over the past few months we've got to know each other more intimately'. These points highlight the complexity, and sometimes possible inconsistency, in how the mentors conceive their roles. It could be that the mentor believed that distance between herself and the novice was one way of sustaining the relationship between them. Alternatively, it could be that she maintained the distance because she had a different notion of 'the relationship' from other mentors.

Finally, the question of why the mentors in this study placed such importance on the relationships with their students needs to be considered. The initial training which the mentors received obviously provided a way for the mentors to think about their role. However, the analysis also suggests that mentors' extrapolations of ideas from school communities and classroom teaching models also play a part in their trying to identify their role in promoting professional growth.

The nature of interrelated development

While many of the mentors discussed their role in terms of the development of their articled teacher, there was another side to the role which a number of them recounted. This focused more on how the mentor herself gained from the experience and how this personal growth related to the growth of the novice. Some indicated how valuable the experience of having an articled teacher in the classroom had been. Some recounted the difficulties of professional isolation, commonly reported by teachers, and how the presence of another professional in the classroom had provided opportunities to share their work.

Some of these mentors reported complex relationships between the role of encouraging growth in the novice teacher and their own professional development. For example, some indicated that having an articled teacher present with them prompts them to think about, and subsequently articulate, the knowledge which is associated with their teaching. This process appears to be prompted either by the mentor simply observing the novice or by contrasting her own teaching behaviours with what she observes through watching the beginner. For example, one mentor commented that 'as soon as I start to explain to her what to do I suddenly think "Gosh, yes, I've done that without thinking"'. Yet another said, 'once you start explaining you realize how much you are carrying in your head'.

It appears that the mentors had different orientations to professional learning and this, in turn, influenced how they viewed the role of mentoring. Given the earlier analysis, indicating the dimensions of professional growth required in novices, it would seem that mentors who have broad views of their own learning would be more likely to encourage growth, in all its dimensions, in their novices.

The interface of school and campus learning

If mentors were to value learning from contexts other than their own, it may be possible for them to draw upon similarities and differences between this knowledge and knowledge in the school situation to provoke incidents of cognitive dissonance for the novice, and hence promote growth.

While the data analysis indicates that very few mentors adopted such strategies, some mentors indicated that they encouraged the articled teacher to 'discuss' what they had learned during their visits to the higher education institution and to build this into their teaching. This was also seen by such mentors as a valuable way of incorporating newer approaches into their own teaching repertoire. Others indicated that they felt that they knew little about what was occurring in campus courses and that this had little to do with the 'nitty-gritty of teaching'.

The importance of challenge in professional growth

The earlier review of research indicated that challenge is essential for professional growth to occur. It is not clear why the mentors in this study generally did not adopt approaches involving open challenge of novices' images of teaching, but a number of reasons may be postulated. It may be that the intensity, or nature, of the relationship established between the mentor and articled teacher may impede such strategies. Neither the mentor nor the articled teacher may wish to place the relationship at risk – the mentor because of the high level of responsibility she feels for the novice and the novice for the level of dependency on the mentor which she may feel. Alternatively, it may be that these mentors felt that the first year of development was too early for such challenge or that coming to grips with the task was itself sufficiently challenging.

From a learning theory perspective, it is possible that the only model for learning and development to which the mentors have access is one which is grounded in classroom teaching. The only adult relationships in the school to which the mentor can relate (such as those among other teachers and helpers in the classroom) are based on friendships and not related to learning. As such, they are inappropriate models for fostering growth in beginning teachers.

From another perspective, since these mentors did not have extensive experience in professional development they had not formulated an appropriate language to talk about alternative ways of viewing classroom contexts. Not only might they have been unaware of the importance of cognitive, affective and behavioural orientations in learning to teach but they may be hampered in bringing about changes in these orientations because of the lack of an appropriate framework in which to do so.

While it seems that these issues require further clarification through longitudinal studies, they also point to possible implications for reconceptualizing teachers' work and school environments as places of learning if the move to school-based teacher education is to continue. While many would claim that costs are the inhibiting factors for school-based teacher development, the professional implications outlined here suggest other less tangible inhibitions.

Coherence in teachers' conceptions

Most of the mentors in this study appeared to have a view of mentoring which they expressed in terms of metaphors and images. These metaphors and images, often drawn from classroom experience, appear to be a focus for them to think about roles, strategies and conceptions of learning to teach. For example, one mentor referred to mentoring as 'enabling', comparing it to an approach to teaching writing:

> ...with our writing with the children we support them as long as they need our support...and gradually the children take over these things, so we are enabling them.

She then explained that being a mentor was 'someone to whom..she (the novice) can talk and put anxieties and joys to', and 'gradually allowing her to do more in the classroom'. The novice was 'usually very aware of why it's gone wrong', and 'it's very much like the children, absorbing a new idea and trying it out'.

There were also some inconsistencies in the way the mentors described their role and the study did not examine the possible inconsistencies between what the mentors said they did and their actual practices. Notwithstanding these possible inconsistencies, the study suggests an overall coherence in the way each mentor conceives the role. This coherence may be important in examining training implications for the future. These coherences may need to be the building blocks for developing mentors' skills and changing their orientations.

Relating teachers' and researchers' conceptions

This study suggests that mentors understand the importance of supporting novices during their formative period. It also indicates that they have a limited language with which to discuss practice and professional growth. While there is variation in understandings amongst the mentors, the data suggest some gaps between the expectations as implied by research and mentors' conceptualizations. The conclusions suggest that mentors need to adopt more of a challenging orientation to their role, drawing on the diversity of approaches to teaching, and that they require a more expansive language with which to discuss professional development and classroom understandings in general.

Conclusions: Possibilities and Caveats

It is clear that the use of mentors as part of school-based training of teachers has real potential; however, this chapter has highlighted a number of implications for school-based training. Because the conclusions are based on one study in primary schools, they should be regarded as tentative.

First, there are caveats concerning changes required to the concept of teachers' work and school climates if the notions of mentoring are to be maximized. The move to school-based training implies that teachers need to change their traditional orientation to their role. For some centuries, teaching, particularly in primary schools, has been identified with teaching young children. Teachers' notions of learning are built on the fact that they teach young pupils. The mentors in this study indicated that they often thought of their mentoring tasks in terms of their teaching but realized the inadequacy of such a model.

The notion of the school as a 'learning community' in which learning occurs at various levels will need to become widely accepted. In such a community open debate amongst all professionals would have to characterize the school environment. Teachers will need to interact with each other, challenging each other and supporting each other in order to sustain that challenge. Many mentors often refer to their happy and friendly school and what is required is the transformation of this climate to sustain professional development for all.

Second, there are implications for re-examining the nature of 'partnerships' between schools and higher education institutions. Staff in both organizations are very busy and it is difficult for each to find time to work together. Of greater importance is the history and feelings each brings with them to their meetings. The irony is that greater professional growth for novice teachers is a real possibility if the differences in orientations of these two groups can be used as the basis of professional challenge and debate. This requires the schools to be less defensive about their practices and look for the reasons why practice and theory often sit uneasily beside each other. In parallel, it requires higher education institutions to value the craft knowledge of teachers and seek ways that it can be legitimated and brought within the mainstream of teacher preparation. In this sense, the initiatives reported by McAlpine *et al.* (1988) to teach novices specific strategies to elicit that craft knowledge while in the higher education institution require further exploration. If the difficulties which these authors report can be addressed, then mentoring has real potential for both the mentor and novice.

Third, there are implications for training programmes for mentors. As noted above, the relationships between a mentor and a novice teacher do not presently find a parallel in schools. Training for mentors to recognize this fact is necessary. However, considerable care needs to be taken in formulating such programmes. The notions of support and challenge and the delicate relationship between these need to be carefully considered. Further, while skill development in areas such as counselling may be necessary, the conceptions that mentors hold and the values and beliefs that they bring to a mentoring context appear to be important factors in determining whether or not these skills are actually exercised. In this sense, the research on teachers' learning, illustrating the powerful images that students bring with them to their training, is perhaps generalizable to all professional development. Development programmes should seek to establish conceptions of mentoring in such a way that the unique combinations of challenge and support necessary to foster growth are realized in mentoring contexts.

REFERENCES

Berliner, D (1987) 'Ways of thinking about students and classrooms by more and less experienced teachers' in Calderhead, J (ed.) *Exploring Teachers' Thinking*, London: Cassell.

Blum, B and Labasco, G (1984) 'The case against the case system', *California Lawyer*, **4**, 30–34.

Brophy, J and Good, T (1986) 'Teacher behaviour and student achievement' in Wittrock, M (ed.) *Handbook of Research on Teaching*, 3rd ed, New York: Macmillan.

Brown, A (1978) 'Knowing when where and how to remember: a problem of metacognition' in Glaser, R (ed.) *Advances in Instructional Psychology*, Hillsdale: NJ: Erlbaum.

Brown, S and McIntyre, D (1988) 'The professional craft knowledge of teachers', *Scottish Educational Review, Special Issue: The Quality of Teaching*.

Calderhead, J (1988) 'The development of knowledge structures in learning to teach' in Calderhead, J (ed.) *Teachers' Professional Learning*, London: Falmer Press.

Calderhead, J (1990) 'Conceptualising and evaluating teachers' professional learning', *European Journal of Teacher Education*, **13**, 3, 153–60.

Calderhead, J (1991) 'The nature and growth of knowledge in student teaching', *Teaching and Teacher Education*, **7**, 5/6, 531–5.

Calderhead, J and Gates, P (eds) (in press) *Conceptualising Reflection in Teacher Development,* London: Falmer Press.

Calderhead, J and Robson, M (1991) 'Images of teaching: Student teachers' early conceptions of classroom practice', *Teaching and Teacher Education,* 7, 1, 1–8.

Daloz, L (1986) *Effective Teaching and Mentoring,* San Francisco, CA: Jossey-Bass.

Department of Education and Science (1992) *Reform of Initial Teacher Training: A consultation document,* London: DES.

Doyle, W (1986) 'Content representation in teachers' definitions of academic work', *Journal of Curriculum Studies,* 18, 4, 365–79.

Edwards, D and Mercer, N (1987) *Common Knowledge: The development of understanding in the classroom.* London: Methuen.

Elliott, R (1992) 'Moving toward teaching: a model of teacher development', paper presented at European Conference on Educational Research. University of Twente, Enschede, The Netherlands, June.

Elliott, R and Lange, J (1991) 'Becoming the reflective professional: evolving models for understanding', paper presented at Australian Teacher Education Association meeting, Melbourne, July.

Eraut, M (1985) 'Knowledge creation and knowledge use in professional contexts', *Studies in Higher Education,* 10, 117–33.

Floden, R and Klinzing, H (1990) 'What can research on teacher thinking contribute to teacher preparation? A second opinion', *Educational Researcher,* 19, 5, 15-20.

Fuller, F (1969) 'Concerns of teachers: a developmental conceptualisation', *American Educational Research Journal,* 6, 207–26.

Hollingsworth, S (1988) 'Making field-based programs work: a three level approach to reading education', *Journal of Teacher Education,* 39, 4, 224–50.

Hollingsworth, S (1989) 'Prior beliefs and cognitive change in learning to teach', *American Educational Research Journal,* 26, 160–89.

Kagan, D (in press) 'Professional growth among preservice beginning teachers', *Review of Educational Research.*

Kober, P (1980) 'The socratic method on trial: are law schools a failure?, *Case and Comment,* 26, 26–35.

Leinhardt, G (1988) 'Situated knowledge and expertise in teaching', in Calderhead, J (ed.) *Teachers' Professional Learning,* London: Falmer Press.

Little, J (1990) 'The mentor phenomenon and the social organization of teaching', in Cazden, C (ed.) *Review of Research in Education,* Washington, DC: American Educational Research Association.

Lortie, D (1975) *Schoolteacher: A sociological study,* Chicago, IL: University of Chicago Press.

McAlpine, A, Brown, S, McIntyre, D and Hagger, H (1988) *Student-teachers Learning from Experienced Teachers,* Edinburgh: The Scottish Council for Research in Education.

McGaghie, W (1991) 'Professional competence evaluation', *Educational Researcher,* 1, 3–9.

Mitchell, J and Marland, P (1989) 'Research on teacher thinking: the next phase', *Teaching and Teacher Education,* 5, 2, 115–28.

Richardson, V (1990) 'Significant and worthwhile change in teaching practice', *Educational Researcher,* 19, 7, 10–18.

Russell, T (1991) 'Critical attributes of a reflective teacher: Is agreement possible?', paper delivered at the Conceptualizing Reflection in Teacher Development Conference, University of Bath.

Schon, D A (1983) *The Reflective Practitioner.* London: Temple Smith.

Shaw, R (1992) 'The nature and conditions of good mentoring practice', in Wilkin, M (ed.) *Mentoring in Schools.* London: Kogan Page.

Shulman, L (1986a) 'Those who understand: knowledge growth in education', *Educational Researcher,* 15, 2, 4–14.

Shulman, L (1986b) 'Opportunities of a mentorship: the implications of the California mentor teacher programe', paper presented at American Education Research Association, San-Francisco.

Shulman, L (1987) 'Knowledge and teaching. Foundations of the new reform', *Harvard Educational Review,* **57,** 1, 1–22.

Teich, P (1986) 'Research on American law teaching: is there a case against the case system?', *Journal of Legal Education,* **36,** 167–88.

Wilkin, M (ed.) (1992) *Mentoring in Schools.* London: Kogan Page.

Zeichner, K and Gore, J (1990) 'Teacher socialisation', in Houston, W (ed.) *Handbook of Research on Teacher Education,* New York: Macmillan.

11 The Wish of Odysseus? New Teachers' Receptiveness to Mentoring

Les Tickle

Introduction

In this chapter I will address a central and critical issue for those concerned with the effectiveness and development of mentoring: the 'receptiveness' of new teachers to the role, conduct and substance of educational practices which come within that term. Drawing on case-study material from 11 teachers in their first year of teaching, I will consider in particular the nature of contacts between new teachers and their tutors in schools. The teachers confirmed what has been reported elsewhere as a range of practical and professional problems, relating to the opportunities (or lack of them) for mutual discourse between mentor and mentored (Cole, 1991; Jacknicke and Samiroden, 1991; Little, 1990; Tickle, 1992d). However, the data which I will draw upon in this chapter take us much further than general considerations about roles and relationships in mentoring. They provide reports from the new teachers themselves of

> Examples of...exchanges between mentors and teachers, now absent from the published literature, (which) might enable us to ground global assessments of perceived effectiveness in concrete instances of communication about teaching (Little, 1990, p. 319).

The purpose of taking, in this instance, the teachers' own accounts of such exchanges is in order to address some issues about 'effectiveness' from *their* perspectives. One of the issues concerns the importance of the personal and individual ownership of knowledge, derived from sources of personal experience. Another is the power of privacy as a perceived necessary condition in both gaining and evaluating the quality of such experience. A third, which derives directly from the first two, is the nature and quality of a particular precondition for 'successful' interactions with tutors, where they do occur. I will use examples from data where 'exchanges' and 'instances of communication about teaching' were, for these particular teachers, paralleled by concern to ensure that experience was their own rather than that of others transferred to them. Other data illustrate the avoidance of, or at least lack of interest in or indifference to, exchanges with tutor-colleagues. Third, data will show that where exchanges were seen as potential sources of learning, the desire for particular, sophisticated kinds of communication about teaching placed tight specifications on what might be seen to be appropriate quality, successful, and hence effective.

The teachers' perspectives illuminate the interactional relationship between 'experienced' and 'novice' professionals in the specific school sites in which the 11 new teachers worked. The sites included first, primary, middle and high schools in a large local education authority in England, in the late 1980s. I researched the experiences of the teachers throughout the year in search of understanding the ways in which they learnt teaching, using qualitative methods of data collection attendant upon the adoption of a symbolic interactionist perspective (see Blumer, 1962; 1969). Those methods included observation and the use of field notes, and tape-recorded discussions and interviews.

It will be clear from the data, I believe, that we need to consider carefully the relationship between mentors and mentored, as part of the experience of learning teaching, around such detailed and carefully focused issues. This will help, I think, to achieve quality in our understanding of specific 'instances of communication', and thus potentially to achieve effectiveness in mentoring's contribution to learning teaching during induction. Calls to develop such understanding have come recently from Jacknicke and Samiroden (1991) and Hargreaves and Tucker (1991). The importance of focusing on specific aspects of the interactions of mentoring is indicated by Cole's (1991) view of collegial support-relationships for new teachers. Cole argues plausibly for self-selected and multiple 'buddies' for new teachers within a 'caring and helping community' ethos. Well, who could doubt the importance of that, or in any case deny it happening? But Cole's argument is based on the premise that appointed or imposed mentor arrangements are at best questionable, and at worst indefensible. In particular, she questions their 'effectiveness in facilitating teacher development' (ibid, p. 425). Having made her case for the more organic arrangements in which relationships will emerge (if the caring and helping community setting is created) she does not address the question of how such buddies, who she clearly regards as multiple mentors, acquire or might develop the capacities needed for effecting teacher development, or what these are beyond the general sense of caring and sharing. All she claims is that teachers in general will engage in 'what comes naturally'.

Consideration of particular transactions in either formal or informal interactions will help us to get beyond general notions of 'good relationships' which 'come naturally'. By moving beyond that idea, and looking beneath the surface of interactions, I believe the data in this report will reveal important characteristics of events which can help us to understand and achieve effectiveness in facilitating professional learning. I shall not claim that the specific issues of the importance of the personal ownership of knowledge, the conditions of privacy, and the particular precondition for successful interactions with tutors, are in any sense exhaustive in illuminating what lies beneath the surface of mentoring relationships. They are presented as an initial exploration of the world which Little would have us explore.

The Mentoring Relationship

In the case of Riverside School reported by Cole, extensive efforts had been made to create a learning community for teachers as well as students. The achievement of that aim was recognized by new teachers employed at the school, who were shown to have close, open and sharing relationships with numerous colleagues, as well as with senior staff responsible for formal assessment of their teaching. The case represents a model of collegiality towards which many would aspire. However, compared with evidence from my own research of 11 other cases, set alongside the reports from Her Majesty's Inspectors of Schools (DES, 1982; 1988), and in the light of other reports in the research literature (see Little, 1990; Jacknicke and Samiroden, 1991 for summaries and reviews) such conditions seem atypical.

Among the teachers I worked with, experiences of relationships with colleagues, and especially with formally designated teacher-tutors, certainly could not be described as close, open or sharing. Lesley rarely saw her headteacher/tutor, and when he left two terms after her appointment she was quite indifferent to the idea of a replacement 'mentor'. With other staff she was careful not to ally herself to any particular faction or individual, or even to be thought to be doing so. Sue regarded her designated tutor as 'the woman in charge of me' who had publicly announced that she 'had her spies out' for information about Sue's performance. Relationships with other staff were superficially friendly, in a casual way, but often affected by cynicism and sarcasm about her having taken up teaching as a career. Anna had several 'tutors' (headteacher, deputy head, two department heads, two advisers) each of whom operated on a basis of occasionally (and superficially in her view) passing comment on details of her teaching. Dave felt that his immediate seniors 'don't understand me', and sought to get his first year completed so as to be fully qualified, and at least formally equal to them. Diane's tutor/headteacher persistently told her off and put her down, to use her terms, to the extent that their relationship broke down completely and Diane left teaching after a term. The only other colleague within school who she could 'talk to' was a welfare assistant. Richard's teacher-tutor was 'given' the role when he was appointed, and was concerned to gain support which would help her conduct it to his advantage. She left the school for maternity leave halfway through the year, and the role was taken over by the headteacher, with whom Richard had a very poor relationship. This is a bleak picutre, but it is not imagined. It was not so bleak for others. Debbie gained considerable support from her year coordinator, though she came to feel isolated as the year progressed and she was left to 'get on with it'. Mike had extensive help from his head of department, though little contact from the designated teacher-tutor. The tutor distanced himself from involvement with Mike after a few weeks, when he judged there were 'no problems' with Mike's classroom performance. Pauline, Kathy and Liz each had both formal and informal supportive relationships with teacher-tutors and other colleagues. Like Debbie and Mike, the opportunities to discuss their teaching, to ask for advice, to share their feelings, were provided by colleagues and used by these teachers – to some extent.

Even in those circumstances, however, there were aspects of that sharing (and the lack of it) which left me puzzled as I evaluated their experiences within their schools and listened to the way the teachers talked about their learning. There were, especially, questions about how the teachers learned in their general (ie, more predominant) state of isolation. There were questions about how such isolated learning was regarded and valued by the teachers, and there were questions about what they made of the interactions with colleagues, and especially teacher-tutors, when they did occur. On the other hand, there were many questions about the ways in which teacher-tutors regarded and conducted their role. Some argued in favour of distanced, passive oversight, and the assurance for the new teacher of being left alone. Others had little option but to allow that, at least for most of the time, given full-time teaching commitments of both parties, and pressure of tasks outside of classrooms. Some saw formal assessment, though not necessarily tutoring, as a predominant concern. Others did not have a conception of the role, and sought to define one through practice by trial and error. I was able to discuss these matters to some extent with both teacher-tutors and the new teachers. The data from discussions with the latter confirmed my impression of a sense of irrelevance of, and hence a degree of indifference to, mentoring provision. This seemed rather puzzling, given the stress which has been laid on the importance of mentoring in so many initial training, internship and induction programmes. In order to illuminate the puzzle I chose to discuss the matter in more detail with five of the teachers, with whom I met every two or three weeks throughout the year in a teachers' centre. It is from their discussions that I will tease out some of the niceties of their relationship to mentoring as a source of learning (as distinct from emotional support, though see Tickle, 1991).

The Teachers' Learning

During the autumn term the teachers talked at length about being *halfway there* as teachers, a term which was connected directly to length of classroom experience. It was compared on the one hand to student-teaching, and on the other to experienced colleagues. By implication being *all the way* was essentially a condition which depended centrally and crucially on the processing of events. It was a matter of experience, as Debbie's rhetorical question suggested:

> Deb: Is that something somebody can actually tell you, or is it one of those
> things that it infiltrates through osmosis, and that eventually,
> through seeing a year's lot of work, you actually get an in-built
> knowledge...? (18.11).

These 'infiltrations' were regarded as essential; they were seen as qualitatively different from being taught. There was a disregard for 'hypothetical' outsider-knowledge in initial training as a means of preparation for 'very real practical issues'. There was a clear assertion, too, that the range of experience needed could not accrue from initial training:

> Deb: I feel that it's maybe inherent in any post-graduate course there are
> things that maybe they can't teach, maybe it's absolutely
> impossible for you to be taught, but there are things that you
> come across, right, in the first week that I wasn't prepared for,
> that I hadn't been prepared for, only in theory...not even a
> theoretical point of view. We've talked about various ways of
> classroom management, and very hypothetical situations, that in
> no way prepared me for having this classroom that was mine, and
> I had to organize it – that no way prepared me – the shock to my
> system having to do that. It didn't prepare me for my first

parents' evening. It hasn't prepared me for the on-going stress
and knowledge how to cope with stress (18.11).

This journey into practical experience included the acquisition of
additional curriculum-subject knowledge, especially for the primary
teachers, and pedagogical expertise, about which the teachers were
self-conscious. They actively pursued such knowledge, seen as directly pertinent to teaching tasks which they were required to undertake: particular periods of history for Sue; aspects of science for Dave;
music for Kathy; the rules of hockey for Debbie. These and others
were largely available in forms of information which did not depend
on colleagues or on experience of teaching. They were preparatory
matter, prerequisite to translation into pedagogical forms suitable for
the pupils. They were the know-what of teaching. Much more problematic was the know-how of a thousand elements, demands which
could only be met by fulfilling tasks directly with the children. These
were far wider than pedagogical strategies.

Liz: Well, I suppose it's things like having to take the children swimming
        on a Thursday and having to leave 14 behind. I, myself, have to
        do all this, I've never taken 20 children on my own before until I
        became a teacher having to do all that sort of stuff, plus keeping
        the others occupied, thinking of things for them to do. We had a
        priest in today, I had to organize the class around that, that sort of
        thing I've never done before and wasn't used to – um, what else,
        I'm sure there's loads – like having to get the Christmas card
        done by a certain time – hand out letters, remembering to do –
        just hundreds of things, little things like that, nothing very big,
        nothing I can't really cope with, but when it all seems to come in
        at once (2.12).

Often these reflections on the problematic nature of teaching, and on
the self in terms of confidence and competence, intuitively detected
gaps, or problems, but could not easily determine or analyse their
nature or what to do about them, because they were so extensive. At
other times the know-how existed 'in principle' but there was a failing
in its applications, and reflection resulted in some feeling of inadequacy, or recognition of the practical limitations to doing the 'best
possible'. Much of what the teachers discussed were 'problems' of
technical know-how which had to be developed and used within the
constraints of time, resources and expectations but which, once identified and acted upon, were readily routinized; academic knowledge
which, once researched and assimilated, was readily accommodated
into teaching programmes. The more problematic realms of knowing
were associated with the making of judgements during teaching, and

what Debbie had called 'knowledge how to cope with stress' – handling all the variables in particular 'cases', and handling one's own responses and reactions in the face of the unpredictable and uncertain.

Each of the teachers saw the need to learn by personal experience, largely without support from others. *Their* curriculum was in some senses self-determined. What seemed to matter was to develop the ability to cope with the anarchy of learning/experience and gradually to control, tame and manage it to best advantage for improving one's teaching. At these stages, the first half of the year, the teachers certainly saw themselves as being *en route* in a status passage in to experience. The route was through uncertain topography, the main features of which were dominated by three elements: the technical knowledge of subject matter, pedagogy and management of those 'hundreds of little things'; the handling of information and making of judgements about the curriculum progress of pupils; and the relationship between one's ideals for teaching and pupils' learning and one's emotional capacities and sense of self whilst travelling the route. The main characteristic of the journey through this topography appeared to be the processing of 'experience' which would mentally map the route, for reference and source of ease for future occasions. It seemed necessary to the teachers that such processing should be done firsthand, in their own account.

Lortie (1975) recognized that the teachers he studied selected from and adapted the ideas of other teachers about 'what to do and how to do it' matters for the classroom, converting the ideas through personal perspectives and application to their situations, and judging them by the criterion of whether 'it works...for me'. Thus he formulated a view of each teacher as 'self-made', even where opportunities for observation and discussion occurred. Confirming this, the teachers with whom I talked reported that where colleagues observed their teaching, or offered advice, they judged the information provided, determined its validity, or its value for them in informing their own practice, and gauged whether it might be applicable to future situations. Alternatively, they sought advice from trusted colleagues, though there were conditions to its 'acceptability'. Debbie could adopt some advice provided it came from a close colleague, with similar 'personality' and 'approach' and provided 'I can see that applying to me'. By that, Debbie meant if she had solicited advice, if she had in the first place considered 'should I have done it like this?', or 'should I do it like that?' Sometimes those questions were prompted by measuring consequences after events; sometimes predicting possibilities to inform potential courses of action, and sometimes in trying to check actions against such intentions. Sometimes the questions arose because of a difficulty in proposing any courses of action. In those cases the key referent was the experience of the trusted colleague:

> Deb: taking on board his (colleague) advice because he's obviously been there, he's obviously been there, he's taught 4th years, he knows those particular children...which is the type of knowledge that I haven't got (18.11).

It was not sufficient simply to defer to the experience of others, however, but to establish it for oneself. Having a guide to the route was not enough; travelling it was essential. Liz identified clearly the need for 'ownership' of the knowledge:

> Liz: I think it's something we've got to go through and find our own method – I know teachers have talked to me about what they do and I haven't been able to take it in because it's not my way, and I think I can only find out my way by trying what works and what doesn't (18.11).

Despite this concern to *go through it,* there was an acknowledgement that advice might arise from others more experienced. However, the delicacy of the advisory dialogue was rehearsed at some length by Liz. She argued cogently that advice after 'failing' an event was stressful and inadequate as a means of support, no matter how well meaning, extensive and eventually effective such advice might be. The crucial feature for her effective learning was to be 'given the right question' in identifying problems in her teaching. She noted the similarity between inadequate principles of learning for her pupils and for herself:

> Liz: I had I suppose constructive comments made after my adviser came in because he assessed the lesson, he's the maths specialist and he assessed the maths lesson, which didn't go too well, investigating, which didn't work out too well, and so he felt able to give me advice and I suppose at the time I found it quite difficult – I mean, nobody likes being criticized or and everybody would rather be told beforehand and then helped over the problem than having to do it and fail and be seen to fail and then get help, which is what happened. I obviously didn't do too well and he went and talked to the head about it and after that I was given a whole lot of support in maths, I went to visit classrooms and the head came into my class and took over and had a special group going out to another teacher and the teacher – you know, a lot of support this way, that he did care about me. But I couldn't help thinking at the time that it was a lot of stress and bother when it would have been nice to have had a chance to talk about it

beforehand, and sorted that out...'worried about my maths, and I'd like a bit of help', before I actually had to fail...and I'd talked to the deputy head about it, but again I wasn't given the right opportunity, I mean, you answer, you speak to people and give them what you think they might be wanting to hear. I mean, the conversation I had with the deputy head wasn't, 'what are the problems you are having at the moment? Tell me how I can help you?' More very general – 'How are things going?' It wasn't that I want to get into a deep discussion about this – it's, 'I want to know generally how things are going?' So, I wasn't really specific about it – I hadn't been given the right question really, I hadn't been fed the right vibes to answer it. I mean, I know this in class, the SMP system is very much a one-way – children have to fail before you can help them – they have to work through the card and get it wrong before you see the problem. You don't teach a topic to the class, explaining the possible problems and then letting them get on with it (23.2).

Here Liz was able to articulate an educational theory about the importance of success in practice, and the importance of prior opportunities, through prompts presented within conditions of dialogue and 'shared' problems. For herself and her pupils she was seeking to avoid failure in trying what works and what doesn't, by having the chance to establish in advance more 'secure' principles for teaching (in this case mathematics). What she identified was the way in which such opportunities to establish theories before testing them were missed. The realms of technical knowledge and the making of judgement, she seemed to be saying, got into crisis because of the 'glossing over' of problems by the deputy head, and her own inability to articulate her ideas in the conditions which pertained. Being given the right question and the right vibes to answer it was, in this self-reflective theory about her own learning, crucial for ownership as well as for the development of understanding *and* experience of success. Dave, too, recognized the after-the-eventness of learning from advice – in this case commissioned comment which might help him understand events better, as a means of developing practice for the future:

Dave: I was fortunate on the one occasion because it is a remedial group and you have one of the teachers in to help with writing and stuff, and he could actually be my evaluator on the situation. (I could say) 'well, this is what happened', or 'you saw that happen now what could I have done?' Sometimes the answer is nothing more, that's it, sometimes you get extra advice. But you know that little tip is useful when the situation occurs; you can store up in your mind for the next occasion – that comes out of something else – somebody else's experiences....And sometimes in that situation you give replies, but think, 'ok, but I can't do that', which is an

> evaluation on evaluation, if you like. You come to a point and say,
> 'no, that's not me'. I find usually, being new, it's always in the,
> sort of, post event that you seek advice, you're never really told
> where some of the problems are unless you have gross problems,
> so you're continually seeking advice after the event, which would
> be better to have that information beforehand, but it doesn't seem
> to be happening that way, so far (16.12).

Sue regarded herself as confident in the classroom, and self-sufficient as a learner, though she discussed details of teaching with the head of department in what she described as a dialogue where they shared ideas. The contrast between being supervised as a student and independent learning as a teacher was a marked one, with an explicit preference for the latter.

Sue: Yes, 'cos this is what interests me, because I feel that what I've partly
          liked about this (year) is that I've been left on my own, and if I've
          learnt, I've learnt on my own terms and not on somebody else
          imposing ideas and strategies and everything upon me – you've
          learned yourself whether it's going in the right direction or the
          wrong direction. So, that is independence – that's self-sufficiency
          may be (2.12).

While independent self-sufficiency in classroom matters was Sue's preferred mode of learning, the others wanted to assert that confidence in framing problems and in setting the agenda for commissioning advice and support in testing strategies in their teaching. Even within that, Liz acknowledged the need to be 'asked the right questions' to unlock her concerns about specific teaching problems, because of a lack of confidence in 'revealing herself'. It was at this point of reflection-in-anticipation of events, at the predictive, planning stage of teaching, where a sense of *going through it* alone began. For Liz, Dave and Debbie it was here where support and advice might have been most effective, subject to their own interpretations and predispositions, in helping them to clarify their aims and proposals. Beyond that stage the implementation of ideas and conduct of practice added to the sense of going through it, alone, as a means of gaining 'experience'.

There was also a different sense to the notion of going through it alone. The teachers reflected on the possible consequences of revealing 'oneself' in the sense of aspects of one's teaching as well as aspects of the emotions. Each of the teachers revealed within the group that they regularly engaged in reflection on revealing or not revealing details of their teaching, of classroom events, of their personal ideas and philosophies, and the ways they felt (see also Hargreaves and Tucker,

1991). They asserted how it was necessary to judge how much to reveal of the rationales (or the uncertainties or vagueness) in their thinking, and whether or not to expose their practice, or their evaluations of practice, let alone their emotions, to the scrutiny of others. So here was a kind of double-bind. The need to learn self-sufficiently was important for reasons of self-esteem, which affected interpersonal relationships with colleagues, and also for micro-political reasons. Yet this was also a denial of the aspiration for dialogue about principles, aims and practice. The power of *going through it* on the route to 'experience' was strong:

Sue: Maybe people aren't that concerned about it (the problem) but you are, and you've got nobody to talk to about it.

Liz: I've got to get through as well as I can without bothering people (and) you can't bare your soul, can you, because it gets trodden all over (18.11).

Yet the bright side of that, certainly for Liz, was the development of confidence, a greater sense of independence and self-sufficiency both in the classroom and in the staffroom. In parts, however, the world remained a private one:

Liz: But there's quite a few things I do and I – it's still because I'm not quite confident about where I stand in the school, I suppose, that I think I'm sneaking in the odd lesson. Today we watched a video version of the book we've been reading, and I feel that's a very good thing to do, to contrast the cartoon version of the story, but again, I kept quite quiet about it, I didn't tell everyone – although I'd be happy to justify why I was doing it, if anyone asked and happy to tell them, but it's just one of those things, I think perhaps when I'm more confident in the school and feel more confident in myself, this is the sort of thing I will go and talk about – do you see the difference? (16.12).

Given this private world, the conversation in the group was much less about how the teachers learnt from colleagues, and more about how they learnt alone. That had a number of notable features which have been reported elsewhere (Tickle, 1992a; 1992b; 1992d). In particular there were factors which made 'second-hand' learning either irrelevant or at best subject to testing and first-hand experience. This confirms Schon's (1983) notion that what is important in learning professional knowledge is the construction of a repertoire of such experience. The way in which this capacity could be realized was thought to be through self-criticism, again in private:

Liz: Having to learn to be able to judge my lessons for myself, being
          self-critical, to work out am I going along the right roads? Why
          am I teaching this lesson – is it leading to anything? Having to do
          that the whole time I think (2.12).

The Wish of Odysseus

In her extensive review of the mentor phenomenon, Little (1990)
helpfully alerts us to the legend in which Odysseus entrusted
Telemachus to Mentor's care; the relationship which required of
Mentor wisdom, integrity and personal investment; and of
Telemachus that he honour the differences in maturity and circum-
stance that separated them (Little, 1990, p.298). She acknowledged
(how could she not?) that by comparison to the legendary image of a
profoundly personal and mutually respectful relationship, mentoring
among teachers is often and predominantly narrowly conceived in
terms of utilitarian purposes – what may be summarized as providing
orientation to school settings, curriculum information, organizational
arrangements, technical assistance, support with resources, or the
assessment of performance. I do not want to suggest that such purposes are ill-conceived, unhelpful or unnecessary; on the contrary (see
Tickle, 1992d). But they do not attend to Bruner's (1977) version of
the legendary relationship, in which,

> ...all forms of assisted learning...depend massively upon participation in a dia-
> logue carefully stabilized by the adult partner. So much of learning depends on
> the need to achieve joint attention, to conduct enterprises jointly, to honour the
> social relationship that exists between learner and tutor...(preface).

So why is there such a difference in conception? Even within the
utilitarian conception why is there such apparent vagueness about the
nature and experience of the mentor role beyond the simply administrative (Ben-Peretz and Rumney, 1991; Cole, 1991; Kremer-Hayon,
1991)? First, it seems, are the conditions, culture and experience of
teaching which Lortie (1975) described, characterized in part by in-
dividualism and individuality, by privacy and privatism, and by implication the business of the personal ownership of experience of 'what
works' for individual teachers. In his portrayal of the route into the
acquisition of professional knowledge, comprising formal schooling
as a student, initial teacher training and 'learning while doing' after
beginning full-time practice, Lortie pointed out the inadequacies of
each phase for the development of a professional culture in which the
problems of teaching might be seen as endemic and universal, rather
than individual and personal. So far as I can tell he was not suggesting

that the question of developing individual competence should not be an issue. Rather, I think, he saw the possibility that if the generally problematic nature of teaching were acknowledged and addressed within the profession in an open and public, as well as a problem-solving way, then collectively and individually it might be possible to improve the quality of teaching.

However, Lortie pointed to some strong influences which restrict such possibilities of professional advancement. He argued that formal schooling as a student, for example, provides powerful, 'recipient', exposure to models of teaching in which individual decision-making and management of situations *appear* to be paramount. He regarded initial training, correctly in my view, as unsophisticated and organizationally brief compared to other professions, and principally constituting a socialization process in the form of status passage from recipient to deliverer, with reinforcement of the same model of individualization. 'Learning while doing' was characterized as being confronted largely alone, confirming teaching as an isolated and individualized activity, and the status passage as being from communal reception of knowledge (though with individualized, competitive receptiveness) to sole, responsible provider. Lortie argued that this individualistic learning of what works by trial and error affects the ways teachers regard themselves in relation to their practice, as individually, personally and even competitively responsible. In contrast, he regarded occupations where knowledge and ignorance are jointly shared, within a framework of community and collective support for the individual, as reducing doubts about personal efficacy and as leading to collaborative approaches in search of solutions to common problems. By implication, he would have the latter kind of arrangement in teaching as a means of transforming the experience of the individual teacher and the professional culture and collective status of teaching. Such a call has been reiterated by Hargreaves and Tucker (1991) on the basis of a recent empirical study of teachers' work.

Arguments in favour of establishing such 'collective support', at least for new entrants to teaching, have a long history in England and Wales, most notably in the McNair Report (1944), James Report (1972), numerous DES proposals, and recently in the HMI Reports *The New Teacher in School* (DES, 1982; 1988). In the USA similar developments have moved apace on the basis of funded projects in numerous locations (see Little, 1990). In each case policy-makers and providers have placed at least the idea, and in some cases the formally designated role, of teacher-tutor or mentor at the pivotal position of professional development for new teachers. However, as Little points out (p.297), 'rhetoric and action have outpaced both conceptual development and empirical warrant'. Not least is the question of how to engender at the interactional level, let alone the school and system level, a perspective on learning teaching which is both communal and public, rather than individually owned and private. The values and assumptions associated with these aspects of teacher culture certainly seemed to be substantially represented among the teacher-tutors associated with the new teachers with whom I worked, and among the teachers themselves (see Tickle, 1992a). Indeed the protection of such characteristics was both explicit in discussing the teacher-tutor role and widely implicit in its conduct and in relationships within it.

Telemachus, on the other hand, was being initiated into a quite different tradition. A characteristic custom among the early Greek warrior class, eventually transmitted to the wider *demos,* was to assemble as equals, as peers, in a circular space in which each could speak freely, and place *issues* in the public domain; issues, that is, as matters of common concern worthy of public debate. This was a formula for a community in which relationships with one another were not defined in terms of domination and submission, but of 'equilibrium, symmetry and reciprocity' (Vernant, 1983, p.185). It is not insignificant that the physical space of the *agora* was devised to facilitate such sharing. Its principles were even incorporated into townships by designers skilled in both political theory and urban planning. Accounts of the adult Telemachus engaging in such public debate, long before those urban developments, are equally significant (Vernant, *ibid*). They make more poignant the role model offered by Mentor, and the relationship to it which was expected of the youthful son of Odysseus. For it is both in that particular relationship and the culture within which it was constructed that there is so much to learn for the sake of the development of teaching, in terms of the practice of individuals and the profession as a whole. Perhaps I can be permitted to speculate that what those earlier participants in dialogue were engaged in was the exercise of social learning by placing experience, ideas and issues in the public domain (a practice which Schon [1971] lamented as missing from the construction of public social programmes in the USA). In the case of teaching, the quest for such public discourse would likely make heavy demands on both mentors and mentored, for they would need to engage with and potentially change individual attitudes and relationships, the conditions which constrain those relationships, and the culture of teaching within which they work and live.

Perhaps in order to do that it will be necessary to develop conceptions about the values and purposes of different kinds of teaching knowledge. Towards that end we have been offered, much more recently, views which might have been acceptable to the Greek warrior class (which might indeed reflect their views). Habermas (1968) for example, defined knowledge as having several branches connected closely with particular kinds of human interests. The technical interest, in his view, is concerned with our endeavour to control and manipulate events. Our practical interest is associated with inter-subjectivity and communication, in reaching mutual understandings and self-understanding in the conduct of our daily lives. An emancipatory interest describes our ability to reflect critically on our own presuppositions and to debate ideas openly (Habermas, 1968, p.313). If Habermas is correct then it is the interconnectedness of these different kinds of knowledge and interests which needs to be attended to. Yet it appeared that the new teachers emphasized to a considerable degree their concern with and reliance on their individual worlds of ideas, thoughts and emotions, as their attention focused in large measure on the external world which they sought to understand, and within which they wrestled for control of events through the manipulation of situations. That was not the only focus of attention but it was a predominant one. In effect they were engaged in a self-reliant, analytical, and technical concern with what worked in practice. The platform for debating underlying theories of teaching, for reaching mutual understanding and self-understanding through discourse, largely eluded them. They unwittingly colluded in creating that elusiveness. There was little opportunity or desire for public debate, or even for exposing thoughts among colleagues. The ability to reflect critically on their own presuppositions, or on those within which they worked, and the development of that ability, appeared to be substantially constrained by the stress which they laid on the importance of personal experience and of privacy. It seemed to be further constrained by the particular ways in which the mentoring role was conducted – both in the 'extreme' cases of relationships breakdown and non-intervention, and in the supportive, constructive, advisory conduct of the role.

The implication of this for learning teaching, for the mentor relationship, and for those new teachers in particular, is the danger that personal, private experience might continue as a dominant, yet narrow, source of knowledge. If that were to happen, then the chance of developing a potentially emancipatory and educative approach to both their practice and the aims and values which underlie it – in short, to develop reflexive attributes of teaching and of professional development – might well be missed. Of course, this is a declaration of my own search for the fulfilment of the wish of Odysseus, or the ideals of Bruner, to be extended to present-day educational practices among mentors and mentored.

REFERENCES

Ben-Peretz, M and Rumney, S (1991) 'Professional thinking and guided practice', *Teaching and Teacher Education*, 7, 5/6, 517–30.

Blumer, H (1962) 'Society as symbolic interactionism', in Rose, A M (ed.) *Human Behaviour and Social Process: An Interactionist Perspective*, London: Routledge and Kegan Paul.

Blumer, H (1969) 'The methodological position of symbolic interactionism', in Hammersley, M and Woods, P (eds) (1976) *The Process of Schooling*, Milton Keynes, Open University Press.

Bruner, J (1977) *The Process of Education*, Cambridge, MA: Harvard University Press.

Cole, A L (1991) 'Relationships in the workplace: doing what comes naturally', *Teaching and Teacher Education*, 7, 5/6, 415–26.

Department of Education and Science (1982) *The New Teacher in School*, London: DES.

Department of Education and Science (1988) *The New Teacher in School*, London: DES.

Habermas, J (1968) *Knowledge and Human Interests*, Frankfurt: Suhrkamp.

Hargreaves, A and Tucker, E (1991) 'Teaching and guilt: exploring the feelings of teaching', *Teaching and Teacher Education*, 7, 5/6, 491–506.

Jacknicke, K and Samiroden, W D (1991) 'Some perceptions of an internship programme', *The Alberta Journal of Educational Research*, 37, 2, 99–118.

James Report (1972) *Teacher Education and Training*, London: HMSO.

Kremer-Hayon, L (1991) 'The stories of expert and novice student teachers' supervisors; perspectives on professional development', *Teaching and Teacher Education*, 7, 5/6, 427–38.

Little, J W (1990) 'The mentor phenomenon and the social organization of teaching', in Cazden, C B (ed.) *Review of Research in Education Number 16*, Washington, DC: American Educational Research Association.

Lortie, D (1975) *Schoolteacher*, Chicago, IL: University of Chicago Press.

McNair Report (1944) *Teachers and Youth Leaders*, London: HMSO.

Schon, D (1971) *Beyond The Stable State*, San Francisco, CA: Jossey Bass.

Schon, D (1983) *The Reflective Practitioner*, New York: Basic Books.

Tabachnick, B R and Zeichner, K (eds) (1991) *Issues and Practices in Inquiry-oriented Teacher Education*, London: Falmer Press.

Tickle, L (1991) 'New teachers and the emotions of learning teaching', *Cambridge Journal of Education*, 21, 3, 319–29.

Tickle, L (1992a) 'Capital T Teaching', in Elliott, J (ed.) *Reconstructing Teacher Education*, London: Falmer Press.

Tickle, L (1992b) 'The first year of teaching as a learning experience', in Bridges, D and Kerry, T (eds) *Delivering In-Service Teacher Education*, Norwich: University of East Anglia.

Tickle, L (1992c) 'The assessment of professional skills in classroom teaching', in *Cambridge Journal of Education*, 22, 1, 91–103.

Tickle, L (1992d) 'The education of new entrants to teaching', unpublished PhD thesis, School of Education, University of East Anglia.

Vernant, J P (1983) *Myth and Thought Among the Greeks*, London: Routledge and Kegan Paul.

12 Correlation in Mentoring: An Enquiry-based Approach

Peter Lucas and Chris True

Introduction

Mentoring should not be seen as exclusively a one-way process in which the 'expert' mentor guides the 'inexpert' and 'deficient' learner. Any learning that takes place should have a dimension of mutuality. We report here on an enquiry in which an experienced PGCE history tutor (Peter) and a new PGCE mathematics tutor (Chris) engaged as part of a three-year TVEI in ITT staff development project (1988–91) in the Division of Education, Sheffield University. We offer this analysis of our experience in the belief that it suggests points that might usefully be considered by mentors in schools, where some of the background factors may well be replicated: ie, adult trainees teaching different subjects from those who are mentoring them, teaching those subjects within an organization which has an explicit rhetoric, and participating (formally or informally) with fellow trainees from other subject areas in professionally focused discussion.

We saw clear parallels between 'active learning', promoted by the TVEI[1], and 'reflective practice', promoted by many ITT institutions, including our own. Both concepts seemed to encourage the notion that individuals should become more responsible for managing their own learning. Students and student teachers were being invited to identify their strengths and weaknesses, to base their conclusions on evidence, to ask questions to strengthen their understandings, and to ascertain the ways in which their relationships with others, and factors within the organization of which they were a part, influenced their effectiveness. We interpreted 'reflection', therefore, not as something redolent of the cloister but as behaviour demanding as much intellectual rigour as could be brought to it, and the nerve and gumption to take whatever measures were needed. 'Reflection', we came to realize, was a 'strong' mode of active learning.

Fidelity[2] requires tutors (and, we might add, mentors) to model the ways they want student teachers to adopt. Thus, because we were expecting our students to be 'reflective', we, too, had to investigate our teaching. Chris had worked briefly with students in another higher education institution, but essentially was coming to his post after having been a head of department in school for 16 years. As tutor, Peter was continuing the process of developing a subject programme on reflective principles. As project coordinator, and during that time also PGCE director, he saw an opportunity to collaborate with a colleague in a non-cognate area and thus to take a cross-curricular initiative in keeping with the spirit of the TVEI, and to extend the basis of support for exploring reflective practice within the team of PGCE tutors.

We have chosen the term 'correlative' to describe our mentoring relationship because it emphasizes the similarities in approach we were working towards; expresses the mutuality of dependence in the affective area of the relationship (that is, each of us gained access to potentially sensitive information about the other as a tutor and as a person); points to the fact that our approach was programmatic, not pragmatic (it had a design); and, finally, indicates the way our subject programmes took on a parallel aspect (that is, we were working separately but with something of a common agenda). This last point had implications for the 'power differential' issue – we did not observe each other teach, nor did our programmes converge, which meant that individual autonomy in the subject seminar and workshop was not threatened and could be preserved.

Chris adopted a similar approach to Peter's in supervision. This step was particularly significant because if reflective practice was to be furthered then an appropriate supervisory style was crucial. Student teachers typically regard block practice as the most important element of the PGCE programme. Traditional approaches to supervision feature strongly the delivery of judgements, which are frequently more negative than positive. Checklists may be ticked, and the way the judgements are stated will vary in terms of the amount of deference to student teachers' feelings. What we tried to do, following Rudduck and Sigsworth,[3] was to establish the following characteristics: a student-set agenda for the observation of the lesson and for the post-lesson debriefing; the employment of evidence in the shape of the supervisor's non-judgemental record of the lesson written during it; and a conscious effort to be aware of the negative impact the power of the tutor-perceived-as-assessor could have and a real attempt to reduce that negative impact on our encouragement of the students to take responsibility for managing their own learning.

Features of the Correlative Approach

Each of us interviewed, in small groups, the other's students, in total 55 – 31 mathematicians and 24 historians. (For one term of the two academic sessions embracing these students, Peter's work as history tutor was undertaken by a local teacher, who was familiar with the PGCE history course, to enable him to concentrate on the coordination of the staff development project and the PGCE programme). Students were invited to consider their university-based subject application courses and our supervision of them on teaching practice from the angle of the encouragement given them to take responsibility for managing their own learning.

To sum up, our correlative approach to the mentoring relationship had these features:

- it was conducted within an overt rationale (reflective practice);
- this rationale was in agreement with the rhetoric of the PGCE programme as a whole;
- it linked two colleagues as fellow learners, not as 'expert' and 'novice';
- each colleague had to transmit, analyse and grapple with the implications of negative as well as positive feedback,
- which meant each had to trust the other with regard to the 'inside' knowledge obtained;
- the bases for discussion weren't impressions, but the detailed evidence of students' reactions and perceptions;
- the gathering of this evidence wasn't casual, but planned;
- a lengthy period of time was involved.

We continue to debrief each other's students, a procedure which has been adopted by all PGCE tutors as part of the Division's student course evaluation activities.

The Impact of the Process

During his first year, Chris compared his position with that of his students. This was at a time when the staff development project as a whole focused on active learning in its conference programme.

I still feel that I am perhaps not being intellectually rigorous enough about things and perhaps (not) thinking carefully enough about the theory because in a sense (during) the last 16 years I have been working in a far more pragmatic way,

he told the project's 'historian'. He felt 'very intellectually drained' because he had 'not been used to working like that really'. It was 'actually, well, only like my students are. I am actually trying to get right down inside what I really think about this, and I find that quite demanding'. He had reassessed what he understood by active learning: the project had 'raised questions to which I have not got a definite answer yet, it is problematic in that sense...'. At the time of interview he had not yet worked out an enquiry: he was 'still looking for a mathematical slant'. In addition to the teaching demands, which he was still getting used to,

> the one part of the job that I have not come to terms with at all really is the research side...that's why I find it rather hard to sort of latch on to something that I really want to do.

Getting organized to bid for money to pursue a publicly worked out enquiry, the proposals for which were to be scrutinized by the PGCE team before the 'go-ahead' was given, was a daunting venture.

It was at this point that Chris and Peter joined forces. This move reflected Smith's[4] observation that,

> more often than not the (mentoring) relationship evolves naturally rather than through the kind of deliberate contracting that an apprenticeship or an internship involves.

During an interview in the second year, referring to 'my initiative', Chris went on to comment:

> I say mine...what happened really was that Peter had an idea and he came to me and the idea appealed to me because it was looking at maths and history, and in that sense it's cross-curricular....

The enquiry was 'a shared thing': 'Peter has accepted my ideas and I have been quite pleased to learn from him as well...'. Chris enjoyed doing the enquiry because it wasn't abstract and being done 'just for the sake of research'. The enquiry

> actually engages me because it is something that I need to think about, about the way I work in here (the university) and the way teachers work in the classroom...I actually see it as part of my evolution as a tutor here....

A year later, noting that the enquiry was 'progressing very well', he commented on its value to him:

> it's been about the way I work with my maths students which has been incredibly useful to me...my individual enquiry is such that my way of working with my students has changed during the course of the enquiry.

His approach was 'still problematic' because there were issues and dilemmas emerging from the way he was trying to work. For him, the enquiry was something he had been 'very interested in'. He wanted 'to hear about what my students think about the way I work with them. Don't get me wrong, I'm still interested in what the teachers say and what the pupils say', but what had been really important had been knowledge and analysis of the students' views. The involvement of the students in this way had been 'a big strength of what we've been doing'. The enquiry had 'certainly' been useful in his professional development. As a result of it he had changed the nature of materials and methodologies to get more coherence between what he was attempting to do and his practice; in brief, to create the conditions in which his students could become more responsible for their own learning.

> Last term...autumn term...was different...from anything I've done in the previous two years in the light of what I've been thinking about as a result of the enquiry.

He made reference to the importance of modelling: '...if I don't give my students responsibility they're not going to give their pupils responsibility...'. He thought that whether it was with his educational studies group or his maths work, he had 'tried to hand over the initiative to my students...'. He recalled that on coming to the department he 'was sure that I used to unwittingly but definitely control. I still control too much, but I have made conscious efforts to hand over the control...' As a result he had 'been more up front about my goals for them in active learning...In the past it's been implicit...'. He cited the way he 'was quite explicit' in the maths course guide 'about the way I was going to work', the clarifying of the intentions and procedures of debriefing students, and the 'much more thorough briefing' of his TP supervisees 'about how I was going to work with them in the one-to-one, whereas in the past...I've not talked about their role in it as much...'.

During one conference, in 1989/90, in which a colleague was reporting back on an enquiry whose grounds were being challenged,

Chris noticed something that, as he later told the project 'historian', surprised him. Acknowledging that he 'would be classed as a scientist' – he was, he emphasized – he found himself having 'far more sympathy with the non-scientific viewpoint'. It appeared to him that the tutor who was doing the challenging 'was trying to apply scientific values to what was essentially a sociological piece of work'. Chris made it clear that he wasn't denying that 'some science' was necessary, but the challenger was exerting what appeared to Chris to be 'inappropriate demands' in this instance. He believed the challenger 'came across very much as a pragmatist'. His own position had changed. Eighteen months previously he

> would have seen myself...perhaps being in the same corner, but now I felt a lot of time for what (T, the tutor being challenged) was saying, about what (T) was looking at and why (T) was looking at it that way. [Even though] for me there is still a tension internally about the validity of anything I do...I have realized that you can perhaps do things in a localized way rather than to make (the) grand sort of enquiries.

In other words, he had found action research of the kind he had been doing a powerful way of improving his understanding of teaching intentions and practice.

Peter had concerns that his position as PGCE director and project coordinator would distort the mentoring relationship, particularly given his strong commitment to reflective practice. He did not seek to 'impose' an approach. Smith[5] has noted that the mentor

> resists certain temptations such as looking at a learner as a possession to be made over in his or her own image or permitting more dependency or intimacy than is constructive.

That the relationship remained healthy was the result of several factors. First, the correlative approach meant that we were mutually dependent on each other in crucial ways. Chris, again in interview:

> ...we actually interrogate each other's method groups and have heard criticism about each other and worked together about it, and not felt, well I've not felt uncomfortable about it.

The procedure we adopted placed discussion squarely on evidence and, no matter how gently points may have been made, reasoning things out. Chris continued:

> ...in that sense he and I have definitely worked closely together in, you know, in a genuine way seeing each other's, well, perceived flaws.... I suspect that I talk

more to him now than I would ever have dreamt of doing because we've worked together and however guarded he is, in a sense I feel that our relationship is quite open....

It was a relationship based on trust. Second, from the start, and within structured opportunities for discussion during the conference programme, Chris was open to other tutors' ideas. In 1988/9 he commented that he was sure there was much to be learned from 'other subject areas', and subsequently was stimulated by the work of a colleague to get his maths students to keep 'learning logs' or diaries (something that Peter had decided not to introduce into the historians' programme) and latterly reconsidering the place of equal opportunities under the stimulus of the practice of one subject team. Working with his colleagues, the essence of the staff development project as far as he was concerned was, as he had commented early in its evolution, 'not a problem because there is no one person with whom I identify'. Third, the enquiry he and Peter were pursuing was, as he had put it, 'a shared thing'. 'Peter has accepted my ideas and I have been quite pleased to learn from him as well...'. He felt he could, legitimately, refer to the enquiry as 'his'.

Reacting to Learners' Explanations

The contemporary modification to the ancient Chinese adage, 'I hear, I forget; I see, I remember; *I make a mistake, I understand*'[6] is an improvement, but as a call to get on with intelligent 'doing' rather than be enfeebled by self-torment, it glosses over the sensitivities at stake. Giving praise is easy and although receiving it might cause blushes, any embarrassment can usually be handled. Giving or receiving criticism, however just, is much harder. Our correlative approach to mentoring reminded us both of the importance of listening to learners and in so doing deepened our understanding of the issues associated with the interpretation of classroom events. Let's consider a common problem in initial teacher training.[7]

When student teachers are asked to consider particular ways in which they have performed in the classroom there is a likelihood that some will use language supervisors do not want to hear (eg, 'In my defence I can say that...'). They may use such terminology even when the supervisor has consciously tried to introduce and phrase questions as 'neutrally' as possible. Often, too, a student will launch quickly into some form of attributionism. Thus weaknesses will be accounted for in terms of the waywardness of pupils (uncontrollable by the class teacher), the pressure put on them by staff to use styles of teaching with which they disagree; the perceived failure of staff in the training institution to have had a seminar/workshop on this or that problem now preoccupying the individual. Other possible causes of weaknesses will include the day and/or time, the temperature, the fact that it's snowing, or that games are under way on the nearby playing field. Typically, in such cases supervisors (ourselves included) may start assessing the student teachers in terms of 'defensiveness'; they are seen as reluctant to face up to the 'truth' that their planning reveals incompetence or that their personal traits cause them to be perceived by pupils as not particularly likeable. This can be seen as serious by 'traditional' supervisors who don't want such 'noise' to get in the way of the acceptance of their judgements, and by those who narrowly interpret 'reflection' as (simply) a willingness to castigate one's own failings as the root of all one's classroom problems. In such an ambience, student 'explanations' can be perceived as 'excuses'. Whatever validity such explanations might have, they may be summarily dismissed in the minds of supervisors rather than intelligently explored. We can, of course, explain these behaviours by reference to such factors as students' feelings of vulnerability in the face of assessment, and supervisors' reluctance to disturb relations between institution and school by tackling issues that go beyond incompetences displayed by the learner. But the crucial point is that too close a focus on 'defensiveness' reduces the rationality in a situation in which the learners ought to be reflecting on any perceived variable where this would help classroom processes to be better understood and more effective actions to be taken. We have referred elsewhere[8] to a student who commented that,

> ...you try and explain why something was happening in such a way and he thinks...you are trying to defend yourself, which implies you have done wrong....

Having to stick rigidly to what they themselves did or did not do within a lesson or in the planning for it, means that insufficient or no consideration may be given to such things as the influence on his or her competency of the student teacher's temporary colleagues, his or her relationships with them or, say, the structure of the school's timetable (eg, overlong lessons, lessons where 'inevitably' pupils will arrive late or in ones or twos).

Whether or not supervisors take account of them, student teachers have to face the implications of what they undoubtedly experience as facts: that Mr Y expresses contempt for role-play; that Miss A always releases her pupils late; that Mr Q does not feel inhibited from interrupting the start of a student teacher's lessons to get to a resources cupboard; that insufficient time was spent in the training institution on, say, the place of questioning. In such circumstances it is no wonder that students can get dismayed when in evaluating their teaching they point to the implications of these facts and are seen as excusing themselves.

Our correlative approach determined that we both became informed as to students' reactions to their subject studies programmes, their views on their tutor's teaching, and the nature of tutor-student and student-student relationships. In our rhetoric we talk of 'focused professional dialogue' in which we hope students will engage. It's a useful phrase, but could be treated as merely a label for what might be rather loosely structured discussion. It's possible to say when recalling what one has been told in such circumstances, 'Maybe that's not what he actually said', or 'Maybe he actually misheard what they were saying, or misinterpreted it'. A phased procedure involving interviews, the solitary analysis of the printed record, and collegial discussion minimizes such evasion. During our 'focused professional dialogue' in the mentoring relationship – discussion using the evidence in the transcripts – we discovered that we were thinking in ways that would cause student teachers to be labelled resistant, and unwilling to look openly at faults in lessons they taught. 'I'm not surprised at that comment; he's been an awkward individual from the start'. 'Three of them aren't really committed to teaching in a state comprehensive'. 'How did we come to accept *them* on the course?' 'I'm getting the backwash from the session they had with X'. 'It's because we have to rush to cover as much as possible before they do the TP'. Such statements may be seen as representing the kind of thoughts we were having. Were these the thoughts of reflective tutors, we questioned. Were we not being just as 'defensive' as some of our students? Were we not making excuses? Was this not evidence of 'conservatism'? There certainly was an instinct to protect ourselves, but beyond that there was also knowledge, which we were able to share, of facts such as the dispositions and behaviours of individual students, of the nature of their relationship with us, and the characteristics of the settings in which we were working.

What we are suggesting is that our correlative approach to mentoring affected our understanding of our role in promoting reflective practice. Essentially, by making each of us reflect collaboratively on our courses within the framework of a 'knowing' other, it helped us to recognize ways in which we were not facilitating the development of students' understanding. Over-sensitivity to evidence of dispositions that were felt to be inappropriate carried the danger of causing us to listen less carefully and evaluate in a less balanced and sympathetic way. We realized that we had to be more sympathetic towards students' explanations, to be prepared to give them greater legitimacy. Had the mentoring relationship not been a correlative one such understanding might not have developed. It would have been easy, for example, for an experienced tutor, without a direct personal stake in the process of evidence gathering and enquiry, to have responded to a colleague in much the same way as a tutor might to a seemingly defensive student teacher. We thus came to a renewed awareness of the significance of the cultural 'embeddedness' and 'high context' nature of teachers' knowledge,[9] features which are so easy for those outside an organization to forget.

For school mentors who are concerned to encourage their student teachers to reflect, there is a dilemma here. They are in a better position than ITT institution tutors to understand in detail the quirks, nuances and particular pressures of their school settings and are therefore able, as it were, to 'speak the same language' as their student teachers. But any genuine exploring of student teacher explanations of where they 'are' with the desirable goal of helping their teaching become steadily more effective, may well lead to the examination of how problems to do with specific colleagues' attitudes and behaviours can be addressed. It may prompt fresh considerations that add to and further complicate the criteria being used when, say, timetables are being prepared and rooms allocated. It may demand that the school's rhetoric, perhaps as expressed in its prospectus and staff handbook, be taken seriously and aspects of a 'staffroom culture' targeted for attention. In short, instead of reflection being narrowly interpreted as '*self*-criticism', it may begin to take on political and ethical dimensions, and the mentoring relationship itself be seen as a catalyst for the wider development of interpersonal relationships and change within the organization. This is exciting, but are school mentors ready to accept the dynamic role that is implied? And what role in this might they want their colleagues in the ITT institutions to play?

Perspectives on Others' Subjects

When we began our enquiry, history and maths appeared to us to be reciprocally distant disciplines. Being able to give up maths after getting a GCSE grade C may lift the spirits of pupils who want to concentrate on history and literary pursuits. A desire to study a 'discipline' they regard as irrelevant, unimportant and doubtfully true, may puzzle maths student teachers. Such reactions are not surprising. Mathematicians solve problems which are of a 'formal' nature. 'Solutions' pursued embrace (to employ Wickelgren's[10] words), complete specification of givens...of the set of operations to be used...of the goals...(and) an ordered succession or sequence of problem states, starting with the given state and terminating with the goal states, such that each successive state is obtained from the preceding state by means of an allowable action....

Such terminology is alien to history which, properly considered, eschews 'correct' accounts.

As a form of knowledge history is differentiated from a number of others because of its prime concern with 'understanding how things come about' rather than with 'producing solutions to problems'.[11]

Healthy, well-founded approaches in history are rooted in painstaking 'thoroughness' in the continual accumulation and recurring analysis of knowledge, not based on a full and detailed description of 'givens'. Historical thinking has to be strictly based on evidence that is trustworthy, it is not the process of obeisance to some set pattern; hypotheses are hesitant, not at all definite, really no better than approaches to goals. Considering past events, historians have to handle many different factors, knowing also that they are ignorant of many others: they can't introduce 'allowable actions'. Furthermore, the concept of empathy has no place among the concepts in mathematics.

Nevertheless, we have become conscious of the ways in which history and maths resemble each other in their subject nature and with respect to the ways they might be taught. Neither of the two is merely concerned with communicating data. Both seek to discover answers to questions. Just as the logic of maths provides a guide to problems, so, too, does the discipline of history; scholars in both search for fresh approaches to the examination of the commonplace. Both want to build up and foster the resolution to ask questions. Both apply themselves to the gathering, analysis and elucidation of data. Both seek out the connections between one thing and another. Exactly as

a neatly packaged, precise, and unforgiving field of academic achievement in which workers cannot be considered as competent unless able to produce instantaneous solutions

summarizes in fanciful terms 'the daily experience of professional mathematicians',[12] the notion of history as a subject lacking intellectual rigour and whose practitioners are obsessed with trivial and irrelevant facts is misguided.

Hedger's and Kent's[13] comments that,

whatever the topic under scrutiny, we believe that it should be introduced through an investigative technique that encourages students to explore situations collectively and to discover results for themselves [and that] this is a process which encourages 'ownership' of ideas and promotes confidence and enthusiasm,

are as applicable to history as maths. Maths activities employing 'real contexts'[14] compare with history activities incorporating source materials and the relating of past events and issues to what is happening today. Lester's advice that

teachers should capitalize on the knowledge their students bring with them from outside of school by having it serve as a basis for the development of mathematical knowledge[15]

remains good when we substitute 'historical' for 'mathematical'. 'When children ask the "why" question in their mathematics classroom, they are on their way to strengthening their number sense';[16] when they say 'Why?' in history, children are developing their purchase on a fundamental value of the discipline.

Such observations haven't to be taken too far. We know, too, that other disciplines share the above characteristics. But we would draw attention to three points in relation to the above, each raising issues for mentors in schools. First, students need to be aware of similarities between their own and non-cognate disciplines. There seems nothing exceptional in saying this, and the introduction of the National Curriculum encourages the possibility. But the tendency in ITT has been for students to become familiar with cognate disciplines, especially those which they may have to teach (eg, historians with geography and English within humanities; physicists with biology and chemistry within science). What is needed is some understanding by them (and their tutors!) of what subjects across the curriculum are requiring of pupils so that they may be less likely to relay negative attitudes towards subjects based on ignorance of what they are about. When, for instance, a maths student teacher says, 'Why should anyone want to study history, it's a waste of time', we might want to consider the desirability of having a person expressing such views enter the teaching profession.

For us, examining the nature of each other's discipline began the process of removing some, at least, of our prejudices and misconceptions. There was a sense of revelation as we realized that there were lines of communication across what had seemed an apparent gulf. As a result, we have felt more strongly challenged to rethink aspects of initial training by this aspect of our enquiry than we have been by reading observations in National Curriculum non-statutory guidance.

How can history student teachers be encouraged to develop what Sprent[17] calls 'a "feeling" for data'? How can maths student teachers be encouraged to use history in their classrooms?[18] Second, each academic discipline, in the way that it is encountered during their undergraduate programmes, is likely to lead its students to hold particular views on, and dispositions towards, academic knowledge and the way it should be taught.[19] This raises questions for initial teacher training, including: are individuals' beliefs about their subjects teased out at the start of the course? Are the relationships between these beliefs and the beliefs others hold about their subjects analysed? And, not least importantly, what is the relationship between subject beliefs held by mentors, tutors and student teachers and their respective attitudes towards the notion of reflective practice? The consideration of such questions will be at least as much the responsibility of school mentors as ITT institutions, not just because of the new criteria for ITT specified in DfE Circular 9/92,[20] but because these questions relate fundamentally to issues associated with appraisal systems, evaluation procedures and school effectiveness. Third, when students from different subjects meet (in school or ITT institution) to discuss general educational issues, how they rate the significance of the act of discussion may vary considerably. For example, history student teachers may feel frustrated if maths student teachers are indifferent to or disregard the worth of attending to problems for which there are no 'solutions'. Maths student teachers may feel annoyed and despairing by a neglect of figures and talk they perceive as 'waffle'. How do we get them to 'come out of their corners' as Chris realized he had done in his reaction to his colleagues' exchange of views?

Conclusion

We have given an account in this chapter of an enquiry-based approach to mentoring which we have described as 'correlative'. Although the mentoring relationship was between tutors in an ITT institution, the background factors were such as to suggest that the approach might have some relevance for the debate on mentoring in schools. On that assumption we have raised several points we believe might usefully be considered by school mentors. We hope that our argument that mentoring should not be seen as a one-way interaction with an 'expert' mentor guiding an 'inexpert' and 'deficient' learner is sufficiently convincing that teacher mentors might consider adopting within their relationships an enquiry stance.

NOTES

This chapter draws on P Lucas and C True (1991) *Active Learning and Reflective Practice: Some Dilemmas and Issues for Students and tutors in Initial Teacher Training,* TVEI Enquiry Report No. 6 (Report for Department of Employment TVEI Unit) Sheffield: University of Sheffield Division of Education. We would like to thank the TVEI Unit in the Department of Employment which funded the staff development project.

1. See Gleeson, D (ed.) (1987) *T.V.E.I. and Secondary Education: A Critical Appraisal,* Milton Keynes: Open University Press; Hopkins, D (ed.) (1990) *TVEI at the Change of Life,* Clevedon: Multilingual Matters; Brandes, D and Ginnis, P (1990) *A Guide to Student-Centred Learning,* Oxford: Basil Blackwell.
2. Noddings, N (1986) 'Fidelity in teaching, teacher education and research for teaching', *Harvard Educational Review,* **56,** 496–510.
3. Rudduck, J and Sigsworth, A (1985) 'Partnership supervision (or Goldhammer revisited)', in Hopkins, D and Reid, K, (eds) *Rethinking Teacher Education,* Beckenham: Croom Helm.
4. Smith, R M (1984) *Learning How to Learn: Applied Theory for Adults,* p.130, Milton Keynes: Open University Press.
5. Smith, *op. cit.*
6. See Ramsden, P (1992) *Learning to Teach in Higher Education,* p.263, London: Routledge.
7. This section is a revisited and extended version of part of a brief article, 'Dilemmas in supervision', by P Lucas and C True, (1991) *Forum,* **33,** 3, 79–81.
8. Lucas and True, *op. cit.*
9. Elbaz, F (1991) 'Research on teachers' knowledge: the evolution of a discourse', *Journal of Curriculum Studies,* **23,** 1, 1–19.
10. Wickelgren, W A (1974) *How to Solve Problems: Elements of a Theory of Problems and Problem-solving,* San Francisco, CA: W H Freeman.
11. Becher, T (1989) 'Historians on History', *Studies in Higher Education,* **14,** 3, p.263.
12. Hedger, K and Kent, D (1987) 'Mathematics and its teaching', *Teaching Mathematics and its Applications,* **6,**2, 49–54.
13. Hedger and Kent, *op. cit.*
14. Hobbs, D (1987) 'Mathematics – an alternative approach', *Teaching Mathematics and its Applications,* **6,** 4, 160–63.
15. Lester, F K Jr (1989) 'Research into practice: mathematical problem solving in and out of school', *Arithmetic Teacher,* **37,** 3, 33–5.
16. Whitin, D J (1989) 'Number sense and the importance of asking "Why?"', *Arithmetic Teacher,* **36,** 9, 26–9.
17. Sprent, P (1988) *Taking Risks: The Science of Uncertainty,* Harmondsworth: Penguin.
18. Fauvel, J (ed.), (1990) *History in the Mathematics Classroom,* The IREM papers, Vol. 1, Leicester: Mathematics Association.
19. See Yaakobi, D and Sharan, S (1985) 'Teacher beliefs and practices: the discipline carries the message', *Journal of Education for Teaching,* **11,** 2, 187–99; Davies, C (1992) 'English Teacher Ideologies: an empirical study', *British Educational Research Journal,* **18,** 2, 193–207.
20. Department for Education (1992) *Initial Teacher Training (Secondary Phase),* Circular 9/92, London: Department for Education.

13 Issues in the Selection and Training of Mentors for School-based Primary Initial Teacher Training

Pie Corbett and Diana Wright

Background

The articled teacher course on which this discussion is based was a two-year school-based postgraduate course for intending primary school teachers. Fourteen students were recruited in 1990 and placed in 12 schools in two LEAs; a further 12 students were recruited in 1991 and placed in 12 different schools in the same LEAs. The articled teachers spent four days each week in school, and one day each week in college. Apart from two six-week placements in other schools, the articled teacher was based in the same school for two years. Headteachers were asked to select a teacher to act as mentor to each articled teacher. A payment of £500 was made to the mentor each year and half a day supply cover provided each week to enable the mentor to organize and support the training of the articled teacher within the school.

Selection of Schools

The importance of the selection of schools for training was formally stated in Circular 24/89 (CATE Criteria). Although the college already had a close relationship with and knowledge of many local schools, the articled teacher course steering committee required more explicit criteria to select participating schools. A significant feature of the original articled teacher scheme was the involvement of LEAs in the development and management of the training course itself. Our course submission stated that: 'The LEA identifies schools on the basis of a whole school management style that can fulfil the range of course expectations as well as a record of recognized good practice'.

As more schools wished to participate in the scheme than could be used, the LEAs drew up a long list from which the schools to be used would be selected. It soon became evident, however, that one very practical detail assumed overriding importance – proximity to the articled teachers' place of residence. In response to a survey by HMI, nine out of the first cohort of 14 articled teachers stated that they could only have considered a training course that placed them in a school near to their home; economic considerations and domestic commitments placed constraints on the daily distance travelled. Consequently, once the successful applicants had been identified, the LEAs had to seek information about the primary schools within easy travelling distance of their homes.

This process raises questions about the procedures the college will require to identify schools to be accredited for initial training under Government Circular 9/92 Annex B. Our College, located in a mainly rural area, currently places students in around 200 primary schools. It will not be easy to obtain current reliable and valid evidence of a school's performance and management record. As a result of this experience we are exploring with the LEA the possibility of including 'suitability for initial training' as a focus for school inspection reports.

Issues for the Headteacher

At the beginning of the scheme we recognized that the headteachers would play an important role. They would be responsible for selecting their key player – the mentor. They would maintain a commitment to the method of training and support the mentor in carrying out their role. The local authorities had attempted to select schools where the headteacher's management style seemed to suit the course – an open, questioning school which was engaged in its own reflective practice and had robust staff development policies. Placing an articled teacher whose business it would be to ask questions and to seek their own answers, into a school which was not used to asking itself questions could cause difficulties.

Before the course began the college tutoring team met with the mentors for a two-day induction programme. Headteachers joined us for the first morning; thereafter, the mentor training took place on one day a term and heads met for a morning each term. The ongoing contact with headteachers proved to be a useful part of evaluating and planning forwards; through these meetings we were able to involve the heads in the planning, thereby developing a genuine partnership that shared responsibility.

It soon became obvious that the headteacher played a crucial role in developing a whole-school mentoring culture. The course could not work effectively if the articled teacher stayed with the same class teacher over an extended period of time. The course required articled teachers to consider children's learning across the whole primary range and to experience a range of styles and approaches. It was necessary that the course was well understood and that aspects of mentoring were carried out by all members of staff. The headteachers had to consider what training opportunities their school could offer, as well as developing a whole-school understanding of the mentoring approach.

It became apparent that schools were approaching their involvement in the training in different ways. Some headteachers delegated all responsibility for the articled teacher to the mentor, while others maintained a close involvement themselves. Some mentors felt that the articled teacher should spend a large part of their training working alongside them in their own classroom, while other mentors negotiated a series of placements with other class teachers in the school. An emerging concern for us was the tension between the role of class teacher and the role of mentor.

We came to realize that there were often advantages to mentoring at a distance. As the course progressed the articled teachers assumed greater responsibility for teaching the whole class. Many articled teachers wanted to change some aspect of classroom organization or try out different approaches to teaching. The course was encouraging the articled teachers to reflect critically on their own teaching but the classroom in which they were working was not their own. Perhaps we had underestimated the sense of ownership and responsibility that primary teachers feel for their own class.

Articled teachers commented upon the difficulties of working with class teachers who seemed to treat them as if they were on a six-week teaching practice – some were reluctant to allow the articled teacher to reflect, to identify their own concerns, to come up with and try their own solutions. Several articled teachers expressed their lack of autonomy through comments such as, 'I would not organize the class like this', and 'The teacher wants me to continue doing it her way'. Tensions arose where teachers began to behave in a 'supervisory' and judgemental manner. In these cases the focus shifted on to pleasing the teacher by performing in the way they required, away from a professional dialogue with the focus upon how children learn. We realized the need to reiterate that in contrast to more traditional courses, articled teachers were in school to *learn* and not just to practise.

At the end of the first year, articled teachers identified the following concerns about the course:

- low status in school;
- difficult relationship with the mentor;
- difficult relationship with the class teacher;
- limited autonomy in school;
- having a different style of teaching;
- having different organizational priorities in the classroom;
- carrying out the 'long studies' required by the course.

This list clearly indicated the need for headteachers to ensure that the articled teacher's concerns were articulated and responded to; the articled teacher needed to feel a valued member of the school community. Mentors needed to help the articled teacher talk through their own needs, to develop their ability to self-evaluate, and to let them become 'their own teacher', rather than imitate someone else's organization and teaching style in order to 'pass'.

It became clear that the articled teachers' development was inextricably linked to the development of the mentor and, as they worked with other class teachers, to the development of the whole school. Articled teachers were limited by or enhanced by the school's development process.

Although many aspects of the importance of the headteacher were perhaps foreseeable, we were surprised to discover that headteachers also played a crucial role in the relationship between articled teachers and mentors, especially where difficulties were encountered. The headteacher acted as a sounding board to both parties, as someone who understood the situation and who might be able to resolve tensions. Difficulties were overcome by airing problems, building in breathing spaces so that the partnerships had chunks of time when they did not teach together, returning to considering the articled teacher's needs and building a programme in negotiation. Where the headteacher was reluctant to act in this role it fell to the college tutor to attempt to bring both parties together to resolve difficulties and forge a way ahead. This did not always work successfully, perhaps because tutors are divorced from the immediate situation and hold little power within it.

Interestingly, it was only at the very end of the two-year cycle, when the first cohort had completed their training, that some heads began to express confidence in understanding the full responsibility of their role in school-based training. This led to several important issues arising – how do schools evaluate the effectiveness of their own role in training, and how do heads carry out their function of assessment effectively? The latter point came again as a surprise, but headteachers expressed the wish to join tutors making visits to schools, thereby broadening their experience and entering into a dialogue about assessment through discussion and observation.

At the end of the second year we identified the following key issues for headteachers:

- there is a need for a whole-school approach to development that includes students in training;
- headteachers need time to develop aspects of their role in training: in assessing students, in developing whole-school policies on training, in managing training, in supporting the mentor in their role;
- class teachers as well as mentors need training to ensure that they understand and can carry out their role in a school-based course;
- schools need to develop procedures for evaluating the effectiveness of their role in training.

Selecting The Mentor

In the course submission we outlined the following advice:

> The headteacher and LEA, in consultation with the college, identifies teachers willing and able to take on the work of mentor. The following criteria are considered when selecting mentors:
> – the teacher is interested and willing to take on the role of mentor for two years.
> – the teacher is willing to attend the training course.
> –the teacher sees her/himself as actively engaged in professional development.
> –the teacher displays a range of styles.
> – the teacher is able to reflect on her/his teaching fluently and with enthusiasm.
> – the teacher will provide an appropriate model and be prepared to provide opportunities to broaden the articled teacher's range of experiences.

During the course we inevitably became interested in the mentors and how they were able – or not – to play an active role in training; how far were they successful in supporting and challenging an articled teacher who was acquiring their own professional understanding and teaching skills. We became concerned to identify what were the skills, attitudes, understandings and processes that needed to be held in mind whilst selecting and training mentors.

During the first year of the course it became evident that the role of mentor was proving difficult for deputy headteachers and those with senior management positions. The role was time consuming and demanding, which meant that either the mentoring or the deputy headship suffered as they tried to juggle two demanding tasks. It began to emerge that there were two sets of people who seemed best placed to take on such a role – those who were relatively new to teaching, and those who had taught for longer but who did not hold senior management positions.

Indeed, the common belief that a mentor should be an 'experienced' teacher was not a view that our experience confirmed. It seemed that mentors who had only recently completed their own training might be well placed to become part of a partnership in learning. In these circumstances, mentor and articled teacher could observe for each other, discuss difficulties as they arose, share and use each other's strengths. Several such partnerships were formed where both parties learned and developed together. In one school, both mentor and articled teacher had previously been employed in industry; a significant strength of this partnership was their common experience of appraisal and regular target-setting – this was reflected in a comprehensive and professional training log.

However, not every new teacher would necessarily be well placed to become a mentor. Through constant defining of the role by mentors, headteachers and articled teachers, a picture of the sorts of skills and approaches required began to emerge, clustered under headings such as:

- organization;
- communication;
- counselling;
- supporting;
- monitoring;
- collaboration;
- problem-solving.

It was interesting to note that the sorts of ideas that were emerging were very similar to the skills and approaches needed by others in management positions, such as curriculum coordinators:

Not being judgemental
Being a good listener
Valuing the offerings and comments of others
Offering a further idea
Viewing the activity as a collaborative one
Being aware of the level of confidence of others in the group

Being prepared to participate and ask questions
Using a 'try out and improve' approach
Reviewing development, clarifying thinking
(Centre for Mathematics Education, The Open University, 1990).

Indeed, during the first term the articled teachers identified a very similar list indicating what they felt to be the ideal qualities of a mentor:

- positive attitude that appreciates and acknowledges our efforts;
- honesty and sensitivity;
- enabling us to develop our own style of teaching;
- offering and exploring strategies, suggesting 'possible ways';
- giving advice rather than judgement;
- showing interest in the college work;
- valuing the contributions of articled teachers;
- open-mindedness;
- knowing that the learning is a two-way process.

We began to wonder whether or not selection would be helped by looking at how prospective mentors worked with their own class. Perhaps there was some sort of carry-over from the mentor's style of teaching into their mentoring? Could we see links between how they approached their work with children and how they approached the role of mentor? Obviously this was difficult to judge, but though this seemed a reasonable proposition we finally concluded that there was no obvious link. It seemed as if working with children did not always bear much relation to how a teacher might work with an adult. Ironically, some infant teachers who allowed their children choice and responsibility were reluctant to do so with the articled teacher. The articled teachers, however, were far clearer that the sort of approach to their own learning that we had developed was also suited to working with children – they began to make connections between their own learning and the classroom.

Part of the mentor's role was to assist the articled teacher to identify their own focus for development, to plan how this might be seen through, facilitate the carrying out of the plan and assist with evaluating the success of the plan. This constant engagement with someone else's development began to have a direct effect upon the mentors in terms of their own development. It also highlighted the need to select a mentor who would enjoy being engaged in learning.

Mentors recognized the benefit of this approach for themselves:

It has helped me look at and think about my teaching constructively – having to justify has made me discard some practices and improve others. I've learned to listen more too!

Such a willingness to learn and develop seemed to be a key factor in selecting mentors.

To summarize this section, we offer the advice we have given recently to headteachers on our B Ed course when selecting mentors to work with groups of students:

The mentor should be:
- interested and willing to take on the role of mentor;
- willing to attend training courses;
- a successful classroom teacher;
- actively engaged in professional development;
- able to liaise successfully with colleagues;
- able to reflect on teaching fluently and with enthusiasm;
- able to organize a range of training opportunities throughout the school;
- able to motivate and raise self-esteem;
- able to form positive relationships;
- able to work with adults in a non-threatening way;
- a good listener;
- flexible enough to allow experimentation and to respond to individual needs;
- well organized and have good record-keeping skills;
- able to help students to self-assess and to develop action plans.

The person you identify does not necessarily need to receive a student into their own classroom. The role of school mentor is to organize and support the training of all students within the school. The mentor does not need to know all the answers to teaching, but needs to be the sort of person who can help trainee teachers to develop their own teaching skills and professional understandings.

Mentor Training

The mentor training began with mentors considering what the role might entail, how it might be carried out and what skills and attitudes might be needed. This activity of 'role definition/clarification' was a regular feature of the course and we worked on the principle that we had to involve the mentors in thinking this through for themselves.

We provided the opportunity for them to share their experiences and we organized short, intense sessions practising key skills.

There was little doubt in our own minds that the ability to actively listen would play a key role in the mentoring. We intended that the mentors should establish and confirm the notion of the reflective practitioner. This would, in part, be done through active listening. By this we intended that the mentors would help the articled teachers *explore* their teaching, *clarify* important issues, *identify* areas of strength and areas for development and form *action plans* for their subsequent teaching and study. This would be done in a non-directive fashion – through open questioning and summarizing. In this way the articled teachers would be put into the position of constantly having to reflect on their experience, learn from their experience and make positive moves forwards. They would be actively engaged in their own development. We hoped that the mentors would act as critical response partners who would develop a relationship based on trust and non-judgemental interest, support and challenge.

The key barrier to adopting this role seemed to be that some mentors found it very hard to listen. Feedback from some articled teachers indicated the value of 'having someone sit and listen and take an interest in what you are struggling to come to terms with'. This was set against the experiences of those whose mentors seemed to have their own agenda and their own swift and ready answers to other people's problems. Indeed, the temptation to provide quick answers from their own store of experience and to pinpoint weaknesses in the articled teacher's teaching proved very strong for some. Some mentors fell into the trap of behaving like an old-fashioned college tutor. For this reason it was vital that the training focused on pushing mentors to clarify and restate their role and to discuss how it might best be accomplished. Mentors were asked to reflect critically on their ability to listen effectively.

To address this need we ensured that each training session had some activity in which the mentors tried out their listening skills and were observed. Mentors worked in groups of three; one carried out a non-directive discussion with a colleague while a third colleague observed. The mentors were told that they were only to ask open questions, with perhaps the occasional probing question; they were to help their colleague to explore, clarify, identify a focus and plan a way ahead. We chose genuine issues for the discussions such as, 'how my mentoring is developing'. We built upon these sessions by considering such areas as the hidden messages in questions and the effective use of summarizing. Mentors discovered different aspects about themselves – one colleague discovered that when she listens she frowns and looks disapproving. 'But I'm really concentrating on what you're saying!', she replied. We were able to explore the importance of body language as well as the hidden messages that seemingly innocent questions and comments can contain.

In each training session we provided an opportunity for mentors to evaluate how things were going as well as consider what might happen next. This took the form of team meetings in which we involved the mentors in feeding-back, reflecting on their own effectiveness and considering how they might progress. It surprised the mentors that from the beginning we did not seem to have the answers. To many questions we would throw the problem back to the group to explore and decide ways forwards. In this way the mentors were constantly engaged in their own growth. We hoped that they might begin to make connections between the way in which we wished to work with them and the ways in which they might work with their articled teacher.

Initially it seemed that the relationships were strong and that both parties were working together effectively. However, as we drew towards the end of the first year there were signs of difficulties emerging. The articled teachers had clearly identified aspects of the course that helped them develop:

- being able to use my own initiative;
- having time to reflect;
- observing different styles of teaching;
- good staff relationships;
- enthusiasm of school for the course;
- steady growth in confidence;
- high expectations;
- being seen as a teacher;
- having a good mentor;

They had also identified aspects that hindered growth, including:

- not knowing when to intervene in someone else's room;
- lack of status;
- lack of confidence;
- exhaustion;
- stress;
- my mentor;
- not knowing how to react to different children;
- losing confidence;
- teaching sessions not going to plan;
- drifting with a lack of focus;

- unrealistic expectations – of myself and of others;
- being treated as a 'helper' and not a teacher.

Mentoring was identified as an aspect that could potentially hinder or assist growth. Many of the relationships experienced difficulty during the fourth term. It seemed that by this point the articled teachers had grown in confidence, had developed understanding about how children learned, what to teach and how they wished to teach – they were really ready to take on more teaching in their own style. In some cases clashes arose as they began to attempt to establish themselves. The demands of the mentor's role had changed and the mentors needed to change with the articled teachers. Initially, the articled teachers had been fairly dependent upon their mentors for basic knowledge about the curriculum and school routines. They had moved from considering procedures into a consideration of how children learn and how teachers teach and this had led them on to develop their own understandings and beliefs. It was crucial that at this point the mentors should build in some breathing space to allow the articled teachers to develop their own ideas in their own ways. This was especially important where the mentor was also acting in the role of class teacher.

A key aspect of the programme was to train mentors in carrying out focused observations. Focused observation is a procedure adopted by all primary initial teacher training courses at the college following a programme of research into the supervision of student teachers (Terrell *et al.*, 1986; Coles and Terrell, 1988). The guiding principle of focused observation is that the articled teacher identifies an aspect of their teaching that they wish to know more about and the mentor observes on their behalf and supports them in an exploration of their teaching, leading to a plan of action. We used video material to practise observing, taking notes and feeding-back. Video extracts showed a teacher carrying out the discussion before the taught lesson where the focus for the observation is agreed upon, the actual taught session and the feedback discussion afterwards. Of course, it was easy to comment critically when watching someone else engaged in mentoring. This gave rise to the notion that we might need more time and other ways of ensuring that mentors can reflect directly upon their own practice. This might be done through the headteacher or deputy acting as mentor to the mentor, through the college tutor acting as mentor, or through regular local support groups of mentors in addition to the college training days. One mentor has tape-recorded his discussions with the articled teacher and reflected upon his role using an action research approach. This has been part of an independent study module for an M Ed. Both articled teacher and mentor felt that the reflections had led to a sharpening and clarification of the sessions. Understanding oneself in relation to another is not an easy task and needs to be supported and challenged.

Another key aspect of the mentor's role was to assist the articled teacher in self-assessing and logging their progress in a professional profile. This profile matched the College Competences for Teaching. We began by asking mentors and articled teachers to create their own profile headings and over a number of training sessions they reconsidered the various categories that they were using. Our concern was to assist both parties in coming to a shared understanding of what teaching entailed, a shared set of competences to which they were committed. In this way we hoped to engage in a genuine debate about what makes good teaching. This activity helped us to reshape our own college criteria, using language more acceptable to teachers in school.

The term 'training' soon became one that we questioned. We could train mentors to fill in forms and to develop certain skills such as observation. However, much of our work was driven by the principle of providing frameworks within which mentors would engage with us in developing an effective course. We questioned whether we were training the mentors or working together in partnership. This led us to consider that the actual training – or mentor development – should not only take part on training days, but should be supported in a range of ways, including:

- conference days in college to develop mentoring skills and to enable mentors to reflect on their role in training;
- informal mentor networks – these became half-day meetings organized and self-generated by mentor groups;
- link tutor visits – these should be as much to consider the mentor's needs as to consider the articled teacher's. The visits should assist the training partnership in becoming more effective;
- headteacher support and appraisal – the head should play a key role in helping the mentor carry out their role effectively;
- accredited course of study – this would provide mentors with a focused opportunity to read, reflect and develop.

We conclude with a summary of key issues for mentor trainers:

Meetings must start before and continue during the training course. The training should:
- be based on engaging the mentors in taking responsibility for evaluating their effectiveness;

- assist in clarifying the changing role – or restating mentors' developing understanding of what the role might be;
- consider organizational matters briefly;
- focus mainly on developing the attitudes, skills and knowledge required to carry out the role effectively;
- develop active listening/good interpersonal skills;
- help mentors understand the need to support and offer challenge;
- help mentors focus upon the trainee's needs;
- emphasize that in primary schools good communciation with other staff is crucial and that 'breathing space' needs to be built in;
- develop the ability to carry out effective 'focused observations';
- assist the mentors and trainee teachers in mapping their own professional growth;
- highlight and share successful practice;
- consider difficulties and potential ways round these;
- establish the notion that a non-judgemental approach may support the articled teachers in becoming 'self-developers' – to become ultimately their own mentors;
- include feedback on the college's role in their development and in the development of the trainee teacher;
- at times include trainee teachers in sessions with mentors so that group principles, understandings and perspectives can be established and shared.

Conclusion

This chapter has summarized some of our thoughts and feelings as we have worked with articled teachers, mentors, class teachers and headteachers during the last two years. Our own thinking has been constantly shaped and reshaped by their enthusiastic and professional engagement in considering together how school-based training might best be done. We have charted some of our thinking and attempted to summarize some of the things we feel we have learned. As such it is a statement that says as much about our own journey as it does about theirs. We are grateful to them for joining us. The mentor's role is complex and subtle. It ultimately has little to do with filling in forms, attending meetings, filling in profiles – it has everything to do with an active engagement between mentor, articled teacher, college and school community. It has everything to do with developing together, to think, to feel, to learn and to grow. It is ultimately to do with the human spirit and how we cherish that within ourselves and within others.

REFERENCES

Cheltenham and Gloucester College of Higher Education (1990) 'Articled Teacher Course Submission;, April.

Centre for Mathematics Education (1990) 'Working with colleagues', Milton Keynes: CME, The Open University.

Department of Education and Science (1989) *Initial Teacher Training: Approval of Courses*, Circular 24/89, London: DES.

Department for Education (1992) *Initial Teacher Training (Secondary Phase)*, Circular 9/92, London: DfE.

Terrell, C and Coles, D (eds) (1988) *Recent Innovations in Initial Teacher Education for Intending Primary School Teachers*, Monograph Number 3, Cheltenham and Gloucester College of Higher Education.

Terrell, C, Mathis, J, Winstanley, R and Wright, D (eds) (1986) *Teaching Practice Supervision in Primary Schools*, Monograph Number 1, Cheltenham and Gloucester College of Higher Education.

Index